High Mountains Deep Valleys

Dedicated to the memory of

David Penman (1936 – 1989)
late Anglican Archbishop of Melbourne

friend, encourager, example

High, Mountains, Deep Valleys

MEDITATIONS AND PRAYERS
FOR THE DOWN TIMES

Edited by Rowland Croucher
and Grace Thomlinson

AN ALBATROSS BOOK

© Rowland Croucher and Grace Thomlinson 1990

Published in Australia and New Zealand by
Albatross Books Pty Ltd
PO Box 320, Sutherland
NSW 2232, Australia
in the United States of America by
Albatross Books
PO Box 131, Claremont
CA 91711, USA
and in the United Kingdom by
Lion Publishing
Peter's Way, Sandy Lane West
Littlemore, Oxford OX4 5HG, England

First edition 1991

National Library of Australia
Cataloguing-in-Publication data

Croucher, Rowland
High Mountains, Deep Valleys

ISBN 0 86760 090 X (Albatross)
ISBN 0 7459 1299 0 (Lion)

1. Meditations. I. Croucher, Rowland

242

Cover photograph: Austral-International Pty Ltd, Sydney
Printed by Kyodo Printing Co. Ltd, Singapore

Contents

Preface

WE BECOME WHAT WE CONTEMPLATE. Contemplation, says Peter Gordon in *Contemplating the Word*, is a tool by which human beings are encouraged:

> to open themselves to the penetrating Word/ Spirit/Life of the Eternal. . . to be set free to live wisely, lovingly and powerfully.

The aim of this book, as of its predecessor *Still Waters, Deep Waters,* is to provide for thoughtful but busy people fifty-two opportunities for serious reflection. Ideally, find a quiet place — an 'oratory' — where you can be uninterrupted. If possible, have no time constraints. Linger there with the Lord. Meander through each chapter and then be still in a listening, receptive attitude. Later, if you practise journaling, write down your personal reflections. Talk about some of these with a spiritual director or soul friend.

Again we have not revealed who wrote what: the Lord speaks to his teachable children in many diverse ways and with many voices.

Thanks again to World Vision of Australia for allowing my assistant Grace Thomlinson and me the time to compile and edit these devotions.

Our desire, as David Steindl-Rast so aptly put it in *Gratefulness: the Heart of Prayer,* is that we may distinguish 'prayer' from 'prayers' and, with hearts that drink deeply from the source of meaning, live gratefully moment by moment.

Rowland Croucher
World Vision of Australia
Box 399C
Melbourne 3001

Theme: Praise

. . .with word and deed

O sing to the Lord a new song
    because he has performed wondrous things!
His right hand and his holy arm have
    gained him victory.
The Lord has made known his salvation;
He has unveiled his righteousness in
    the sight of the nations.
He has remembered his loving-kindness and
    his faithfulness to Israel's descendants.
All the ends of the earth have
    witnessed the salvation of our God. . .

Let the sea in its vastness roar in praise,
    the world and its inhabitants!
Let the rivers clap their hands
    and the mountains sing praises together
    before the Lord, for he is coming to
    judge the earth.
He will judge the world with justice,
    the peoples with unfaltering fairness.

               Psalm 98: 1-3 and 7-9, Berkeley

1

In the beginning, God

There is a God in heaven. . . God is with you.

God conceals himself. . . God reveals mysteries.

The Lord is King; the people tremble. . . He has pity on the weak and poor.

The high and lofty One who inhabits eternity. . . inhabits the praises of Israel.

The world and all that is in it belong to the Lord. . . the cattle on a thousand hills. . . Rich as he was, he made himself poor for your sake.

God is ready to judge the living and the dead. Our God is a consuming fire. . . He will save his people from their sins.

I am your God — let nothing terrify you! God remembers those who suffer. God is wise and powerful! Praise him for ever and ever. He reveals things that are deep and secret; he knows what is hidden in darkness, and he himself is surrounded by light. How deep is God's wisdom and knowledge! Who can explain his decisions? Who can understand his ways?. . . All things exist through him and for him.

The Lord's unfailing love and mercy still continue, fresh as the morning, as sure as the sunrise. The Lord is all I have, and so I put my hope in him.

In view of all this, what can we say? If God is for us, who can be against us? Nothing can separate us from God's love. God, the source of my happiness.

(Daniel 2: 28; Isaiah 45: 14-15; Daniel 2: 29; Psalm 99: 1 and 72: 13 — all GNB; Isaiah 57: 15, RSV; Psalm 22: 3, KJV; Psalm 24: 1 and 50: 10; 2 Corinthians 8: 9; 1 Peter 4: 5 — all GNB; Hebrews 12: 29, RSV; Psalm 130: 8; Isaiah 41: 10; Psalm 9: 12; Daniel 2: 20 and 22; Romans 11: 33 and 36; Lamentations 3: 22-24; Romans 8: 31 and 38; Psalm 43: 4 — all GNB)

The novelist Katherine Mansfield, an atheist, woke up one lovely morning at her villa in the south of France, looked out her window at the beauty of it all, and said: 'How I wish there were someone to thank!'

There is, Katherine. And God heard you. . .

Who is God? Where is God? What is God like?

When you come into contact with the God depicted in the Bible, you'd better be ready for some surprises. We define reality in terms of our limited experience and, if that experience was flawed by bad relationships, 'bad luck' or bad life-management, we may create expectations about God that are also flawed. We know only in part and see through a glass darkly. So our 'God-talk' suffers from severe limitations.

Who is God? The German mystic Gerhard Tersteegan wrote: 'A god understood, a god comprehended, is no god.' After all the words and theories, preachings and theologies, God is still incognito and beyond our comprehension. 'We cannot see light,' wrote C.S. Lewis in *The Four Loves*, 'though by light we can see things. Statements about God are extrapolations from the knowledge of other things which the divine illumination enables us to know.'

The Eastern Orthodox tradition has always held that God in his essence is unknown; he is discerned through his works and words.

'God' is not a static noun but a dynamic verb. It's like trying to understand a train trip by studying the timetables: you have to take the journey to experience it. Nicolas Berdyaev, the Russian philosopher, reminds us that theological doctrine is not necessary for faith, but that faith is necessary for theological doctrine. Believing is seeing.

According to Paul the apostle, the God of the Bible is one who can make the things that *are* out of things that *are not*: he can make the dead come to life again. God is the sum of all possibilities.

God is love and God is just. God's justice, says C.S. Lewis, is his love labouring to make us lovable. When our sin is abhorrent to us as it is so manifestly to God, we may understand a little of his holy anger against that

which is destroying us. He has given us ten commandments (not ten suggestions) to preserve a moral
environment in which humans can survive. God's kindness and severity (Romans 11: 22) are joined together in
the Bible, and what God has joined together let not the
Pharisees or the sentimentalists separate (even if there is
great mystery here). The judge of all the earth will act
justly, he can do it without our help, and that's comforting.

Where is God? In heaven, in sacred places and religious
celebrations, yes, but also within us, as the ground of our
being (Tillich), in ordinariness and in crisis, in the
variegated beauty of creation, in others and uniquely in
Jesus of Nazareth — 'God was in Christ'. We think about
God in terms of transcendence — ('out-thereness') — *and*
immanence ('down-hereness'). God is not merely far away,
beyond the bright blue sky; he is closer than breathing,
nearer than hands and feet. God is the life in every living
thing — Justin Martyr says he is 'present in all his works
though still unseen' — but as Creator he is greater than
the sum of all his creation.

But the more urgent questions are: 'Where is God when
it hurts?' and 'Is God deaf?' From biblical times, God's
apparent absence or silence have puzzled and pained his
people. In Samuel Beckett's *Waiting for Godot*, 'God', we
assume, does not come. Since Auschwitz we wonder if
we can still praise him. And today, in many parts of the
world, his servants are ridiculed, tortured and killed. And
the cries of the martyrs are still louder than those protesting the injustices done to those martyrs.

God is not deaf; he is listening. He suffers with his
people and hears their cries. 'Where was your God when
my son was killed in a car accident?' asked the distraught
mother. The pastor quietly replied, 'The same place he
was when *his* son was killed.'

What is God like? Our hunger for God was articulated
by Philip: 'Lord, show us the Father, that is all we need'
(John 14: 8). Jesus' answer was breathtaking: 'Whoever
has seen me has seen the Father' (John 14: 9). What is
God like? He is like Jesus. Jesus is God for you, near
you. Your faith depends on him from start to finish

(Hebrews 12: 2). He cannot stop loving you. He thinks you're beautiful, he delights in you, so in the joy and comfort of this total acceptance, make room for surprise and hope and wonder and the unexpected and, above all, the warm certainty that you are loved for ever.

And never forget, as an old mystic said, if you have God and everything else you have no more than having God only; and if you have everything else and not God you have nothing.

❧❦❧

No philosophical theory which I have yet come across is a radical improvement on the words of Genesis, that 'In the beginning God made heaven and earth.'

C.S. Lewis, *Miracles*

Some people want to love God in the same way as they love a cow. You love it for the milk and the cheese and for your own profit. So do all people who love God for the sake of outward riches or inward consolation. But they do not love God correctly, for they merely love their own advantage.

You are looking for something along with God, and you are behaving exactly as if you were making of God a candle so that you could look for something. When we find the things we are looking for, we throw the candle away. Whatever you are seeking along with God is *nothing*. It does not matter what it is — be it an advantage or a reward or a kind of spirituality or whatever else — you are seeking a nothingness and for this reason you find a nothingness.

Meister Eckhart

God is a lover different from human lovers, who give a gift which is exterior to them. God is working in all his gifts, giving of himself as a sign of his love. Creation is an ongoing process and God is patiently working from inside each creature in the potentiality he has poured into that finite creature. He is the ground of being directing all creatures to their full actuality. . .

George A. Maloney, *Alone with the Alone*

The God of the gospel is the God. . . who again and again discloses himself anew and must be discovered anew. . . In this he is, without doubt, a God wholly different from other gods. Other gods do not seem to prohibit their theologies from boasting that each one is the most correct or even the only correct theology. . .

The God of the gospel is no lonely God, self-sufficient and self-contained. . . He is *our* God. He exists neither *next to* us nor merely *above* us, but rather *with* us, *by* us and, most important of all, *for* us. . . The content of God's Word is his free, undeserved Yes to the whole human race, in spite of all human unreasonableness and corruption.

Karl Barth, *Evangelical Theology*

People become like their gods. It is not that we, since the creation of the world, have created gods in our image. Rather we have imagined the sort of gods who might be useful for us. If we want to conquer our enemies, our god will be warlike; if we need to feel okay when we've done wrong, then our god will be appeased through sacrifices.

The gods of the American Zuni Indians are kindly and beneficent; so these people have no sorcery, they dance a lot and life is a constant celebration. The Ojibwa gods, on the other hand, have to be bargained with and bribed; their religion is fear motivated; life is selfish and there is an abundance of black magic. . .

The god of the Pharisees is stern and legalistic, so life for them is governed by 'decency', authority and duty, and their preaching aims to induce guilt. The God of Jesus loves sinners, so Jesus enjoys partying, life is zestful and spontaneous, the kingdom is one of feasting, of joyful celebration. For the Pharisees 'repentance precedes acceptance'; with Jesus it was the other way around.

William Temple once wrote: 'If your conception of God is radically false, then the more devout you are the worse it will be for you. . . You had better be an atheist.' A legalistic religion is a heavy burden to carry. Jesus' religion carries us. . .

Rowland Croucher

The appropriate stance in relation to the Holy One is utter openness and flexibility and high sensitivity. We humans must prepare for God's coming with silence, emptiness and receptivity.

To me, God is the Holy One whose other name is Surprise. The willingness to let the Ultimate assume whatever form he will and come in whatever manner he chooses is absolutely crucial, and it must be coupled with our trust that God wants to become known to us and is able to communicate with us, if we will allow it on those terms. . .

The bumper sticker 'Let God be God' states the most important imperative of life. What could be more important, really, than letting one's god be the true God — letting the one who is God by nature function as one's God in fact? Every day of our lives the God who made us does battle with the gods we have made. . . Only the Creator can fully satisfy and genuinely fulfil a creature. As St Augustine said so long ago, 'You have made us for yourself, O Lord, and our hearts are restless until they rest in you.'

John Claypool

The self we love is not the self God loves; the neighbours we do not prize are his treasures, the truth we ignore is the truth he maintains, the justice we seek because it is our own is not the justice that his love desires. The righteousness he demands and gives is not our righteousness, but greater and different.

He requires of us the sacrifice of all we would conserve and grants us gifts we had not dreamed of. . . repentance and sorrow for our transgressions rather than forgetfulness; faith in him rather than confidence in ourselves; trust in his mercy rather than sight of his presence; instead of rest, an ever-recurrent torment that will not let us be content; instead of the peace and joy of the world, the hope of the world to come. He forces us to take our sorrows as a gift from him and to suspect our joys lest they be purchased by the anguish of his Son incarnate again in every neighbour. He ministers indeed to all our good, but all our good is other than we thought.

H. Richard Niebuhr, *The Meaning of Revelation*

There is only one good definition of God: the freedom that allows other freedoms to exist.

John Fowles, *The French Lieutenant's Woman*

. . .God is still the God who evokes reverence and awe. It is a distorted Christianity which in the midst of the joy of the heavenly journey forgets the awe and the dread. . . 'Our God is a consuming fire' (Hebrews 13: 16).

Michael Ramsay, *Be Still and Know*

[When young I used to say to myself] 'If God does not punish me for my sin, he ought to do so.' I felt that God was just, and that he knew that I did not wish him to be anything else but just; for even my imperfect knowledge of God included my recognition that he was a just and holy God. If I could have been certain of salvation by any method by which God could have ceased to be just, I could not have accepted even salvation on those terms; I should have felt that it was derogatory to the dignity of the Most High and that it was contrary to the universal laws of right.

Charles Haddon Spurgeon, *Great Texts of the Bible*

'I love you,' said a tiny voice. I looked around. No-one was there. Just a chain link fence with a sign that said 'Humpty Dumpty Nursery.'

Then I saw a little girl, almost hidden, perched in a bush. Her friendly, chocolate-covered smile peeped out among the leaves. I felt warm inside. . . like a squeezed teddy bear.

She loves me, eh? But she doesn't know me.

But wait. She wasn't evaluating me; she was expressing herself.

God says, 'I love you.' But we don't believe it. How could he love us? He knows us. We forget God's declaration isn't a judgment about us, but a revelation about him.

Wes Seeliger

Late have I loved you, O beauty so ancient and so new;
late have I loved you.
For behold you were within me, and I outside;
and I sought you outside and in my ugliness fell
upon those lovely things that you have made.
You were with me and I was not with you.
I was kept from you by those things,
yet had they not been in you, they would not have
been at all.
You called and cried to me and broke upon my deafness;
and you sent forth your light and shone upon me,
and chased away my blindness.
You breathed fragrance upon me,
and I drew in my breath and do now pant for you:
I tasted you and I now hunger and thirst for you;
you touched me, and I have burned for your peace.

St Augustine of Hippo

Lord God, Creator, Saviour and friend, I see glimpses of your creative beauty in the stars, in the mountains, in trees and birds and flowers. The sun sings your praises, the moon gives you glory, the oceans, storms and thunder join the mighty chorus to extol your majesty.

You are the One in whom I live and move and have my being: you are not a remote unfeeling deity but, amazingly, are deeply concerned about all my ways. I, even I, can experience your healing presence in my valleys, my lonely nights and my grievings.

In my waywardness when I am inclined to self-destruct, your grace covers a multitude of sins. Your will is my peace. To obey you is perfect freedom. Your energising power gives my life purpose and meaning, and the promise of your nearness offers renewing hope. Thankyou for your gifts of fresh new mornings, work and play, laughter and cheerfulness, rest and sleep. Above all, thankyou for your word to guide me, strength to love, the fellowship of your people and the sure promise of eternal life.

Lord, may I give you the same place in my heart that you have in the universe.

Eternal God, the light of the minds that know you, the joy of the hearts that love you and the strength of the wills that serve you; grant us so to know you, that we may truly love you, and so to love you that we may fully serve you, whom to serve is perfect freedom, in Jesus Christ our Lord.

St Augustine of Hippo

A Benediction

Prayer

> May the 'Lord of all being, throned afar'
>> be enthroned within ~~you~~. us
> May he whose 'glory flames from sun and star'
>> be glorified in your life. lives
> May the 'centre and soul of every sphere'
>> be centre of all your thinking
>> and speaking and acting.
> May the One who is near each loving heart
>> stay close by ~~you~~, for ever.   Amen.

2

High praises from low places

Why are you downcast, O my soul? Why so disturbed within me? Put your hope in God, for I will yet praise him, my Saviour and my God.

As for me, I will always have hope. . .

Do not be anxious about anything, but in everything, by prayer and petition, with thanksgiving, present your requests to God.

Be joyful always; pray continually; give thanks in all circumstances, for this is God's will for you in Christ Jesus.

About midnight Paul and Silas were praying and singing hymns to God, and the other prisoners were listening to them.

Sorrowful, yet always rejoicing.

In all our troubles my joy knows no bounds.

He put a new song in my mouth, a hymn of praise to our God. Many will see and fear and put their trust in the Lord.

I will sing of your strength, in the morning I will sing of your love; for you are my fortress, my refuge in times of trouble.

I will praise you, O Lord my God, with all my heart; I will glorify your name forever. For great is your love towards me; you have delivered my soul from the depth of the grave.

(Psalm 42: 11; Psalm 71: 14; Philippians 4: 6; 1 Thessalonians 5: 16-18; Acts 16: 25; 2 Corinthians 6: 10; 2 Corinthians 7: 4; Psalm 40: 3; Psalm 59: 16; Psalm 86: 12 and 13 – all NIV)

As creatures of the world we share in its sorrows, strains

and struggles. So often we are subject to its din and disturbance, its wars and its woes to the point where our personal lives may become clouded or cluttered with doubts and difficulties, problems and pain, sorrows and suffering. At such times there is always a choice to live under or over the circumstances, to concentrate on self or refocus on God, to worry or worship.

Worry can't change the past, but it can ruin the present and the future. It won't empty tomorrow of its sorrow, but it will empty today of its joy. Worry is the only game in which if you guess right, you don't feel any better. It's like a rocking chair that gives you something to do, but doesn't get you anywhere. It is unbelief parading in disguise, trying to interfere with God's plans.

Worship on the other hand is, as William Temple says:

to quicken the conscience with the holiness of God,
to feed the mind on the truth of God,
to purge the imagination by the beauty of God,
to open the heart to the love of God,
to devote the will to the purpose of God.

'It is never more helpful to us than when it is most difficult to offer, and it is certainly most acceptable to God when it costs us the most' (Fred Mitchell).

When we choose to worship, we and our circumstances are usually transformed. Furthermore, as we determine to do it, it may be easier for others to find God and difficult for them to forget him.

We become '. . .more than conquerors through him who loved us' (Romans 8: 37, NIV).

❦

We were created for God's pleasure, to express his worthiness, to give him pleasure (Revelation 4: 9-11). We are made for worship.

Editorial, *Restore*

To worship God must be the consuming passion of the heart, whether we express it in old ways or new ways, in silence or with shouts, in stillness or with dancing.

Graham Kendrick, *Real Worship*

As we praise and worship, God steps out of his mystery into our history and we move from our history into his mystery.

Source unknown

All too often our faith is earth-bound and we find it hard to believe that God can do anything that our minds cannot explain. It is only as we spend time worshipping God, concentrating on the nature of his Person — especially his greatness and love — that our faith begins to rise.

Like a plane soaring through the dark rain clouds into the fresh beauty of the sunshine, so our faith rises, stimulated by worship and by the new vision of God that worship brings, until we begin to believe that God *can* work in ways that may be beyond our present understanding.

Throughout the early chapters of Acts we find the constant blend of worship and wonders, praise and power. . . There are countless examples in the Bible and in Christian biography where a sustained time of praise prepares the way for the Lord to demonstrate his power.

David Watson, *Fear No Evil*

Praise releases the power of God into our lives and circumstances, because praise is faith in action. When we trust God fully, he is free to work, and he always brings victory. It may be a victory that changes circumstances, or a victory *in* the circumstances.

M.R. Carothers, *Power in Praise*

Praise clarifies your vision. The focus of your attention is drawn from the complexity of the problem to the adequacy of God's resources; from the urgency of your need to the power of the Lord to meet your need. As you praise him, you begin to remember how he has helped you on other occasions and your faith rises in expectancy. The more you praise, the smaller the mountain you are facing appears in the light of God's greatness. Almost unconsciously you are casting your burden on the Lord (Psalm 55: 12).

. . .Praise lifts your eyes from the battle to the victory, for Christ is already Victor, and you have the Victor in your heart that you might have his victory in your life and in your prayer.

. . .Praise honours God, brings joy to the angels and strikes terror in any evil spirit which may be around. Praise clears the atmosphere, washes your spirit, multiplies your faith and clothes you with God's presence and power.

. . .If the Lord is inhabiting the praises of his people, the influence of the enemy must be driven away. Satan and his demons fear the presence and authority of Jesus. Praising Jesus puts the demon hosts to flight. Expect Satan to run from you (James 4: 7). . . Praise is the Christian's heavy artillery. Praise is a strategic way to victory.

W.L. Deuwel, *Touch the World through Prayer*

When we magnify God, we view the circumstances around us differently. When we focus on all the greatness and goodness of God, it lifts us out of our surroundings and gives us an eternal perspective and a view into the heavenly realm. That perspective helps us to deal with our circumstances more objectively, because it shows us reality from God's perspective.

Gary Browning, *Restore*

Worthy of praise from every mouth,
of confession from every tongue,
of worship from every creature
Is thy glorious name, O Father, Son and Holy Ghost;
Who didst create the world in thy grace
and by thy compassion didst save the world.
To thy majesty, O God, ten thousand times ten thousand
bow down and adore,
Singing and praising without ceasing, and saying,
Holy, holy, holy, Lord God of hosts;
Heaven and earth are full of thy praises;
Hosanna in the highest.

Nestorian Liturgy

Gracious Father, I have made my decision: I will, by your grace, worship you and seek to glorify your name. Please make me a transformer. May I be used by your Spirit to make a difference wherever I am.

May great glory come to your name as saints unite in worship and sinners trust the Saviour.

Through Jesus Christ our Lord. Amen.

W. Wiersbe, *Real Worship*

A Benediction

I know whom I have believed, and am convinced that he is able:

. . . to do immeasurably more than all we ask or imagine,

. . . to make grace abound,

. . . to help those who are being tempted,

. . . to save completely those who come to God through him.

Therefore

Praise the Lord, O my soul;

all my inmost being, praise his holy name. Amen.

Depart. . . and hide yourself

And the word of the Lord came to him, 'Depart from here and turn eastward, and hide yourself by the brook Cherith, that is east of the Jordan. You shall drink from the brook, and I have commanded the ravens to feed you there.' So he went and did according to the word of the Lord; he went and dwelt by the brook Cherith that is east of the Jordan.

And he said, 'Go forth, and stand upon the mount before the Lord.' And behold, the Lord passed by, and a great and strong wind rent the mountains, and broke in pieces the rocks before the Lord, but the Lord was not in the wind; and after the wind an earthquake, but the Lord was not in the earthquake; and after the earthquake a fire, but the Lord was not in the fire; and after the fire a still small voice.

Have you not known? Have you not heard? The Lord is the everlasting God, the Creator of the ends of the earth. He does not faint or grow weary, his understanding is unsearchable. He gives power to the faint, and to him who has no might he increases strength. Even youths shall faint and be weary, and young men shall fall exhausted; but they who wait for the Lord shall renew their strength, they shall mount up with wings like eagles, they shall run and not be weary, they shall walk and not faint.

For thus said the Lord God, the Holy One of Israel, 'In returning and rest you shall be saved; in quietness and in trust shall be your strength.'

And Jesus, full of the Holy Spirit, returned from the Jordan, and was led by the Spirit for forty days in the wilderness.

And from time to time he would withdraw to lonely places for prayer.

In these days he went out into the hills to pray; and all night he continued in prayer to God.

And he took them with him and withdrew privately to a town called Bethsaida.

(1 Kings 17: 2-6, RSV; 1 Kings 19: 11-12, RSV; Isaiah 40: 28-31, RSV; Isaiah 30: 15, RSV; Luke 4: 1-2a, RSV; Luke 5: 16, NEB; Luke 6: 12, NEB; Luke 9: 10b, NEB)

Then the word of the Lord came to Elijah, 'Depart from here and turn eastward, and hide yourself by the brook. . .' (1 Kings 17: 3). Can't you hear the prophet protesting: 'Go hide myself! But, Lord, I'm a public man! I've gotta be where the action is. How about some more of that palace assignment? Didn't you just love what that prophecy did to Ahab? Wow! We really shook him up, didn't we? So, what do you mean, "Go hide yourself"? Why, Lord, it doesn't make sense when there is so much work to do and so much life to experience.'

That is how Elijah might have responded to his new 'assignment' if he were the typical Western activist Christian of the late twentieth century.

Yet it is possible that, in trying to 'be strong for the Lord', we who are the people of God neglect the wellspring of real power — to be with our Lord in the quiet place. It 'is in the stillness and in staying quiet that our strength lies', says Isaiah, not in a whirlwind of activity and an abundance of noise. Retreat — a time apart from life's action simply to be in the quiet presence of God — has sustained Christians for centuries. Out of the quiet monasteries flowed the life and truth that brought stability when the walls of civilisation crumbled in the Dark Ages. Out of the imposed stillness of a prison cell has power arisen in the likes of a John Bunyan or an Aleksandr Solzhenitsyn. Out of retreat comes a cure for the malaise of our day; where, in the words of Frodo Baggins from Tolkien's *The Lord of The Rings*, 'merely to be there was a cure for weariness, fear and sadness'.

Retreat brings a 'spot of rebirth', Evelyn Underhill says. Retreat times can provide spiritual rebirth, quicken what has grown dull and dead in us and make us more effective in our work. In genuine retreat, that which is foundational to the spiritual life finally becomes central: namely, our relation to God.

John Casteel notes that 'the purpose of retreat is the deepening of communion with God. . . the offering of ourselves to God in such a way that he can draw us into closer communion with himself — and through this communion grant us richer community with other persons in Christ and a truer understanding of ourselves. The root of this purpose is to be found in the Great Commandment, "Thou shalt love the Lord thy God", and the second is like it, "Thou shalt love thy neighbour as thyself".' Therefore, he cautions the Christian contemplating retreat to remember that 'the true retreat does not aim either "to get work done", or "to enjoy a holiday". Its focus is not upon a task, a subject, a problem, or pleasurable inspiration. The centre and justification of retreat is found only in *communion* — in a coming to oneself, a participation with others in Christ, a being in prayer with God.'

What is retreat for? To strip away the press of the crowd, the rush of activity, the sights, sounds and lights of our unreal life so that we can drive a stake into our purpose for being: 'To glorify God and fully enjoy him for ever'.

❧

Frodo was now safe in the Last Homely House east of the Sea. That house was, as Bilbo had long ago reported, 'a perfect house, whether you like food or sleep or storytelling or singing, or just sitting and thinking best, or a pleasant mixture of them all.' Merely to be there was a cure for weariness, fear and sadness.

J.R.R. Tolkien, *The Lord of the Rings*

I came back here, and here I have been. I have done this and that. I have written some more of my book. And, of course, I make up a few songs. They sing them occasionally: just to please me, I think; for of course, they aren't really good enough for Rivendell. And I listen and I think. Time doesn't seem to pass here; it just is. A remarkable place altogether.

J.R.R. Tolkien, *The Lord of the Rings*

A first retreatant lately told me that when she confessed to her husband what she intended to do, he took his pipe out of his mouth and said earnestly: 'Go, my dear. Go by all means! You're just about due for a spot of rebirth.' That man, it seems to me, had a very clear idea of one function of a retreat: its power of causing the rebirth of our spiritual sense, quickening that which has grown dull and dead in us, calling it out into light and air, giving it another chance.

Evelyn Underhill, *Light of Christ*

Now those who control the modern factory — wiser in their generation than the children of light — know what all this means in the exhausting and impoverishing of human material, in nervous tension, apathy, unrest. So there is no good factory without its welfare department, its rest room, its opportunity for quiet. To withdraw the worker at times from the clatter and pressure is to increase the quantity and quality of the work. So I sometimes think retreats should be regarded as a bit of spiritual welfare work; quite essential to the organisation of the church, and specially to the efficiency of its ministers. I am sure that were the making of at least a yearly retreat an absolute obligation of the priesthood, this would be a far more direct way of renewal than some of those now proposed.

I don't mean by this to recommend the retreat for merely practical reasons — because it makes the effective active Christian even more active and effective than before. I would rather recommend it because it puts in the foreground and keeps in the foreground that which is, after all, the first interest of religion — so easily lost sight of — the one thing needful — the soul's relation to God.

Evelyn Underhill, *Light of Christ*

We knew as a fellowship that our mission as the church in the world would be in peril if this outward movement

did not have a corresponding movement of retreat.
Elizabeth O'Connor, *Call to Commitment*

Many people seek fellowship because they are afraid to
be alone. Because they cannot stand loneliness, they are
driven to seek the company of people.
Dietrich Bonhoeffer, *Life Together*

We needed to learn to live from a quiet centre.
Elizabeth O'Connor, *Call to Commitment*

Later the soul will bring forth fruit exactly in the measure
in which the inner life is developed in it. If there is no
inner life, however great may be the zeal, the high intention, the hard work, no fruit will come forth; it is like a
spring that would give out sanctity to others but cannot,
having none to give; one can only give what one has. It
is in solitude, in that lonely life alone with God, in
profound recollection of soul, in forgetfulness of all created
things, that God gives himself to the soul that thus gives
itself whole and entire to him.
Charles de Foucauld

Alone you stood before God when he called you; alone
you had to answer that call; alone you had to struggle
and pray; and alone you will die and give account to God.
You cannot escape from yourself; for God has singled you
out. If you refuse to be alone you are rejecting Christ's
call to you.
Dietrich Bonhoeffer, *Life Together*

The one therefore that intends to attain to the more inward
and spiritual things of religion, must with Jesus depart
from the multitude and press of people. No-one doth
safely appear abroad but he who can abide at home. . .
Who so therefore withdraweth himself from his acquaintance and friends, God will draw near unto him with his
angels. . .
Shut thy door upon thee, and call unto thee Jesus, thy
beloved. Stay with him in thy closet; for thou shalt not
find so great peace anywhere else. . .

Seek a convenient time of leisure for thyself, and meditate often upon God's loving-kindness. Meddle not with things too high for thee, but read such things as may rather yield compunction to thy heart than occupation to thy head.

Thomas à Kempis, *Of the Imitation of Christ*

I believe the retreat as a part of our normal spiritual routine will yield on the whole its fullest results when we regard it more often and more generally, in Abbot Delatte's beautiful phrase, as an opportunity of 'steeping our souls in the beauty of the mysterious'. To dwell quietly and without self-occupation in the atmosphere of God is surely the best of all ways of redressing the balance between the temporal and eternal sides of our life.

Evelyn Underhill, *Light of Christ*

Lord of the still small voice:
 It is no wonder that so often I can't hear you
  for the roar of the crowd that is in my world,
  for the rush of the schedule,
  for the sounds of a never-silent age
  that is full up with music boxes blaring.
 I'm weary of the noise and the hustle,
  yet I can't stop;
  No — that isn't right: rather, I won't stop
  to discover the renewal of being
  quiet in your presence.
 Yet how can I imagine
  that if in your incarnation you had to get away
  to be with your Father in peace,
  that I shouldn't need to get apart with you
  before I come apart without you?

Lord of my soul:
 May deep call to deep;
  may your voice call to my spirit stirring it to life.
 As a lover calls out 'come away with me',
  so I hear you calling me to yourself;

where I can know the embrace of your love
being set free in the intimate moment
with you alone.
May I no longer run from aloneness with you,.
but rather run to it with heart open wide.
May I no longer fear the quiet,
but rather delight in the gift of silence with you.
Lord of all:
Present to me a place where I can meet you
as a blessing of your grace.
Protect the time you alot to me
that no intrusion would come to assassinate
the precious moments of stillness with you.
Prick my heart that I may never forget, even once,
that it is you I need to fill the void in me.
Provide that retreat I so desperately need
in days of stillness,
in hours of quiet,
in minutes of rest and peace,
even in seconds when your presence is so real
that it transforms my soul.
So meet me; by your grace.   Amen.

A Benediction

May the peace of God, which transcends all human understanding, keep constant guard over your heart and mind as they
rest in knowing the love of God through Christ Jesus. And the
blessing of God Almighty, Father, Son and Holy Spirit rest upon
and abide within you now and always. Amen.

The food of God

And God spoke all these words: 'I am the Lord your God who brought you out of Egypt, out of the land of slavery. You shall have no other gods before me. You shall not make for yourself an idol in the form of anything in heaven above or on the earth beneath or in the waters below. You shall not bow down to them or worship them; for I, the Lord your God, am a jealous God.'

Present the offerings made to the Lord by fire, the food of their God.

The true worshippers will worship the Father in spirit and truth, for they are the kind of worshippers the Father seeks.

But you are a chosen people, a royal priesthood, a holy nation, a people belonging to God, that you may declare the praises of him who called you out of darkness into his wonderful light.

Through Jesus, therefore, let us continually offer to God a sacrifice of praise — the fruit of lips that confess his name.

Woe to them! They have taken the way of Cain; they have rushed for profit into Balaam's error; they have been destroyed in Korah's rebellion. These men are blemishes at your love feasts.

To him who overcomes, I will give some of the hidden manna.

(Exodus 20: 1-5; Leviticus 21: 6; John 4: 23; 1 Peter 2: 9; Hebrews 13: 15; Jude 11 and 12; Revelation 2: 17 — all NIV)

God himself first identified the offerings of the priests as his food. It's not that God needed actual meat and grain to eat. The satisfaction he sought ascended to him through the obedience of prescribed worship laid down in the tabernacle sacrifices. He wanted worship. As often as his people expected to eat, God expected his meals of praise.

Whereas demons demanded sacrifices of others as a basis for their food, God prepared his own menu — Christ. All of the work at the altar pictured God's work in Christ. The implied message is clear: God wants to be richly rewarded with worship. It is like food to him. He wants it lovingly prepared, generously offered and faithfully renewed. Nothing but Christ satisfies him.

God's method is simple: feed the people on the truths of the work of Christ and they in turn should praise him for what he has done. In the wilderness, God's singular menu of manna strengthened the people to offer him food. Now, since the cross, no better food than Christ can be found for God's servants because he is the essential ingredient of elective worship.

Those who commune with God know the value of Jesus' flesh and blood, but so do God's enemies. Demons who have been robbed of the human attentions they crave have not been able to stop the church from filling God's plate, but in many cases they have managed to spoil the taste. Tainted food will not do for God.

Offering God the praise he deserves for the unmatchable work of Christ is the true worshipper's daily work and this is God's food. For this he bought us and for this we must live. In a sense God is leading us to join him in truly living on love: his love to us in Christ and our love to him for Christ. Here is a feast of love for every day.

❧❧

Old Testament saints understood that sacrifice was central to worship and it is wrong to assume that Christian worship is not also sacrificial. Although our Lord Jesus made the one final sacrifice for our sins, never to be repeated, we are to offer what Peter calls 'spiritual sacrifices acceptable to God by Jesus Christ'. And this can be done only when one's whole attention is focused upon God, 'lost in wonder, love and praise'. Then, in fact, the worshippers receive far more than they can ever give, because the paradoxical fact is that there is no experience more completely blessed than true, spiritual worship. But it is absolutely crucial to keep these matters the right way around. Come to give, not to get. It is the only proper way!

Stuart A. Frayne, *What is Worship?*

As we come before God, we shouldn't come with empty hands. We should bring him a sacrifice! This does not mean an animal sacrifice, for Christ himself has offered himself as our sacrifice for all time. But the Old Testament principle is still true. We should bring God something. Often people get nothing out of worship because they don't come to give something to God first. The sacrifice we should bring is the sacrifice of thanksgiving and praise. And when we bring praise to God we find his presence draws near to us in a special way. Praise him that he is a great God! Praise him that he is King over all gods, the Lord over all the earth! Praise him for what he has made — the majestic mountains, the deep valleys, the rolling seas! Let's thank, praise and honour him for who he is! This focuses our attention on him and prepares our hearts for worship.

Ian Malins, *Come Let Us Worship*

Break thou the bread of life,
    Dear Lord, to me,
As thou didst break the bread
    Beside the sea.
Beyond the sacred page
    I seek thee, Lord;
My spirit pants for thee,
    O living word!

Thou art the bread of life,
    O Lord, to me,
Thy holy word the truth
    That saveth me.
Give me to eat and live

With thee above,
Teach me to love thy truth
For thou art love.

Mary Artemisia Lathbury and Alexander Groves

Soren Kierkegaard. . . watched his contemporaries in nineteenth century Denmark go to church ritualistically and participate much as they would in a theatre. The worshippers saw themselves as essentially spectators. They understood the clergy and the choir to be the main performers in the service and, if God were present at all in the process, he was a remote prompter, off in the wings somewhere. In this frame of reference, of course, the whole interaction was horizontal. It was people watching other people do certain rituals, with little depth, little awe, little real involvement on the part of the individual worshippers. To this whole way of conceiving worship, Kierkegaard thundered: 'Not so!' A church and a theatre are not similar processes at all. To worship is to do something quite different than going to a concert or a play. For one thing, the worshipper is the prime actor and God is the audience. The role of the clergy and choir is that of prompters, standing alongside the process reminding and suggesting. Worship is not something done by the clergy for the worshippers' perusal, but something worshippers do for God out of their own depths.

John Claypool, *Worship as Involvement*

To us a human is primarily food; our aim is the absorption of its will into ours, the increase of our own area of selfhood at its expense. But the obedience which the Enemy demands of humans is quite a different thing. One must face the fact that all the talk about his love for them, and his service being perfect freedom, is not (as one would gladly believe) mere propaganda, but an appalling truth. He really *does* want to fill the universe with a lot of loathsome little replicas of himself — creatures whose life, on its miniature scale, will be qualitatively like his own, not because he has absorbed them, but because their wills freely conform to his. We want cattle who can finally become food; he wants servants who can finally become his children. We want to suck in, he wants to give out. We are empty and would be filled; he is full and flows over. Our war aim is a world in which Our Father Below has drawn all other beings into himself: the Enemy wants a world full of beings united to him but still distinct.

Screwtape in C.S. Lewis, *The Screwtape Letters*

I'm deathly afraid of personal spiritual deterioration, of having a name that I'm alive when I'm really dead. . . The present crisis won't be solved by Christians who get their food and weapons secondhand. It will be solved by people who walk with God, who feed on his word, who have strength for the battle, and who know how to use the sword of the Spirit. We need a return to the old-fashioned spiritual disciplines of life.

Warren Wiersbe, *The Integrity Crisis*

We're here to be worshippers first and workers only second. We take a convert and immediately make that new Christian a worker. God never meant it to be so. God meant that a convert should learn to be a worshipper, and after that he or she can learn to be a worker. . . The work done by a worshipper will have eternity in it.

A.W. Tozer, *Great Quotes & Illustrations*

I want deliberately to encourage this mighty longing after God. The lack of it has brought us to our present low estate. The stiff and wooden quality about our religious lives is a result of our lack of holy desire. Complacency is a deadly foe to all spiritual growth. Acute desire must be present or there will be no manifestation of Christ to his people. He waits to be wanted. Too bad that with many of us he waits so long, so very long, in vain.

A.W. Tozer in *The Best of A.W. Tozer*

Heavenly Father, I rejoice in the immutable, absolute truth of your word. In your grace, keep me from knowing only the letter of truth and sound doctrine. Let it enter my spirit, let it control my mind, let it stabilise and energise my emotions. I will to apply your truth aggressively and to depend upon its power to defeat all of my enemies. Through the intercessory work of the Holy Spirit and in the name of my Lord Jesus Christ, I thank you for hearing this petition. Amen.

Mark Bubeck, *The Adversary*

Grant, almighty God, that as we are inclined not only to superstitions, but also to many vices, we may be restrained by thy word; and as thou art pleased daily to remind us of thy benefits, that thou mayest keep us in the practice of true religion. O grant that we may not be led astray by the delusions of Satan and by our own vanity, but continue firm and steady in our obedience to thee, and constantly proceed in the course of true piety, so that we may at length partake of its fruit in thy celestial kingdom, which has been obtained for us by the blood of thine only begotten Son. Amen.

John Calvin

A Benediction
May the Father show you his mercy by enriching you in the grace which enlightens your eyes to the greater glories of Jesus so that you may be refreshed in the communion of the Father's love and overflow with praise and thanksgiving. May the Spirit of Truth capture your mind and heart with an ever deepening knowledge of the holy. Amen.

5

A God who works wonders

[The brothers] left Egypt and went back home to their father Jacob in Canaan. 'Joseph is still alive!' they told him. 'He is the ruler of all Egypt!' Jacob was stunned and could not believe them.

When the Lord brought us back to Jerusalem, it was like a dream! How we laughed, how we sang for joy! Then the other nations said about us, 'The Lord did great things for them'. Indeed he did great things for us. . .

[Jesus] said this and showed them his hands and his feet. They still could not believe, they were so full of joy and wonder. . .

So Peter was kept in jail, but the people of the church were praying earnestly to God for him. . . Peter knocked at the outside door, and a servant-girl named Rhoda came to answer it. She recognised Peter's voice and was so happy that she ran back in without opening the door, and announced that Peter was standing outside. 'You are mad!' they told her. But she insisted that it was true. So they answered, 'It is his angel'. Meanwhile Peter kept on knocking. At last they opened the door, and when they saw him, they were amazed.

. . .the Son of God, who loved me and gave his life for me.

I do have faith, but not enough. Help me to have more!

(Genesis 45: 25 and 26; Psalm 126: 1-3; Luke 24: 40 and 41; Acts 12: 5, 13-16; Galatians 2: 20; Mark 9: 24 — all GNB)

It was the first lecture of the diploma course and I was

briefly surveying the history and religion of Israel. When I recounted the story of God's decisive intervention at the time of the Exodus, there was a sudden exclamation of 'How marvellous!' from one of the forty or so students crowded into the class. Startled by such an unusual occurrence in a normally sedate group, I traced its source to a frail-looking young man — he looked as though the proverbial puff of wind would blow him over. A few minutes later, when we came to the point where God, in his grace, made a covenant with Israel, he exclaimed, 'That's terrific!'

Back in the staff common room I confided to my colleagues that we had something of an oddity in the first year diploma class. That was when I discovered that Richard — his name — was in fact an acute asthmatic who was so frail that he had never attended school; his entire education had been by a personal tutor who had encouraged dialogue and interaction.

Sadly, Richard quickly adapted to the 'hallelujah-less, take-it-for-granted' atmosphere so characteristic of so much of our Christian community. We know the story, perhaps too well, and it fails to excite us. But God is a God of miracles; all things are possible with him (Luke 1: 37) and he *does* surprise and delight us. So often he works for us in *ways that appear almost too good to be true*.

It was so with Jacob. There was nothing he could have wished for more than to know that Joseph, his long-lost son, was alive. The joyous assertion of the brothers (Genesis 45: 26) was, for him, too good to be believed. But Joseph *was alive!*

Or consider Israel in exile in the iron grip of a conqueror who had devastated its land, destroyed its capital and decimated its population. It seemed like a dream when God moved the heart of a heathen king (Ezra 1) and the captives, their long exile over, were back in Judea once more (Psalm 126). *But it was not a dream* and the God who controlled events on the international scene then is the same today.

Even our prayer life can be permeated by a strange mixture of faith and unbelief. Picture that prayer meeting in Jerusalem (Acts 12) when Peter was under sentence of death: the earnest petitions, the remembrance of God's miraculous interventions in the past. Yet when Peter, very much alive and well, arrived on the doorstep, those godly prayer-warriors were incredulous, unable to accept what God had done! Knowing how often we pray without any conviction of a divine response, we are hesitant to criticise those disciples, but God *does* work in answer to prayer!

Think, too, of the bleak despair and hopelessness of the disciples after the death of their Master. They were shattered men. How they must have longed for the tumultuous events of those days to be reversed and for their Lord to be restored to them! If ever there was a thing too good to be true, this was it! Luke 24: 41 (RSV) has the strange, almost contradictory statement — 'they still disbelieved for joy'.

But it *did* happen! Jesus was alive! He had broken forever the bonds of sin, death and the grave! He had answered decisively that age-old question, 'Is there a way out into the unknown — a bridge into eternity?' Yes, there is. Jesus has pioneered that way and we may travel it.

All these miracles are well documented historical facts. But there is a miracle which takes place in our personal experience, the miracle of Christ's redeeming love for the individual: 'the Son of God loved *me* and gave his life for me' (Galatians 2:20). How impossible that must seem! I can comprehend that 'God loved the world' (John 3: 16) — the world is a big place, with millions of people. But for the Son of God to love me — just one amongst five thousand million people in the world today — in a universe so immense! It seems too good to be true. But this is the glory of the gospel and its message of redeeming love. It reaches right down to the individual, it is personal and we can both accept it and rejoice in it.

'What is man, that you think of him;
mere man, that you care for him?' (Psalm 8: 4, GNB)

P.S. And Richard? He longed to serve Christ amongst young people, but in a few brief years after leaving college his frail body gave up the struggle. I can well imagine what he has been exclaiming since! 'How marvellous!

That's terrific!' *There is so much more!*

❄❄❄

The validity of the Christian faith rests on one supreme miracle: the cornerstone upon which the whole superstructure of Christianity rises or falls, depends on the truth of this miracle — the resurrection of Jesus Christ. . .

No other religion has ever dared to put forth this challenge, has ever dared to make its appeal *to* miracles, and rest its appeal *on* a miracle.

Kathryn Kuhlman, *I Believe in Miracles*

So often we pray with such little belief in the efficacy of prayer that we are 'astonished' when the answer comes. How we need the word of Mark 11: 34, 'When you pray, believe that you receive. . . and you shall have. . .' Other conditions being satisfied, this believing before receiving is a mighty prayer secret.

Guy H. King, *A Day at a Time*

Each of us is created in God's own image, and it means that, though we are creatures and full of sins and defects, there is the deep-down likeness between us and God, and our destiny is to be with him. When we say that God loves us we mean that he cares for each single one of us as if there is no-one else for him to care for.

He cares for you in all that unique individuality which is yours. He wants *you* to be with him forever, to share with you all that he has to share.

The wonderful thing about man is that he is described as being in God's own image. Not that God and man are identical in all respects — far from it. God remains the Creator, and we always remain creatures, utterly dependent upon him. Yet there is a true affinity between God and man. Man has powers of memory, thought, consciousness, purpose, appreciation of beauty, appreciation of truth, moral distinction between right and wrong, and a rare potential of freedom. Above all, he has the possibility of really knowing God, and having fellowship with God.

Michael Ramsey, former Archbishop of Canterbury

It is a thing most wonderful,
almost too wonderful to be,
That God's own Son should come from heav'n,
And die to save a child like me.
And yet I know that it is true. . .'

William Walsham How

God commends his love —
Greater could not be —
While I was a sinner,
Jesus died for me.

George Goodman

Why did he love me? I never can tell.
Why did he suffer to save me from hell?
Nothing but infinite grace from above
Could have conceived such a story of love

G.R. Harding Wood

Here might I stay and sing,
No story so divine;
Never was love, dear King!
Never was grief like thine!
This is my friend,
In whose sweet praise
I all my days
Could gladly spend.

Samuel Crossman

What can I offer the Lord
for all his goodness to me?

Psalm 116: 12, GNB

Love so amazing, so divine,
Demands my soul, my life, my all!

Isaac Watts

We may have as much of God as we will. Christ. . . bids
us take all we want. If a man is admitted into the bullion
vault of a bank and told to help himself and comes out
with one cent, whose fault is it that he is poor? Whose

fault is it that Christian people generally have such scanty portions of the free riches of God?

Alexander Maclaren

Lord, I thank you for the gift of love; indeed I am fearfully and wonderfully made. I praise you for all that goodness and tender mercy which have surrounded me all the days of my life; for those divine interventions, both great and small, which have marked out the days and years of my pilgrimage.

Above all, I thank you for the miracle of the new birth in your Son, my Saviour, Jesus Christ, that in him I am a new creation. Like Paul, I confess myself to be the chief of sinners, but you loved me and you have bound me to yourself, eternally, by your love and grace. I cannot fully understand such love, but I can and do rejoice in it; I cannot begin to comprehend why you should choose such a person as I am to serve you, but I gratefully accept that role as your servant — and the servant of all, for the sake of Jesus Christ.

Help me never to take you for granted; never to lose sight of the wonder of your love; never to cease to respond sacrificially to your love; never to lose the hope of seeing the miracle wrought out in my life worked out in the lives of those about me, however unresponsive they may seem to be.

A Benediction
Go into this day in the consciousness that the Lord God Almighty invited you to walk with him. May the humility which marks out the person who walks daily with God be accompanied by a sense of your thrill and wonder at the way in which the Almighty works in your life and in his world — today.

Send my roots rain

(Gerard Manley Hopkins)

But I desire to speak to the Almighty and to argue my case with God. . . Though he slay me, yet will I hope in him; I will surely defend my ways to his face. . . Now that I have prepared my case, I know I will be vindicated. Can anyone bring charges against me? If so, I will be silent and die. Only grant me these two things, O God, and then I will not hide from you: Withdraw your hand far from me, and stop frightening me with your terrors. Then summon me and I will answer, or let me speak, and you reply. How many wrongs and sins have I committed? Show me my offence and my sin. Why do you hide your face and consider me your enemy? Will you torment a wind-blown leaf? Will you chase after dry chaff?

Then Job replied to the Lord: 'I know that you can do all things; no plan of yours can be thwarted. You asked, "Who is this that obscures my counsel without knowledge?" Surely I spoke of things I did not understand, things too wonderful for me to know. You said, "Listen now, and I will speak; I will question you, and you shall answer me." My ears had heard of you, but now my eyes have seen you. Therefore I despise myself and repent in dust and ashes.'

My God, my God, why have you forsaken me? Why are you so far from saving me, so far from the words of my groaning? O my God, I cry out by day, but you do not answer, by night, and am not silent.

Yet you are enthroned as the Holy One; you are the praise of Israel. In you our fathers put their trust; they trusted and you delivered them. They cried to you and

were saved; in you they trusted and were not disappointed.

But I am a worm and not a man, scorned by men and
despised by the people. All who see me mock me.
They hurl insults, shaking their heads: 'He trusts in the
Lord; let the Lord rescue him. Let him deliver him, since
he delights in him.'

(Job 13: 3, 15, 18-25; Job 42: 1-6; Psalm 22: 1-8 — all NIV)

'It's not fair,' my five-year-old daughter used to declare.
And I had to agree with her that life is very seldom fair.
But we have the conviction that God, at least, ought to
be fair. If we serve him faithfully, there should be the
rewards of service, some blessing, some recognition that
we are doing well. On the other hand, we agree with
David that evil men ought not to prosper. The schemers,
the manipulators, the self-seekers ought to be punished as
they deserve.

Yet anyone who has been some distance on the Christian
way knows that it does not always work out that way.
Often our best efforts meet with disappointment and
failure so that others say to us, 'Is it really worth it? What
are you achieving?' I suppose we should not be surprised
at this situation, for Jesus never promised us 'success' as
a result of our ministry; quite the reverse. And there are
plenty of examples in scripture of those who walked by
faith, yet saw no mighty 'results'.

It doesn't make us feel any better about it. How can
God treat us this way, when we have tried with our whole
hearts to obey and serve him? Is it his fault or ours?

God does not defend himself or answer our complaints.
But he does come close to us and reveal himself to us.

❦

I struck the board and cried, 'No more;
I will abroad.
What? shall I ever sigh and pine?
My lines and life are free; free as the road,
Loose as the wind, as large as store.

Shall I be still in suit?
Have I no harvest but a thorn
To let me blood and not restore
What I have lost with cordial fruit?
Sure there was wine
Before my sighs did dry it; there was corn
Before my tears did drown it;
Is the year only lost to me?
Have I no bays to crown it,
No flowers, no garlands gay? All blasted,
All wasted?
Not so, my heart; but there is fruit,
And thou hast hands.
Recover all thy sigh-blown age
On double pleasures: leave thy cold dispute
Of what is fit and not; forsake thy cage,
Thy rope of sands
Which petty thoughts have made; and made to thee
Good cable, to enforce and draw,
And be thy law,
While thou didst wink and wouldst not see.
Away; take heed;
I will abroad.
Call in thy death's head there; tie up thy fears.
He that forbears
To suit and serve his need
Deserves his load.
But as I raved, and grew more fierce and wild
At every word,
Methought I heard one calling, 'Child!'
And I replied, 'My Lord.'

George Herbert, 'The Collar'

Thou art indeed just, Lord, if I contend
With thee; but, sir, so what I plead is just.
Why do sinners' ways prosper? and why must
Disappointment all I endeavour end?
Wert thou my enemy, O thou my friend,
How wouldst thou worse, I wonder, than thou dost
Defeat, thwart me? Oh the sots and thralls of lust

Do in spare house more thrive than I that spend,
Sir, life upon thy cause. See banks and brakes
Now, leaved how thick! laced they are again
With fretty chervil, look, and fresh wind shakes
Them; birds build — but not I build: no, but strain,
Time's eunuch, and not breed one work that wakes.
Mine, O thou Lord of life, send my roots rain.
Gerard Manley Hopkins, 'Thou art indeed just'

Sometimes the establishment of this degree of prayer
comes by way of a painful inward struggle and aridity;
what St John of the Cross has described as 'the night of
the senses' — a period of distress and obscurity in which
it seems to the soul that it is losing all it had gained of
the life of prayer. . . It meets and must conquer many
resistances in the active mind, must cut for itself new
paths; and this may involve tensions and suffering and
the apparent withdrawal of the ordinary power of prayer.
Evelyn Underhill, *Collected Papers*

The mystics down the centuries have often referred to 'the
dark night of the soul'. This describes those periods when
God seems strangely silent and absent in spite of personal
need. We wonder what he is doing, why he is withholding his presence from us. We pray to him, but the heavens
seem as brass and we feel trapped by the prison of our
own dark moods. 'The greatest test of a Christian's life
is to live with the silence of God,' wrote Bishop Mervyn
Stockwood in a letter to me recently. How far can we
keep trusting God when we have no experience of his
love? Is it enough to take him at his word when we feel
no reality behind those familiar phrases?
David Watson, *Fear No Evil*

It's no fun, Lord, I can't keep anything for myself,
The flower that I pick fades in my hands.
My laugh freezes on my lips.
The waltz I dance leaves me restless and uneasy.
Everything seems empty,
Everything seems hollow,

You have made a desert around me.
I am hungry and thirsty,
And the whole world cannot satisfy me.
And yet I loved you Lord; what have I done to you?
I worked for you; I gave myself for you.
O great and terrible God,
What more do you want?

Child, I want more for you and for the world.
Until now you have planned your actions,
    but I have no need of them.
You have asked for my approval, you have asked for
    my support,
    You have wanted to interest me in your work.
But don't you see, child, that you were reversing the
    roles.
I have watched you, I have seen your goodwill,
And I want more than you now.
You will no longer do your own works, but the will
    of your Father in heaven.

Michel Quoist, *Prayers of Life*

I know now, Lord, why you utter no answer. You are
yourself the answer. Before your face, questions die away.
What other answer would suffice?

C. S. Lewis, *Till We have Faces*

---

*Lord, all our lives we have been taught to believe that when we
needed you, you would always be there. We have grown up
with the idea that if we seek to do your will, you will surely
bless us. But it doesn't always work out that way. It is so
hard to understand that we may be in your will and yet fail.
It is so difficult to stand by and see others riding the crest of
the wave while we struggle and flounder. We confess that we
resent it. We blame them. We blame you. We blame ourselves.
We demand explanations. We sink into waves of depression
until we are near drowning in our own tears.*

*In our hearts we know we cannot put you on trial. You do
not have to defend yourself. But in your love, O Lord, draw*

near to us. Fill our emptiness with your presence, so that we do not need to be filled with the gratification of success. Make us content to be yours, and to leave the answers in your hands.
  Amen.

A Benediction
Now may the God, who blesses us in ways we do not always recognise — who himself, in Jesus, bore the pain of rejection and desolation, who through the Holy Spirit draws near to fill our emptiness — send the rain to seep through to our roots and bring us to life again. Amen.

7

Our watchword is security

(William Pitt)

Leave your country, your people and your father's household and go to the land I will show you. . . So Abram left, as the Lord had told him.

[The Lord] protected them and cared for them, as he would protect himself. Like an eagle teaching its young to fly, catching them safely on its spreading wings, the Lord kept Israel from falling.

'Good teacher, what must I do to inherit eternal life?'. . . 'One thing you lack,' [Jesus] said. 'Go, sell everything you have and give to the poor, and you will have treasure in heaven. Then come, follow me.' At this the man's face fell. He went away sad, because he had great wealth. 'We here,' [Peter] said, 'have left everything to become your followers.' Jesus said, 'I tell you this: there is no-one who has given up home, brothers or sisters, mother, father or children, or land, for my sake and for the gospel, who will not receive in this age a hundred times as much — houses, brothers and sisters, mothers and children, and land — and persecutions besides; and in the age to come eternal life.'

God is our refuge and strength, an ever present help in trouble. Therefore we will not fear, though the earth give way and the mountains fall into the heart of the sea, though its waters roar and foam and the mountains quake with their surging.

The steadfast love of the Lord never ceases, his mercies never come to an end; they are new every morning; great is thy faithfulness.

Do not be anxious about anything, but in everything, by prayer and petition, with thanksgiving, present your requests to God.   And the peace of God, which transcends all understanding, will guard your hearts and your minds in Christ Jesus.

The inheritance to which we are born is one that nothing can destroy or spoil or wither.   It is kept for you in heaven. . .   This is cause for great joy, even though now you smart for a little while, if need be, under trials of many kinds.   Even gold passes through the assayer's fire, and more precious than perishable gold is faith which has stood the test.   These trials come so that your faith may prove itself worthy of all praise, glory and honour when Jesus Christ is revealed.

(Genesis 12: 1 and 4, NIV; Deuteronomy 32: 10 and 11, GNB; Mark 10: 17, 21 and 22, NIV; Mark 10: 28-30, NEB; Psalm 46: 1-3, NIV; Lamentations 3: 22 and 23, RSV; Philippians 4: 6 and 7, NIV; 1 Peter 1: 4-7, NEB)

'Our watchword is security!' Thus proclaimed the eighteenth-century Earl of Chatham, William Pitt. It is not difficult to imagine a scene in which this confident assertion might have been made in a stirring speech to parliament. Was Pitt making a policy statement on behalf of a political party in a time of national vulnerability, or was he boasting of some military or commercial success? Was it an optimistic cry of determination, or an expression of a vain hope? The context has been lost, so we can only speculate these two centuries later. But somehow we can resonate with these words: *our* watchword is security, too.

Security is that which keeps us untroubled by danger or apprehension, safe against attack and confident concerning the future. And, deep down, most of us search for it. We long for predictability, reliability, stability — most of the time anyway, even if we are ardent seekers of adventure. We prize the notion that we should be able, by careful planning and good fortune, to survive the vagaries of life that will inevitably buffet our small corner of the world somehow, some time.

We tend to go to great lengths to procure whatever security we can. We lock our houses against burglars to make sure we do not lose what we already have, and we insure our possessions and our health — and even our lives — just in case the unthinkable should happen to us. We set aside financial resources for our retirement, old age or just a 'rainy day', and fret about the effects of unpredictable interest rates and stock market volatility on our investments. We hold tightly to our jobs, even if they are not lucrative and prestigious, because they are a symbol of our future well-being. We search for meaningful relationships that we hope will provide support and comfort for whatever joys and sorrows life brings us. And we hope, perhaps against hope that, whatever politicians and super-powers may decide to do, our community, our nation and our world will not crumble beneath us.

Sometimes we have, paradoxically, to lose our security before we can find it. Perhaps we suffer some deep loss — a person, a marriage, employment, health — and our once-comfortable lives become suddenly insecure, unpredictable. It is at such times that we have special opportunities to take our eyes from what the world considers to be the basis of security to renew our vision of what God sees as the basis of security: 'Do not worry about your life, what you will eat or drink; or about your body, what you will wear. . . Who of you by worrying can add a single hour to your life?. . . Seek first [your heavenly Father's] kingdom and his righteousness, and all these things will be given to you as well' (Matthew 6: 25, 27 and 33, NIV). In times of prosperity and contentment that may sound like glib, idealistic advice, but in times of adversity and hopelessness there is nothing else worth clinging to.

Our watchword *is* security — the security of knowing that nothing can separate us from the love of God and the completion of his purposes in our lives and in the universe.

❦

In our production-orientated society, being busy, having an occupation, has become one of the main ways, if not *the* main way, of identifying ourselves. Without an occupation, not just our economic security but our very identity is endangered. . .

More enslaving than our occupations, however, are our preoccupations. To be *pre*-occupied means to fill our time and place long before we are there. This is worrying in the more specific sense of the word. It is a mind filled with 'ifs'. We say to ourselves, 'What if I get the flu? What if I lose my job? What if my child is not home on time? What if there is not enough food tomorrow? What if I am attacked? What if war starts? What if the world comes to an end? What if. . .?' All these 'ifs' fill our minds with anxious thoughts and make us wonder constantly what to do and what to say in case something should happen in the future. Much, if not most, of our suffering is connected with these preoccupations. Possible career changes, possible family conflicts, possible illnesses, possible disaster and a possible nuclear holocaust make us anxious, fearful, suspicious, greedy, nervous and morose. They prevent us from feeling a real inner freedom. Since we are always preparing for eventualities, we seldom fully trust the moment. It is not an exaggeration to say that much human energy is invested in these fearful preoccupations. Our individual as well as communal lives are so deeply moulded by our worries about tomorrow that today hardly can be experienced.

Henri Nouwen, *Making All Things New*

Happy the ones, and happy they alone,
They, who can call to-day their own:
They who, secure within, can say,
'Tomorrow do your worst, for I have lived today.'

John Dryden, 'Horace'

Jesus does not respond to our worry-filled way of living by saying that we should not be so busy with worldly affairs. He does not try to pull us away from the many events, activities and people that make up our lives. He does not tell us that what we do is unimportant, valueless or useless. Nor does he suggest that we should withdraw from our involvements and live quiet, restful lives removed from the struggles of the world.

Jesus' response to our worry-filled lives is quite different. He asks us to shift the point of gravity, to relocate the centre of our attention, to change our priorities. Jesus wants us to move from the 'many things' to the 'one necessary thing'. It is important for us to realise that Jesus in no way wants us to leave our many-faceted world. Rather, he wants us to live in it, but firmly rooted in the centre of all things. Jesus does not speak about a change of activities, a change in contacts or even a change of pace. He speaks about a change of heart. This change of heart makes everything different, even while everything appears to remain the same. This is the meaning of 'Set your hearts on his kingdom first. . . and all these other things will be given you as well.' What counts is where our hearts are. When we worry, we have our hearts in the wrong place. Jesus asks us to move our hearts to the centre, where all other things fall into place.

Henri Nouwen, *Making All Things New*

Contemporary culture is plagued by the passion to possess. The unreasoned boast abounds that the good life is found in accumulation, that 'more is better'. . . Furthermore, the pace of the modern world accentuates our sense of being fractured and fragmented. We feel strained, hurried, breathless. The complexity of rushing to achieve and accumulate more and more frequently threatens to overwhelm us; it seems there is no escape from the rat race.

Christian simplicity frees us from this modern mania. It brings sanity to our compulsive extravagance, and peace to our frantic spirit. . . It allows us to see material things for what they are — goods to enhance life, not to oppress life. People once again become more important than possessions. Simplicity enables us to live lives of integrity in the face of the terrible realities of our global village. . .

Turn your back on all high pressure competitive situations that make climbing the ladder the central focus. The fruit of the Spirit is not push, drive, climb, grasp and trample. Don't let the rat-racing world keep you on its treadmill. There is a legitimate place for blood, sweat and tears; but it should have its roots in the call of God, not

in the desire to get ahead. Life is more than a climb to
the top of the heap.

Richard Foster, *Freedom of Simplicity*

To the Christian, the quest for success in certain areas can
be hazardous. The pitfalls are many and the temptations
to sin, subtle. In our culture so much emphasis is placed
on material things that it is easy to think of success only
in terms of money, possessions, power or prestige. But is
this all there is to success? Should the search for achievement be confined to them? Should not the Christian also
think of being successful in those qualities of human existence that have eternal value? It seems to me that we
can *only* satisfy our deep need for fulfilment by being
successful in honesty, charity, patience, spirituality and the
development of desirable personality characteristics.

Archibald D. Hart, *The Success Factor*

When I reached El Aboid Sidi Seik for the novitiate, my
novice master told me with the perfect calm of a man who
had lived twenty years in the desert: '*Il faut faire une
coupure, Carlo.*' I knew what kind of cutting he was talking
about and decided to make the wrench, even if it were
painful.

In my bag I had kept a thick notebook, containing the
addresses of my old friends; there were thousands of them.
In his goodness God had never left me without the joys
of friendship. If there was one thing I really regretted
when I left for Africa, it was not being able to speak to
each one of them, to explain the reason for my abandoning
them, to say that I was obeying a call from God and that,
even if in a different way, I would continue to fight on
with them to work for the kingdom.

But it was necessary to make the 'cut' and it demanded
courage and great faith in God. I took the address book,
which for me was the last tie with the past, and burnt it
behind a dune during a day's retreat. I can still see the
black ashes of the notebook being swept away into the
distance by the wind of the Sahara.

But burning an address is not the same thing as destroying a friendship, for that I never intended to do; on the contrary, I have never loved nor prayed so much for my old friends as in the solitude of the desert. I saw their faces, I felt their problems, their sufferings, sharpened by the distance between us.

Carlo Carretto, *Letters from the Desert*

Sometimes you need to feel that you are lost, sinking, desolate, alone, if you want to feel for sure that God is there, hands holding you even in your mini-hell. . . I do not recommend hell, not even a mini-hell, to anyone. Hell, anyone's hell, hurts too much. So if you can feel God in your mini-heavens of all-rightness, be content. But there is a chance that you may have to make your bed in hell, some time, and you may feel as if you had fallen there before your time, alone, helpless, everything gone wrong at the core, instant God-forsakenness.

If you do, or when you do, you may, as I did, feel God closer to you than when everything was heavenly. God is there, ahead of time, before you get there, waiting, hands open, to hold you when you are sure you are sinking. You will feel his presence, feel his strength, feel the courage that comes from his support, if you just let him hold you. And when you do feel him, you will know that it will be all right with you, at that moment, later, or any time. . . You will know it, too, when you feel yourself falling out of reach of the human hands you need, falling away from them and landing in God's hands. You will feel, at bottom, that no-one but God himself is holding you and you will know that, in spite of everything, it all is right with you.

Lewis Smedes, *How Can it be Right When Everything is all Wrong?*

O God, our help in ages past,
our hope for years to come,
our shelter from the stormy blast,
and our eternal home:
under the shadow of thy throne
thy saints have dwelt secure;

sufficient is thine arm alone,
and our defence is sure.

Isaac Watts

Lord, you are my constant companion.
There is no need that you cannot fulfil.
Whether your course for me points to the mountaintops of glorious ecstasy or to the valleys of human suffering, you are by my side, you are ever present with me.
You are close beside me when I tread the dark streets of danger.
And even when I flirt with death itself, you will not leave me.
When the pain is severe, you are near to comfort.
When the burden is heavy, you are there to lean upon.
When depression darkens my soul, you touch me with eternal joy.
When I feel empty and alone, you fill the aching vacuum with your power.
My security is in your promise to be near me always, and in the knowledge that you will never let me go.

adapted from Leslie F. Brant, 'Psalm 23'

A Benediction

To him who is able to keep you from falling, and to bring you faultless and joyful before his glorious presence — to the only God our Saviour, through Jesus Christ our Lord, be glory, majesty, might and authority, from all ages past and now and for ever and ever! Amen.

Jude 24-25, GNB

Holy, holy, holy

In the year of King Uzziah's death I saw the Lord Yahweh seated on a high throne; his train filled the sanctuary; above him stood seraphs, each one with six wings: two to cover its face, two to cover its feet and two for flying. And they cried out to one another in this way, 'Holy, holy, holy is Yahweh Sabaoth. His glory fills the whole earth.'

Who among the gods is your like, Yahweh? Who is your like, majestic in holiness?

Play music in Yahweh's honour, you devout, remember his holiness and praise him.

Each of the four animals had six wings and had eyes all the way round as well as inside; and day and night they never stopped singing: 'Holy, holy, holy is the Lord God, the Almighty; he was, he is and he is to come.'

And they made coats of fine linen of woven work for Aaron. . . And they made the plate of the holy crown of pure gold, and wrote upon it in a writing, like to the engravings of a signet, *Holiness to the Lord*.

Be holy in all you do, since it is the Holy One who has called you, and scripture says: Be holy, for I am holy.

(Isaiah 6: 1-3, JB; Exodus 15: 11, JB; Psalm 30: 4, JB; Revelation 4: 8, JB; Exodus 39: 27 and 30, KJV; 1 Peter 1: 14-15, JB)

When Joseph was being enticed by Lady Potiphar, he responded to her, 'How could I do such a wicked thing and sin against God?' Joseph had a lofty view of God's holiness, a view sadly on the decline in our age. The question often asked these days is, 'Where do I have to draw the line?' We want to know how far we can accommodate the world without offending our God.

Can we, the people of a holy God, be content with any less than the highest standards for our own lives? We need to examine ourselves for those areas where we have compromised with the world's systems. Daily we need to ask, 'Have I lowered my standards to gain peer approval rather than purge my life of every unchristlike trait?' The prayer of our heart ought to be that of an aged saint: 'Lord, make me as holy as a saved sinner can be.'

Two college boys were trying to smuggle a goat, the school mascot, into their dormitory room. Going up the stairwell one boy said to the other, 'What about the smell?' His room-mate replied, 'He'll just have to get used to it!' College boys may be content to take such a laissez-faire attitude to a dirty environment, but our holy God will not.

In the Old Testament, the Lord had a temple for his people; in the New Testament he has a people for his temple. And a holy God is entitled to the highest possible standards from us if we are to be his habitation.

We are not commanded to be mighty and wise, as God is mighty and wise, but 'be holy as I am holy'. The declarations of his power are to enforce our subjection, those of his wisdom to encourage our direction by him; but this only to attract our imitation. . . We do not so glorify God by elevated admirations, or eloquent expressions, or pompous services of him, as when we aspire to conversing with him with unstained spirits, and live for him in living like him.

Stephen Charnock, *The Existence and Attributes of God*

What people are waiting for from the church, whether they realise it or not, is that the church of today show them the gospel. Our contemporaries want to meet Christ who is alive today; they want to see him with their eyes and touch him with their hands. Like those pilgrims who approached Philip one day, they say to us, 'we want to see Jesus'. Our contemporaries want a meeting face to face with Christ. The challenge for us Christians is that they demand to see Christ in each one of us; they want us to reflect Christ as clearly as a pane of glass transmits the rays of the sun. Whatever is opaque and besmirched in us disfigures the face of Christ in the church. What the unbeliever reproaches us with is not that we are Christians, but that we are not Christian enough: that is the tragedy.

Cardinal Suenens

We are never duly touched and impressed with a conviction of our insignificance, until we have contrasted ourselves with the majesty of God.

John Calvin

We must have the conviction that it is God's will that we seek holiness — regardless of how arduous and painful the seeking may be. And we must be confident that the pursuit of holiness results in God's approval and blessing, even when circumstances make it appear otherwise.

Jerry Bridges, *The Pursuit of Holiness*

If I ask myself 'What things must I rather die for than betray?' then I will know what things for me are holy.

John Baillie, *Our Knowledge of God*

Study leads to precision, precision leads to zeal, zeal leads to cleanliness, cleanliness leads to restraint, restraint leads to purity, purity leads to holiness, holiness leads to meekness, meekness leads to fear of sin, fear of sin leads to saintliness, saintliness leads to the possession of the holy spirit, the holy spirit leads to life eternal, and saintliness is greater than any of these.

Rabbi Phineas b. Jair

It is not the importance of the thing, but the majesty of the Lawgiver, that is to be the standard of obedience. . . Some, indeed, might reckon such minute and arbitrary rules as these (in Leviticus) as trifling. But the principle involved in obedience or disobedience was none other than the same principle which was tried in Eden at the foot of the forbidden tree. It is really this: Is the Lord to be obeyed in *all* things whatsoever he commands? Is he a holy Lawgiver?

Andrew Bonar, *A Commentary on Leviticus*

It is holy wrath, the wrath of the Holy One about the failure to stress the holy, about our rebellion against God's holy will, which is the truth. But this wrath is not an emotion which resembles anything we know in human experience; it is the inevitable necessary reaction of the will of God to all that opposes him. God takes the fact that he is God 'seriously' — and this is the only thing that is wholly serious, and from which all that is really serious is derived. 'God is not mocked.' Both the negative and the positive aspects of the divine energy of will are inseparable from the divine being of God. What kind of God would he be if he did not care whether people took him seriously or not? Since God takes himself absolutely seriously, he gives seriousness to life. If God did not take himself seriously, what else could be taken seriously?

Emil Brunner, *The Christian Doctrine of God*

God wants us to walk in *obedience*, not victory. Obedience is oriented toward God; victory is oriented toward self.

Jerry Bridges, *The Pursuit of Holiness*

Father, who is like you in all the universe? You are:
  awesome in holiness,
   pristine in purity,
    radiant in righteousness,
     majestic in glory,
      drenched in splendour.
We confess that we have not lived up to your image which we bear. By comparison all our righteousness is as filthy rags. Forgive us for lowering our standards and being content to be less holy than you are.
Father, we thank you that in Jesus Christ that image can be

renewed. We praise you that by your matchless grace we can be recreated into your image by receiving the righteousness of Jesus Christ anew through Calvary. Open our eyes today to see our lives as you see them, to see the contamination in our words and deeds and attitudes. Sanctify us through and through. Imbue us with your glory and splendour in Christ Jesus that your name may be magnified through our lives today. Amen.

A Benediction

May the thrice-holy God of Israel be with you this day as you go forth under the banner of his Name to reflect his splendour before the world. May his strength empower you, his wisdom guide you, his honour motivate you as you live in greater holiness for him. Amen.

Pick up your tab

In the beginning God created the universe.

In the beginning was the Word.

For God loved the world so much that he gave.

Love the Lord your God. . . and. . . your neighbour as you love yourself.

Shameless nation, come to your senses. . . Turn to the Lord, all you humble people of the land, who obey his commands. Do what is right, and humble yourselves before the Lord.

At that time the kingdom of heaven will be like this. Once there were ten girls who took their oil lamps and went off to meet the bridegroom. Five of them were foolish and five of them were wise.

Once there was a man who had to go on a journey; he called his servants and put them in charge of his property. He gave to each one according to his ability: to one he gave five thousand silver coins, to another he gave two thousand, and to another he gave one thousand. Then he left on his journey. After a long time the master of the servants came back.

Peter spoke up and said to Jesus, 'I will never leave you, even though all the rest do!'

'When, Lord, did we ever see you hungry and feed you, or thirsty and give you drink? When did we see you a stranger and welcome you in our homes, or naked and clothe you? When did we ever see you sick or in prison, and visit you?'

(Genesis 1: 1, GNB; John 1: 1, NIV; John 3: 16, GNB; Matthew 22: 37 and 39, GNB; Zephaniah 2: 1 and 3, GNB; Matthew 25: 1-2, 14, 15 and 19, GNB; Matthew 26: 33, GNB; Matthew 25: 37-39, GNB)

Christianity is not a private religion, but the religion of Jesus and those who profess it are accountable to him. No more or less.

Some who want to avoid accountability often say, 'My faith is my own — a very private matter. I don't have to associate with other Christians or share my faith or go to church because you can be nearer God's heart in a garden than anywhere else on earth.' It's not as easy or as nice as that. To be part of the Body of Christ is to be responsible to him and responsible for each other.

Those who have a 'private faith' wouldn't dream of claiming a 'private science', or 'private economic system' or 'private rules of the road'. Jesus enunciated principles by which to confess and practise faith in him. One cannot claim to be Christian if they are not respected and acted out.

Love one another, as I have loved you. Go and make disciples, baptise them and teach them to obey. When you have a feast, invite the poor, the crippled, the lame and the blind. You cannot serve both God and money. Whoever does not receive the kingdom of God as a little child will not enter it.

The basic unit of the Methodist revival was the Class Meeting. Once a week, converts met in a small group of about twelve. In true Wesleyan style, they followed an agenda in the form of questions. An early one was, 'Does anyone overtake another in a fault?' If any had observed 'unchristian' behaviour in another class member during the week, he or she was accountable to report it and each accountable to have it reported and correct it. Such admonition was not destructive, but referred to by Charles Wesley in one of his hymns as 'building each other up'.

He bids us build each other up
and gathered into one
to our high calling's glorious hope
We hand in hand go on.

Dorothy Day (longtime editor of the US *Catholic Worker*

and a social activist) always recognised the authority of her church although she took God as her ultimate authority and acted according to that conscience.

She and her bishop, Cardinal Spellman, often differed on the nation's role in peace and war. She wrote, acted and preached the pacifism she believed in. Yet she never doubted that the cardinal was her superior, the representative of the unity of her local faith community. She always asked for her bishop's blessing even when she went a different way.

Quentin Questnell, *The Authority for Authority*

My work has life and death implications. Efficiency is paramount.

I recently visited the USA to observe and update my professional status. One of the new trends I discovered and implemented on my return was a system of higher accountability. All work done was immediately identifiable by the laboratory scientist responsible for it.

I came back with lots of strategies to upgrade efficiency, but discovered that after introducing the accountability procedures, the efficiency of our lab increased dramatically. It was not necessary to introduce any other efficiency techniques.

Neville Farmer

I believe the church can be renewed because it provides us with the greatest reservoir of people *committed* to God anywhere. Granted there are many unregenerate with apathy, neglect and indifference, and the introverted. There are irrelevant things and people. It is within the church, however, that one finds the most people who are sensitive and can be led to be sensitive to the radical call of God and to what God is doing in the world today.

Findley B. Edge, *The Greening of the Church*

Can church members be more than strangers? Yes, the church is primarily God's people. We don't just go to church, we *are* the church. When the Bible speaks of Christians being brothers and sisters, it isn't being poetical.

The essence of being the church is that it is God's literal family, God's tribe, God's clan.

The church is community. . . the possibilities of community are immense. The energy for *faithful* living generated when brothers and sisters support each other, share one another's burdens, weep with those who weep, laugh with those who laugh, is a strong tool for the kingdom.

Community makes it possible to take risks that right action demands. To share resources and loosen the hold of affluence on our lives. To be persons and not just roles to each other. To admonish and encourage each other. To develop openness and caring. To seek God's wisdom together is *to be accountable* to one another, to co-operate in the mutual love of servanthood. Each of these is a process and not a finished state.

Owen Salter, 'Can Church Members be
More Than Strangers?'

Being an individual isn't wrong. But *individualism* is that way of seeing things in which we put the highest value on ourselves and our best interests — and that is idolatry.

To become a Christian is to admit rebellion; in other words, to admit that we have made ourselves the most important thing in our lives. Conversion is turning away from this behaviour, surrendering control and submitting our wills in obedience to God.

This new harmony with God must then spill over into all relationships.

Brad Lovegrove, *The Cult of the Individual*

It is comparatively easy to put on the shoe of community. But when the shoe starts pinching it gets a little harder.

Accountability is one of the spots where community fits a bit uncomfortably. It means we strive to be answerable to our brothers and sisters for the way we live our lives; for the way we spend our money; for the quality of our commitment to Christ; for the balance between our callings and our activities (family, work, church, sport); for our struggle to overcome sin.

The other side of accountability is liability. We not only ask our brothers and sisters to share in our decisions, we agree to share in theirs; to hold them to what they decide; to support them when they fail, forgiving and strengthening as the Father does.

On Being

You don't have to live *in* a community to live *in* community. I do not know what your destiny will be, but one thing I do know — the only ones among you who will be really happy are those who have sought and found how to serve.

Albert Schweitzer

Lord,
I just read that thirty-nine thousand children in your global family die every day. Every day, Lord! That's hard to believe. Thirty-nine thousand! We are horrified if one jet crashes and kills three hundred people. If five people are shot by a crazed gunman in the street, it makes headlines for days.

Why don't we feel more accountable for these unknown children? I want to make a difference, but it is so frustrating to know what and how to do it.

Keep me trying, Lord. Keep a healthy tension between my frustration and the magnitude of the task. Help me to influence my family, my people, my local community and political decision-makers in conversation, letter writing and, if I have the opportunity, my own public statements.

Don't let me give up. I want to be accountable. Amen.

Lord Jesus,
This day I seek the tranquillity of your special presence. How did you do it Lord? You kept peace when all around was at war. You were able to love those who hated you. You were able to forgive those who maliciously used you. You trusted those you knew would let you down.

How did you do it, Lord? And yet I'm glad you did. It gives me hope that today even I can:
pray for those I'm angry with

forgive those who cannot forgive me
love the unlovely
pastor those who have criticised me
*speak the truth in love to those who have told half-truths
about me.*

*Thank you, Lord, for modelling ministry. Help me to hold
my own accountable to yours. Amen.*

A Benediction

*Now go to meet the day. It is the one the Lord has made.
It is his gift to you. Walk in it as his servant and may his
peace and tranquillity attend all your ways.*

10

The compassionate life

The Lord has told us what is good. What he requires of us is this: to do what is just, to show constant love, and to live in humble fellowship with our God.

Jesus went through all the towns and villages, teaching in their synagogues, preaching the good news of the kingdom and healing every kind of disease and sickness. When he saw the crowds, he had compassion on them, because they were harassed and helpless, like sheep without a shepherd.

Be compassionate as your Father is compassionate. Do not judge, and you will not be judged yourselves; do not condemn, and you will not be condemned yourselves; grant pardon, and you will be pardoned.

You have a permanent place in my heart, and God knows how much I miss you all, loving you as Christ Jesus loves you.

You are God's chosen race, his saints; he loves you and you should be clothed in sincere compassion, in kindness and humility, gentleness and patience. Bear with one another; forgive each other as soon as a quarrel begins. The Lord has forgiven you; now you must do the same. Over all these clothes, to keep them together and complete them, put on love.

Your life in Christ makes you strong, and his love comforts you. You have fellowship with the Spirit, and you have kindness and compassion for one another. . . The attitude you should have is the one that Christ Jesus had. . .

'Which of these three, do you think, proved himself a neighbour to the man who fell into the brigands' hands?' 'The one who took pity on him,' he replied. Jesus said to him, 'Go and do the same yourself.'

We love because God first loved us. If someone says he loves God, but hates his brother, he is a liar. For he cannot love God, whom he has not seen, if he does not love his brother, whom he has seen. The command that Christ has given us is this: whoever loves God must love his brother also.

(Micah 6: 8, GNB; Matthew 9: 35-36, NIV; Luke 6: 36-37, JB; Philippians 1: 7-8, JB; Colossians 3: 12-14, JB; Philippians 2: 1 and 5, GNB; Luke 10: 36-37, JB; 1 John 4: 19-21, GNB)

Compassion is an 'okay' kind of word isn't it? We like to think of ourselves as a compassionate people who really are mostly good, gentle and understanding. We should like to think that the compassionate life was simply the human way of living. But being human and being compassionate are not the same. All the conflict, war, hatred, injustice and oppression in the world remind us that authentic compassion is not a response natural to every human.

True compassion is tragically rare. Competition and not compassion seems to be the rule of life.

As followers of Jesus we need to hear his call: 'Be compassionate as your Father is compassionate.' This is a radical dimension of Christ's call to us. It goes against our competitive nature. Indeed, we only begin to understand compassion when we understand that our Father has first loved us. Because he is compassionate towards us, we may grow in compassion and reach out to others.

Christian compassion must be more than an emotional 'gut' reaction. It is often appropriate that we feel a deep anger at the sin, cruelty and injustice in our world. But true compassion will always move from emotion to action, in the spirit of the obedient and suffering Servant of God.

Compassion must involve action, and yet prayer is central to authentic compassion for others. Prayer will lead us into the mysteries of suffering and enable us to reach out even to our enemies in compassion. Prayer calls us to be aware of the world in which we live and present it with all its horrors, violence, needs and pain to a God who is Compassion.

Yet we are always aware that the evil, failure and hurt needing to be confronted by compassion has an echo in our own hearts. Our own sin, hurt and overwhelming need constitute a painful reminder of how we, too, need to receive from lives full of compassion.

❧❧

One day, the three of us visited the late Senator Hubert Humphrey to ask him about compassion in politics. . . The Senator, who had just finished talking with the ambassador of Bangladesh and obviously expected a complaint, a demand or a compliment, was visibly caught off guard when asked how he felt about compassion in politics. . . But then, after having adapted himself to the somewhat unusual situation, Senator Humphrey walked back to his desk, picked up a long pencil with a small eraser at its end, and said in his famous high-pitched voice: 'Gentlemen, look at this pencil. Just as the eraser is only a very small part of this pencil and is used only when you make a mistake, so compassion is only called upon when things get out of hand. The main part of life is competition; only the eraser is compassion. . . in politics compassion is just part of the competition.'

H.J.M. Nouwen, D.P. McNeill,
D.A. Morrison, *Compassion*

The life of Jesus illustrates the three vital elements of compassion in action. The first element is true understanding. . .

Compassion is born from true understanding. Matthew noted that Jesus had compassion on the crowds because 'they were like sheep without a shepherd, harassed and helpless'. . . Compassion means that we have two cross hairs in the sights of our understanding: the fact that people are beings created by God in the image of God and the fact that people have fallen and live in a fallen world. Where the two lines cross is the centre of the sphere of compassion.

The second element of Christian compassion is outrage. If we see what is wrong as God sees it, we will feel about it as God feels. . . to be moved with compassion denotes a gut reaction, an intense visceral emotion; and suggests strong anger at the situation which has reduced people to their present circumstances. . .

The third element of Christian compassion is identification. The Latin root for 'compassion' is parallel to the Greek root for sympathy; both refer to deep fellow feelings 'with' or 'alongside' someone. Identification is at the heart of the incarnation.

Os Guinness, *The Dust of Death*

Just as our neighbour is in need and lacks that in which we abound, so we were in need before God and lacked his mercy. Hence, as our heavenly Father has in Christ freely come to our aid, we also ought freely to help our neighbour through our body and its works, and each one should become as it were a Christ to the other that we may be Christs to one another and Christ may be the same in all; that is, that we may be truly Christians.

Martin Luther, *Christian Freedom*

I quoted something I had heard a preacher say to Len, a Canning Town Christian. The preacher had said, 'What we want in this country is a voice.' I asked Len what his comments were. 'You'd have to have lips and a mouth and a body as well, wouldn't you?' he said.

David Sheppard, *Built as a City*

The bowels of compassion: a wonderful old phrase.
They ought to be kept open.

Norman Douglas, *An Alumanac*

If you think of your fellow creatures, then you only want to cry; you could really cry the whole day long. The only thing to do is to pray that God will perform a miracle and save some of them. And I hope I am doing that enough.

Anne Frank, *The Diary of Anne Frank*

The great news we have received is that God is a compassionate God. In Jesus Christ the obedient servant, who did not cling to his divinity, but emptied himself and became as we are, God has revealed the fullness of his compassion. He is Immanuel, God-with-us. The great call we have heard is to live a compassionate life. In the community formed in displacement and leading to a new way of being together, we can become disciples – living manifestations of God's presence in this world. The great task we have been given is to walk the compassionate way. Through the discipline of patience, practised in prayer and action, the life of discipleship becomes real and fruitful.

H.J.M. Nouwen, D.P. McNeill, D.A. Morrison, *Compassion*

Father, I confess my great need of your compassion. My failures, doubts, temptations and fears threaten to overwhelm me. Life seems to be a never-ending competition and I often feel as though I don't even know the rules. You understand and love me as you do all your children. Reach out to me so that in the depths of my being I may know your compassion. Thankyou that in the life, teaching and suffering of your Son I learn that you are a God of compassion.

In my mind I know that to follow you means that I must live a life of compassion. But my heart is often so hard and my body so slow to help others, even when I become indignant over their plight. Show me that it is precisely because of my poverty and pain that I may be able to help others. Just as you love me, so may I love others. Amen.

A Benediction
May the Father who is Compassion, the Son who is still moved by the sight of the wounded people and the Spirit who is the Comforter transform our competitive souls into compassionate lives. Amen.

11

Love that gives itself away

(Anders Nygren)

This is love: not that we loved God, but that he loved us and sent his Son as an atoning sacrifice for our sins.

You, O Lord, are loving.

This is how we know what love is: Jesus Christ laid down his life for us. And we ought to lay down our lives for our brothers. God is love; he who dwells in love is dwelling in God, and God in him. This is for us the perfection of love, to have confidence on the day of judgment, and this we can have, because even in this world we are as he is.

God demonstrates his own love for us in this: While we were still sinners, Christ died for us.

A new commandment I give you: Love one another. As I have loved you, so you must love one another. All will know that you are my disciples if you love one another.

Let no debt remain outstanding, except the continuing debt to love one another, for he who loves others has fulfilled the law.

For the whole law is fulfilled on one word, 'You shall love your neighbour as yourself.'

Love contains no fear — indeed fully-developed love expels every particle of fear, for fear always contains some of the torture of feeling guilty. This means that the person who lives in fear has not yet had love perfected.

(1 John 4: 10, NIV; Psalm 62: 12, NIV; 1 John 3: 16, NIV; 1 John 4: 16b and 17, NEB; Romans 5: 8, NIV; John 13: 34, NIV; Romans 13: 8, NIV; Galatians 5: 14, RSV; 1 John 4: 18, Phillips)

What is this thing called love? A four letter word, easy to say, but incredibly hard to do. And not all that easy to understand, since (in English at least) the word is used in so many different ways. It carries an enormous freight on its small shoulders: it can be love for God, or for truth, or for having one's back scratched; it can be love for one's family, or for chips with vinegar, or a love affair in illicit circumstances. Has it been so inflated by over-use that it is now devalued?

If love now means everything and therefore nothing, we have a problem. For the apostle John says that God *is* love! What a risk John took even if the Greeks did have at least four words for love! The biggest danger is that people will make a 'dislectic' mistake and conclude that Love (capital 'L') is God. A transcendent sexual experience, a sweet revelation of family life, a friendship that passes the love of women, and behold, they think they have been visited by a divinity. And like a god, such love issues commands which they obey to the letter: selfish, mean, manipulative and treacherous acts are defended because it was 'love' that told us to do them.

But John took the risk: 'God', he said, 'is love'. John did more than that, he 're-minted' the word and gave it a character so radical as to shake all ancient (and modern) ethical systems. He taught that love is to give yourself away for the benefit of others regardless of whether or not they attract you or deserve your goodwill. John learned such love at the foot of the cross where God's love-gift of himself was poured out for those who put him there (1 John 3: 16).

The love that gives itself away comes from God. He and such love are inseparables, the 'Siamese twins' of the universe. This love 'has flooded our innermost heart through the Holy Spirit he has given us' (Romans 5: 5, NEB) and what he has worked into us must now be worked out in daily living. Such love is a gift to be received, but making it work will cost us all that we have and all that we are.

If we had not seen the love that is revealed in the cross of Christ, we should not have known what love, in the Christian sense of the word, is. We should doubtless have known what love in general is, but not what love in the highest and deepest sense is, not what divine love, *agape*, is. What, then, has the cross of Christ to tell us about the nature and content of agape-love? It testifies that it is a love that gives itself away, that sacrifices itself, even to the uttermost.

Anders Nygren, *Agape and Eros*

The model of suffering love is God himself. Why, a reasonable angel might ask, did the Creator not give up millennia ago on these stupid rebels? Why does God not call a halt to the frustrations of human history? Why does he not let us finish ourselves off with the doomsday bomb? Why does he not come quickly himself to turn the world into his perfect kingdom? Why does he wait so long before taking decisive action? The answer: God is love. Love suffers long.

Lewis Smedes, *Love within limits*

For the love of God is broader
than the measures of man's mind;
and the heart of the Eternal
is most wonderfully kind.
If our love were but more simple
we should take him at his word;
and our lives would be illumined
by the goodness of our Lord.

William Faber

In the Bible, love is much more a matter of will and of action than of feeling. Feeling may come into it, but it is not the central thing. Love in the Bible is a steady direction of the will towards another's lasting good. Love means coming to help in time of need; it means saving activity. In the parable of the good Samaritan, when the Samaritan saw the wounded man, he came to his help; a kindly feeling of pity would not have been any use; what was needed was action to save a life. Jesus told that parable not only to show us how we ought to act, but also to show us what God is like, and to make clear to us that God also acts to save.

Stephen Neill, *The Christian's God*

On the whole, God's love for us is a much safer subject to think about than our love for him. Nobody can always have devout feelings and, even if we could, feelings are not what God principally cares about. Christian love, either towards God or towards others, is an affair of the will. If we are trying to do his will we are obeying the commandment, 'Thou shalt love the Lord thy God'. He will give us feelings of love if he pleases. We cannot create them for ourselves, and we must not demand them as a right. But the great thing to remember is that, though our feelings come and go, his love for us does not. It is not wearied by our sins, or our indifference; and, therefore, it is quite relentless in its determination that we shall be cured of those sins, at whatever cost to us, at whatever cost to him.

C.S. Lewis, *Mere Christianity*

The love of our neighbour is the only door out of the dungeon of self, where we mope and mow, striking sparks, and rubbing phosphorescences out of the walls, and blowing our own breath in our own nostrils, instead of issuing to the fair sunlight of God, the sweet winds of the universe.

George Macdonald, 'Love thy neighbour'

If lovelessness actively repels people from the church and the gospel, thus being the biggest single obstacle to effective witness in a community or a nation, it also evacuates the Christian of his significance before God. He becomes a nonentity, a cipher. God cannot use the loveless Christian for his glory, even if he is gifted with prophetic speaking; even if he is able to understand and explain the deep things of God, man and Satan, even if he is knowledgeable about the vast field of truth and experience; and even if he has the incisive and bold measure of faith envisaged by Jesus himself — the faith that moves mountains. William Barclay, *Flesh and Spirit*

Love sees possibilities that apathy and indifference cannot see. This works on many levels of life. Driven by self-giving love to seek a happier personhood for another, we are able to hear signals in the other person that hint at a will to change. Love keeps us open to possibilities within the loved one. It is only when we lose patience or no longer even care that we say: 'he's hopeless'. At another level, when we experience the love of God, we feel possibilities for newness on every side. The Spirit of God is the agent of love within us. When God takes us into love's embrace — when all our sins are forgiven, when all our blemished past is accepted, and when we face our future as a tomorrow bathed in the atmosphere of divine love — we are reborn in hope. Desire is transformed into expectancy. We know all things are *possible*. The love of the Spirit communicates the wellspring of hope.

Lewis Smedes, *Love within Limits*

When I want to be free at all costs
I am already beginning to bind myself
When I pursue my own wishes
I throw myself in chains
I do what I don't want to do
I am at my own mercy
And when I finally consider myself free
Freedom becomes a burden
Because I must make decisions
Which I am unable to make
And my freedom turns into a new prison
I can only find freedom
In the ropes that bind me
To you

Ulrich Schaffer

Many waters cannot quench love; rivers cannot wash it away.

Song of Songs

Lord, we might have known that you would be love! If you had not poured yourself into the tiny frame of the Babe of Bethlehem and then gone on to pour yourself out on the cross, somehow this truth about you may just have penetrated our darkened minds. If we had summed up all the best and noblest thoughts that ever came into our thinking, all the beauty, truth and goodness that is possible, and then if we had pushed it to the ultimate, we should perhaps have just managed to see the dim outlines of love. No doubt we would have badly distorted the picture and got much of it wrong, but our poor hungry hearts would somehow have recognised that when we were in touch with love we were in touch with truth, with reality, with you.

But Lord, you did not leave us to guess and to grope in the darkness. You came down to where we were: Love translated into flesh and blood, Love active and living in the dusty lanes and by-ways of the world. You gave yourself utterly all day and every day until on the cross there was nothing more to give. And then Love, which crashed headlong into human sin and selfishness, crashed through into victory and the power of an endless life. Risen Jesus, Risen Love, you reign for ever and ever. Amen.

A Benediction

May the Father's love which gave to the uttermost and spared nothing in its downreach towards men and women, and may the Son's love which touched and healed and bled and died for us, and may the Spirit's love which is poured into our hearts, bless, preserve and keep us in time and in eternity. May the presence of the living God and the power of his crucified love move us and change us and turn us upward to him and outward to others now and forever. Amen.

Two friends, one soul

(Euripides)

My commandment is this: love one another, just as I love you. The greatest love a person can have for his friends is to give his life for them. And you are my friends if you do what I command you. I do not call you servants any longer, because a servant does not know what his master is doing. Instead, I call you friends, because I have told you everything I have heard from my Father. You did not choose me; I chose you and appointed you to go and bear much fruit, the kind of fruit that endures. And so the Father will give you whatever you ask in my name. This, then, is what I command you: love one another.

Dear friends, let us love one another, because love comes from God. Whoever does not love does not know God, for God is love. And God showed his love for us by sending his only Son into the world, so that we might have life through him. . . We love because God first loved us. If someone says he loves God, but hates his brother, he is a liar. For he cannot love God, whom he has not seen, if he does not love his brother, whom he has seen. The command that Christ has given us is this: whoever loves God must love his brother also.

We were God's enemies, but he made us his friends through the death of his Son. Now that we are God's friends, how much more will we be saved by Christ's life! But that is not all; we rejoice because of what God has done through our Lord Jesus Christ, who has now made us God's friends.

(John 15: 12-17; 1 John 4: 7-9, 19-21; Romans 5: 10 and 11 — all GNB)

Friendship with God is the ultimate friendship. In Jesus Christ, he reveals his nature as 'full of grace and truth'; by his Spirit, he awakens our desire to know him and respond to his love.

One of the fruits of the divine friendship is a new intimacy with our brothers and sisters. Like pieces of metal attracted to a magnet, we find that as we are drawn closer to God, we are simultaneously drawn closer to each other. As our barriers of fear and mistrust are gradually broken down, we find that we want to reach out to others and offer them our gifts.

We offer ourselves to each other in a spirit of servanthood, aware that each one is sent to us by God and reveals a different aspect of God's nature. The one may wash our dusty feet, another may allow us to pour the ointment of our tenderness on his wounds. There will be times of laughter and sharing, times of silence when together we adore our mutual friend.

During his earthly ministry, Jesus loved his friends deeply and regarded them as gifts from God. They, in turn, comforted him with their love and encouraged him by their growth toward maturity. At the most crucial times of his life, he desired their company and support — on the mountain of transfiguration, in the garden of Gethsemane, at Calvary. His final prayer was that his friends would be one with each other and with God.

Committing ourselves to our friends in a covenant relationship will be costly: genuine Christian love, according to Morton Kelsey, is 'forged against the anvil of our selfishness and possessiveness, of our anger and our fear'. To be true friends we may have to confront others with the way they hurt us, and with the way we perceive they could be hurting themselves.

As long as we have the intention to love, God will take our faltering attempts and transform them, using the process as a means towards union with himself. As we rest in our friend of friends, we will find that it is the Lord himself who is loving through us.

The intimate relationships in my life have been the source of the revelation of the mystery of Jesus. Through relationship I came to experience incarnation — goodness and transcendence enfleshed in human form.

Teresa M. Boernig, *Prayer and Relationship*

Your friend is your needs answered.
He is your field which you sow with love and reap with thanksgiving.
And he is your board and fireside.
For you come to him with your hunger, and you seek him for peace. . .

And let there be no purpose in friendship save the deepening of the spirit.
For love that seeks aught but the disclosure of its own mystery is not love but a net cast forth; and only the unprofitable is caught. . .

And in the sweetness of friendship let there be laughter, and sharing of pleasures.
For in the dew of little things the heart finds its morning and is refreshed.

Kahlil Gibran, *The Prophet*

I have described the goal of life as a deep and lasting relationship to God. But this relationship cannot be understood apart from two other relationships which are bound up with it: with other people and with ourselves. Indeed, the relationship to God, to other people and to ourselves forms a trinity in unity. Each relationship requires and depends upon the others, so that if one is defective the others will be defective too. It is through other people's love that God's love is first mediated to us.

Christopher Bryant, *The Search for God in Depth*

When we honestly ask ourselves which persons in our lives mean the most to us, we often find that it is those who, instead of giving much advice, solutions or cures, have chosen rather to share our pain and touch our wounds with a gentle and tender hand. The friend who can be silent with us in a moment of despair or confusion, who can stay with us in an hour of grief and bereavement, who can tolerate not-knowing, not-curing, not-healing and face with us the reality of our powerlessness, that is the friend who cares.

Henri Nouwen, *Out of Solitude*

The real cure for loneliness is the healing interaction of two personalities.

Katie F. Wiebe, *Alone: A Search for Joy*

While each of us has a personal journey to complete, there is no need for us to travel alone. If we travel together we are able to encourage each other. Our journeying involves us offering heart hospitality to others. . . It is ours to provide a free and empty space without evoking a sense of owing, a space uncluttered with personal furniture. . . Providing a free and empty space for others, we commit ourselves to accepting the strangeness of strangers. Each brings a gift, themselves. In our openness, we are challenged by each guest, changed by them unpredictably. . . It is thus that we entertain angels unawares, even Christ himself. We are most aware of his presence when the Christ in others reaches through to and engages the Christ in us.

Graeme L. Chapman, *Being Together in the World*

One cannot collect all the beautiful shells on the beach. One can collect only a few, and they are more beautiful if they are few. . . We can have a surfeit of treasures — an excess of shells, where one or two would be significant.

Anne Morrow Lindbergh, *Gift from the Sea*

One of the critical problems in society is the absence of trust. Men and women cannot trust because they do not have enough friendship in their life. If there were more friendships in the world there would be more trust, and the level of tension in societal relationships would decrease almost automatically.

Andrew M. Greeley, *The Friendship Game*

Sometimes I wonder if it is wise to work directly at

relationship. What matters is to be centred oneself, always ready for the moments or hours of meeting when they come. Then the relationship can be trusted to take care of itself. . . Meeting is of course always something of a miracle, and cannot be planned nor explained. Mercifully, real, vibrant meetings which always entail the presence of the mysterious 'third'. . . befall us as a grace, and stand out like beacons, and no forceful removal of barriers will, of its own accord, bring them about.

Irene Claremont de Castillejo, *Knowing Woman*

Every time I am given this unexpected awareness towards some other creature and feel this current of communication between us, I am touched and activated by something that comes from the fiery heart of the divine love, the eternal gaze of the Father towards the Son, of the Son towards the Father.

John V. Taylor, *The Go-Between God*

Community is that place where we enter into the presence of each other and the Lord who called us there, as fully and totally as we do in the engagements with ourselves and God. It is a place that calls me to abandon myself to you, for in so doing I discover myself. It is a place where I am available to you as I have learned to be with God and, because of my availability with you, I learn to be available to God. It is a place where I am totally present to you, aware of you and listening to you with the totality of my being. It is a coming together because Christ has called us to be committed to him and to each other through his gift of koinonia.

William Clemmons, *Discovering the Depth*

No friendless man. . . can be truly himself;
What a man looketh for in his friend and findeth. . .
is his own better self.

Author unknown

Self-revelation is both the indispensable core of personality expansion and the essential gift-giving of friendship. We become fuller, richer, warmer, more humane human beings precisely to the extent that we are able to enter into friendship relationships. The more we permit the lover to know us, the more worthy of his love we become; as his searching gaze probes even deeper into our personality, he discovers riches of which no-one else was ever aware and in which we scarcely dare to believe. But, because he sees within us, we actually become the good that he sees. By reinforcing the very tentative inclinations of the beloved, the lover actually creates his beloved. We become that which the lover wants us to be, and he becomes that which we want him to be. When he reacts positively to our tentative, fragile, yet courageous self-revelation, with warmth and affection and encouragement, we discover resources in ourselves of which we had always dreamed but whose reality we could not believe. The lover, in other words, is a person who makes our dreams about ourselves come true.

Andrew M. Greeley, *The Friendship Game*

No matter how much we love a person, accept him, give him support, have a warmth and affection for him; no matter how much we help him in so many ways, unless we can actually call him forth so that he is himself exercising the uniqueness God gave him, then the love is incomplete; he is not free; he is less than fully human.

Gordon Cosby, from a sermon,
'The Calling Forth of the Charisma'

Lord, I need friends. . .
  to ease my loneliness;
  to speak peace to me when I am distressed;
  to walk with me when I am unsure of the way;
  to provide a safe place where I can discover my
  true self.

I need friends. . .
  who will laugh with me as well as pray with me;
  who will embrace me without wanting to possess me;
  who will explore their truth with me as it is

continually revealed.

I need friends. . .
who will reflect you, Lord, as you reflect your
Father;
who will recognise and call forth the Christ in me
as I do the same for them,
so that in mutual giving we may become
the persons you have always seen us to be. Amen.

A Benediction
May God who gives patience, steadiness and encouragement
help you to live in complete harmony with each other — each
with the attitude of Christ toward the other. And then all of
us can praise the Lord together with one voice, giving glory to
God, the Father of our Lord Jesus Christ.

(Romans 15: 5-6, LB)

13

Accepting diversity

Those who depend on obeying the Law live under a curse. . . the Law has nothing to do with faith (Paul). If [faith] is alone and includes no actions, it is dead (James).

We have many parts in the one body, and all these parts have different functions. In the same way, though we are many, we are one body in union with Christ, and we are all joined to each other as different parts of one body.

Christ is like a single body, which has many parts; it is still one body, even though it is made up of different parts. God put every different part in the body just as he wanted it to be. . . There would not be a body if it were only one part! There are many parts, but one body.

What we see now is like a dim image in a mirror. . . What I know now is only partial. . . Meanwhile these three remain: faith, hope and love; and the greatest of these is love.

So, then, let us stop judging one another. . . aim at those things that bring peace and that help to strengthen one another.

And now I give you a new commandment: love one another. As I have loved you, so you must love one another. If you have love for one another, then everyone will know that you are my disciples.

Accept one another, then, for the glory of God, as Christ has accepted you.

Above all, keep your love for one another at full strength, because love cancels innumerable sins. Be hospitable to one another without complaining. Whatever gift each of you may have received, use it in service to one another, like good stewards dispensing the grace of God in its varied forms.

(Galatians 3: 10, GNB; James 2: 17, GNB; Romans 12: 4-5, GNB; 1 Corinthians 12: 12-13, 18-20, GNB; 1 Corinthians 13: 12-13, GNB; Romans 14: 13 and 19, GNB; John 13: 34-35, GNB; Romans 15: 7, GNB; 1 Peter 4: 8-10, NEB)

Snoopy was typing a manuscript, up on his kennel. Charlie Brown: 'What are you doing, Snoopy?' Snoopy: 'Writing a book about theology.' Charlie Brown: 'Good grief. What's its title?' Snoopy (thoughtfully): 'Have You Ever Considered You Might Be Wrong?' This points up a central Christian dictum: God's truth is very much bigger than our little systems.

Our Lord often made the point that God's fathering extended to all people everywhere. He bluntly targeted the narrow nationalism of his own people, particularly in stories like the good Samaritan. Here the 'baddie' is a hero. It's a wonderful parable underlining the necessity to love God through loving your neighbour — and one's neighbour is the person who needs help, whoever he or she may be. But note that love of neighbour is more than seeking their conversion, then adding a few acts of mercy to others in 'our group'. Jesus' other summary statements about the meaning of religion and life in Matthew 23: 23 and Luke 11: 42 involve justice too: attempting to right the wrongs my neighbour suffers.

'Ethnocentrism' is the glorification of my group. What often happens in practice is a kind of spiritual apartheid: I'll do my thing and you do yours — over there. Territoriality ('my place — keep out!') replaces hospitality ('my place — you're welcome!'). I like Paul's commendation in Philippians 2: 19-21 of Timothy 'who really cares' when everyone else was concerned with their own affairs.

Sometimes our non-acceptance of others' uniqueness has jealousy or feelings of inferiority at their root. You have probably heard the little doggerel, 'I hate the guys/ that criticise/ and minimise/ the other guys/ whose enterprise/ has made them rise/ above the guys/ that criticise/ and minimise. . .'

In our global village we cannot avoid relating to 'different others'. Indeed, marriage is all about two different people forming a unity in spite of their differences. Those differences can of course be irritating — for example when a 'lark' marries an 'owl' (but the Creator made both to adorn his creation).

Even within yourself there are diverse personalities. If you are a 'right brain' person, why not develop an interest in 'left brain' thinking?

The Lord reveals different aspects of his truth to different branches of the church. What a pity, then, to make our part of the truth the whole truth. Martin Buber had the right idea when he said that the truth is not so much *in* human beings as *between* them. An author dedicated his book to 'Stephen. . . who agrees with me in nothing, but is my friend in everything.' Just as an orchestra needs every instrument, or a fruit salad is tastier with a great variety of fruits, so we are enriched through genuine fellowship with each other.

A Christian group matures when it recognises it may have something to learn from other groups. The essence of immaturity is not knowing that one doesn't know, and therefore being unteachable. No one denomination or church has a monopoly on the truth. How was God able to get along for 1500, 1600 or 1900 years without this or that church? Differences between denominations or congregations — or even within them — reflect the rich diversity and variety of the social, cultural and temperamental backgrounds from which those people come. But they also reflect the character of God whose grace is 'multi-coloured'.

If you belong to Christ and I belong to Christ, we belong to each other and we need each other. Nothing should divide us.

❧❦

Diversity is a hallmark of life, an intrinsic feature of living systems in the natural world. The demonstration and celebration of this diversity is an endless rite. Look at the popularity of museums, zoos, aquariums and botanic gardens. The odder the exhibit, the more different it is from the common and familiar forms around us, the more successful it is likely to be. Nature does not tire of providing oddments for people who look for them. Biologists have already formally classified 1.7 million species. As many as 30 to 40 million more may remain to be classified.

David Ehrenfeld, 'Thirty million cheers for diversity'

We cannot easily forgive another for not being ourselves.

Emerson

I will buy with you, sell with you, talk with you, walk with you, and so following; but I will not eat with you, drink with you, nor pray with you.

Shylock, *The Merchant of Venice*

Truth is what people kill each other for.

Herbert Read

After three days of discussion at Marburg, the Reformers agreed on fourteen articles, but could not be reconciled on the fifteenth concerning the Eucharist. This led to a division between the Lutheran and Reformed churches which continues to this day. It is reported that when Luther refused to shake hands with Zwingli in farewell, the Swiss reformer left with tears in his eyes. His attitude throughout had been most brotherly.

Arthur Gunn, 'Ulrich Zwingli, the unknown reformer'

If Jesus ever came down to earth again, the Spaniards would dance with joy, the Italians would start singing, the French would discuss whether his visit was timely and the Germans? Well, they would present him with a schedule.

Cardinal Sin, of Manila

Different groups within the Christian church are at odds with one another because their models of the Christian life, its beginnings and its fullness, are so diverse. One group of genuine believers can never remember a conscious conversion to faith in Christ; another insists that a datable experience of being 'born again' is essential; a third says that a second distinct experience of 'baptism of the Holy Spirit' is necessary for Christian maturity. When we 'test the spirits' in the lives of representatives among these groups, we often find an equal level of spiritual vitality — or deadness! — in each sector. The Christian life is being offered in diverse packages, but what is inside is the same — newness of life in Christ. Nonetheless, the different groups enjoying this life are readily offended by another's packages. One person's piety is often another's poison.

Richard Lovelace, *Dynamics of Spiritual Life*

Inevitably, law reduces things to a common denominator. Under grace, everything is completely different. Individual difference is encouraged. . . Each Christian becomes an authentic witness, since each has their own experience of Christ, incommensurable with that of any other person, since all genuinely personal experiences are individual and unique. Each has his or her own irreplaceable contribution to the life of the whole. Each has an instrument to play, a gift to offer to the harmony of the whole orchestra.

Stephen Neill, *On the Ministry*

We can no longer doubt that there are many different expressions of Christianity within the New Testament. These patterns. . . did [not] always complement each other; on the contrary, they not infrequently clashed, sometimes fiercely. . . The language forms were different, often so different that the words of one believer could not serve as the vehicle of faith of another, or even for himself in different circumstances. . . So, if we have been convinced of the unity of first-century Christianity, we can hardly be less convinced of its diversity.

James D.G. Dunn, *Unity and Diversity in the New Testament*

[The church of the next century must be] a church which allows considerable diversity of outlook and expression and does not insist on rigid uniformity. We should not be afraid of diversity within the church. The fact is that people have different temperaments, and these require a variety of expression of faith and worship. But there is another more profound reason for pluralism within the church. This is that no one of us and no one point of view can comprehend the fullness of the mystery of God. We know him only in part, and we can see him only from a perspective which is formed by our historical, cultural and sociological heritage as well as by our personal experience. The pluralism within the church is far from being a simply negative thing and need not be divisive.

Archbishop Keith Raynor

'The very idea of diversities compatible with communion. . . or of the sufficient minimum of doctrine to be held in common if unity is to be preserved. . . is the object of all my research.' It should also be an object of vital interest to all Christians. The diversity which always has existed in the church is still, theoretically, valued and not merely tolerated. Where differences did not inhibit communication by leading to an isolated sectarianism, communion was not sundered; folk lived out, and died for, the one faith before it found uniform expression in creeds and conciliar definitions. If the same faith is being lived, varying formulations of it (which may have equally respectable apostolic origins) must be reconcilable.

Yves Congar, *Diversity and Communion*

With regard to the question of a 'minimal creed', what might it affirm? Here's a suggestion: We affirm: 1. One God: Father, Son and Holy Spirit; 2. Jesus Christ as my Saviour, my Lord and my God; 3. The scriptures as authoritative in all matters of faith and conduct; 4. Love for, acceptance of and full fellowship with all who thus confess their allegiance to Christ through Christ; 5. Our commission to continue the holistic ministry of Christ in evangelism and social action to a lost world.

Rowland Croucher, *Recent Trends Among Evangelicals*

Jacques Ellul, noting that in many of the conflicts of our time sincere Christians are to be found on both sides, welcomes this fact, for he claims that their Christianity can unite them across political and partisan divisions, so lessening the hostility of those divisions and preparing the way for eventual reconciliation.

John Macquarrie, *The Humility of God*

Jesus brings together Jew and Gentile and from them both produces one new kind of person. . . It is not that Jesus makes all the Jews into Gentiles, or all the Gentiles into Jews; he produces a new kind of person out of both, although they remain Gentiles and Jews. Chrysostom, the famous preacher of the early church, says that it is as if one should melt down a statue of silver and a statue of lead, and the two should come out gold. The unity which Jesus achieves is not achieved by blotting out all racial and national characteristics; it is achieved by making all people of all nations into Christians. . . Christianity produces people who are friends with each other because they are friends with God.

William Barclay, *Galatians and Ephesians*

---

*Lord God our Creator, when you made all creatures great
    and small in their rich diversity
    you were so delighted
And when you made human beings (in your image) to
be so diverse, they must represent somehow the rich
    diversity of the Godhead itself.
Lord, our Redeemer, when Jesus Christ died to draw all
    unto him, it was in prospect of heaven being populated
    by people from every tribe, language, nation and race.*

*Lord, help me to appreciate all this richness;
    may my theology not be too eccentric, peripheral to the
    central concern of the gospel which is to increase love
    for God and others.
So teach me how to stay close to you, close to
humankind,
    and make it the goal of my life to bring God and
    humankind together.*

Help me to move from law (with its tendency to reduce
everything to a common denominator) to grace
(where individual differences are celebrated)
May my view of myself be conditioned more by my being
bound up in life with others, rather than my
separateness from them.
Help me to be big enough to be all things to all people, to
help in their saving to keep the bridges between me
and others in good repair. . .

Cure thy children's warring madness
Bend our pride to thy control;
Shame our wanton selfish gladness,
Rich in things and poor in soul.
Grant us wisdom, grant us courage,
Lest we miss thy kingdom's goal.

H.E. Fosdick

Gather us in, thou love that fillest all;
Gather our rival faiths within thy fold.
Rend each one's temple-veil and bid it fall,
That we may know that thou hast been of old;
Gather us in.
Gather us in: we worship only Thee;
In varied names we stretch a common hand;
In diverse forms a common soul we see;
In many ships we seek one spirit-land;
Gather us in.
Each one sees one colour of thy rainbow-light,
Each looks upon one tint and calls it heaven;
Thou are the fullness of our partial sight;
We are not perfect till we find the seven;
Gather us in.

G.E. Matheson

A Benediction

May God be merciful to us, and bless us;
look on us with kindness,
so that the whole world may know your will;
so that nations may know your salvation.

May the peoples praise you, O God;
may all the peoples praise you!

Psalm 67: 1-2 (GNB)

Theme: Protection

. . .in the valleys

The Lord is my shepherd; I shall want nothing.
   He makes me lie down in green pastures,
and leads me beside the waters of peace;
   he renews life within me,
and for his name's sake guides me in the right path.
Even though I walk through a valley dark as death
I fear no evil, for you are with me,
   your staff and crook are my comfort.

You spread a table for me in the sight of my enemies;
   you have richly bathed my head with oil
   and my cup runs over.
Goodness and love unfailing, these will follow me
   all the days of my life,
   and I shall dwell in the house of the Lord
   my whole life long.

Psalm 23: 1-6, NEB

The mountain *in* the valley

My God, my God, why have you forsaken me?

Let us fix our eyes on Jesus, the author and perfecter of our faith, who for the joy set before him endured the cross, scorning its shame, and sat down at the right hand of the throne of God. Consider him who endured such opposition from sinners, so that you will not grow weary and lose heart.

'The stone the builders rejected has become the capstone; the Lord has done this, and it is marvellous in our eyes'.

[Jesus]. . . said: 'If anyone would come after me, he must deny himself and take up his cross and follow me. For whoever wants to save his life will lose it, but whoever loses his life for me and the gospel will save it.'

For as in Adam all die, so in Christ all will be made alive.

Praise be to the God and Father of our Lord Jesus Christ! In his great mercy he has given us new birth into a living hope through the resurrection of Jesus Christ from the dead, and into an inheritance that can never perish, spoil or fade — kept in heaven for you.

For to me, to live is Christ and to die is gain.

I have been crucified with Christ and I no longer live, but Christ lives in me.

Or don't you know that all of us who were baptised into Christ Jesus were baptised into his death? We were therefore buried with him through baptism into death in order that, just as Christ was raised from the dead through the glory of the Father, we too may live a new life.

I tell you the truth, if you have faith as small as a

mustard seed, you can say to this mountain, 'Move from here to there' and it will move. Nothing will be impossible for you.

(Matthew 27: 46; Hebrews 12: 2-3; Mark 12: 10-11; Mark 8: 34-35; 1 Corinthians 15: 22; 1 Peter 1: 3-4; Philippians 1: 21; Galatians 2: 20; Romans 6: 3-4; Matthew 17: 20 — all NIV)

We like to distinguish between 'mountain-top' and 'valley' experiences in life, pursuing (or is it stumbling upon?) the former at least occasionally, and hoping to avoid the latter as much as possible. The scripture readings above remind us, however, of the links between the two. Jesus, at the very moment of forsakenness, achieved the pinnacle of salvation history. The pain and shame, the foolishness of the cross, undoubtedly imposed a traumatic 'valley' experience on his body, mind and spirit, and yet in God's economy this moment was the peak of the divine drama that was to mark a watershed for humanity.

It can be the same for us. Like the prodigal son, we can experience times of personal lostness, life 'in the pits'; and we can also, in the midst of those hard times, 'come to ourselves' and discover whole new vistas of the human spirit, new depths of self-knowledge, new opportunities for growth, and finally 'getting life together'.

Wilfred Noyce, the British mountaineer-poet, wrote after the 1953 Everest expedition that, despite the danger, the frostbite and exhaustion, 'In the last resort a man goes beyond his physical body, relying on resources of the spirit which may be further explored but which will never, I hope, be accurately charted. . . Everest was not climbed by limbs and oxygen, but with the help of [resources of the spirit].' Here was a man who, literally in the valley below the towering mountain, wrote in his diary, 'Is it friendly or sinister? Whichever it is, it's *enormous*. Feel a little lonely and appalled' — and then went on to climb the daunting slopes! His valley-fears became mountain-top exhilaration.

When it comes to life in the Spirit, the Christian has enormous God-given resources on which to draw. An

Easter-faith doesn't hinge on institutional religion and its formal practices, but on the invasion of despair and discouragement by resurrection. Behind the mess we have made of this world is a loving Creator who justifies the ungodly, gives life to the dead, and calls into existence things that do not exist (Romans 4). It is this 'unreasonable' faith which has the capacity and power to penetrate our valley-times with mountain-top experiences; it is this God of surprises who can turn the darkness of our despair into the brightness of a creative joy in life. Christ *is* risen! He is risen indeed!

Two men died on the same day, one on a hill, one in a valley. He who died on the hill prayed for the men who killed him, and during his terrible suffering he had compassion for his mother. His name was Jesus. The other man killed himself on the tree that he had chosen. His name was Judas.

Corrie ten Boom, *Each New Day*

[Jesus] calls her name — 'Mary'. I have never heard a word shaped with such tenderness. The woman answers him with the most beautiful word of faith ever known: 'Master!' From my place in the garden I am filled not only with breathless wonder that he is risen, but with a yearning for this encounter to happen to me, too. . . And then I realise that my longing has been granted, for Christ is alive today and he stands upon every path and turning of my life. He comes straight to me, too, his presence so loving that I seem to hear him speak my name. This is God's Easter gift to each of us. . . We can recognise him deep in our heart and hear his voice as he gently calls our name. And as we raise our head to answer, Easter is truly born. *Master!*

Sue Monk Kidd, 'Easter Sunday'

'Peace I leave with you, my peace I give unto you: not as the world giveth, give I unto you. . .' By such gentle ways we are led till we come to the place where we understand

that it is not enough to accept the will of God in the sense
of ceasing to wish it were different, and taking it peace-
fully. We must go further than that. We are not wholly
loyal till we learn to welcome it. Stormy wind fulfilling
his word — by the time the wind blows upon us it is his
wind for us.

Amy Carmichael, *Gold by Moonlight*

In our distorting fear we are tempted to invoke the power
of the resurrection as a short cut to new life. We want
our Easter without having to go through Good Friday.
We choose to overlook the lesson of Palm Sunday: that
when we offer our hosannas to Jesus and proclaim him
king *before* we are prepared to experience the pain of his
dying and of our own dying with him, our shouts become
hollow. . . the road goes through Calvary and there is no
other. Before his resurrection brings new life to us, before
we can tolerate the gifts of his rising, something in us has
to die. It may well be something which has been very
important to us. . . When we seek to evade the hurt, we
lose the goal.

Graeme Griffin, 'Faith and Fear'

Just as the New Testament in speaking of the victory of
Christ cannot detach the resurrection from the cross which
precedes it and the exaltation to which it leads, so in
proclaiming the church as participator in the new life of
the risen Christ it cannot separate the resurrection from
the gift of the Holy Spirit. . . By that Spirit, the God 'who
raised Christ Jesus from the dead' gives [us] life.

Neville Clark, *Interpreting the Resurrection*

The most fundamental idea which lies behind the Passion-
sayings is the steadfast belief of Jesus that the purpose
and experience of his passion lay deep in the providence
of God. He did not look upon his sufferings as chance
events, or as a stroke of fate, or simply as a tragedy
compassed by men. On the contrary, his experiences were
events determined in the counsels of God. . . Jesus interpreted his suffering, death and resurrection positively, as
active elements in his Messianic vocation. . . [as] an

achievement to which his life is dedicated.

Vincent Taylor, *Jesus and His Sacrifice*

The cross of Jesus Christ was this world's darkest hour. For a few days it appeared as though God had been defeated and all hope was destroyed. But the cross was matched by the resurrection. Jesus rose again from the dead. His body was restored to pulsating vitality. This was not a fanciful identification of the disciples' wishes with reality; it was an historic event to which they were 'eyewitnesses' — they saw him, touched him, talked with him. And this was the supreme exhibition of the victory of good over evil. Hopelessness was transformed into hope, darkness became light, defeat became victory.

Charles Ohlrich, *The Suffering God*

In the deserted, moon-blanch'd street,
How lonely rings the echo of my feet!
Those windows, which I gaze at, frown,
Silent and white, unopening down,
Repellent as the world; — but see,
A break between the housetops shows
The moon! and, lost behind her, fading dim
Into the dewy dark obscurity
Down at the far horizon's rim,
Doth a whole tract of heaven disclose!

Matthew Arnold, 'A Summer Night'

Moyst with one drop of thy blood, my dry soule
Shall (though she now be in extreme degree
Too stony hard, and yet too fleshly,) bee
Freed by that drop, from being starv'd, hard, or foule,
And life, by this death abled, shall controule
Death, whome thy death slue. . .

John Donne, 'Resurrection'

Generations have trod, have trod, have trod;
    And all is seared with trade; bleared, smeared with toil;
    And wears man's smudge and shares man's smell: the soil

Is bare now, nor can foot feel, being shod.

And for all this, nature is never spent;
    There lives the dearest freshness deep down things;
And though the last lights off the black West went
    Oh, morning, at the brown brink eastward,
    springs —
Because the Holy Ghost over the bent
    world broods with warm breast and with ah!
    bright wings.

Gerard Manley Hopkins, 'God's Grandeur'

When the one
who looked upon the weeping Peter
looks upon you,
you will be inebriated with the *wormwood*
of as twofold bitterness:
remorse for yourself
and compassion for Christ,
so that having atoned with Peter
for the guilt of your crime,
with Peter
you will be filled
with the spirit of holiness.

Bonaventure, 'The Tree of Life'

. . . to say 'Jesus is risen; he is risen indeed!' has meaning
only when we also say 'Adam is fallen; he is fallen indeed!'
Falling and rising, darkness and light, death and life are
great opposing themes in the tale of humankind as told
in the Bible. Like truth and falsehood, beauty and ugliness, goodness and evil — singly any one of these ideas
has no meaning; it has to be seen over against its opposite.
So it is with the rising of Jesus.

John Bodycomb, 'The Prototype'

He comes to us as one unknown, without a name, as of
old by the lakeside he came to those men who knew him
not. He speaks to us the same word: 'Follow me!' and
sets us to the tasks he has to fulfil for our time. He
commands. And to those who obey him, whether they

be wise or simple, he will reveal himself in the toils, the conflicts, the sufferings which they shall pass through in his fellowship; and, as in an ineffable mystery, they shall learn in their own experience who he is.

Albert Schweitzer, *Quest of the Historical Jesus*

There is only one means to ensure our suffering, and that is to understand his, to hook onto his, to remember ours *is* his.

Louis Evely

It is good for us to encounter troubles and adversities from time to time, for trouble often compels a man to search his own heart. It reminds him that he is an exile here, and that he can put his trust in nothing in this world. It is good, too, that we sometimes suffer opposition, and that men think ill of us and misjudge us, even when we do and mean well. Such things are an aid to humility, and preserve us from pride and vainglory. For we more readily turn to God as our inward witness, when men despise us and think no good of us.

Thomas à Kempis, *The Imitation of Christ*

Whoever turns his face fully to the Mercy Seat
and with faith, hope and love,
devotion, admiration, exultation,
appreciation, praise and joy
beholds him hanging on the cross,
such a one makes the Pasch, that is, the passover,
with Christ. . .
experiencing
as far as is possible in this wayfarer's state,
what was said on the cross
to the thief who adhered to Christ;
today you shall be with me in paradise.

Bonaventure, 'The Soul's Journey into God'

God of all salvation, healing and wholeness, you formed us in your own image, you created us male and female, you willed our union and harmony, you commanded us to love you and to love each other, you entrusted the earth and all that dwells here to our care. We confess that we live as though we have lost all consciousness of your blessings. We confess that too often we have Golgotha faces rather than the animated urgency of Emmaus. Come and invade our darkness with the warm life-giving light of your Spirit. Raise us to new life, breathe your holy inspiration into us, fill us with your peace, lift our burdens and straighten our paths. Grant us the gift of your reconciling presence, so that even in the valleys of life we may discover the mountain on which to worship you. In the name of Christ, our risen Lord. Amen.

A Benediction

May the love of the risen Lord draw you to himself.
May the power of the risen Lord strengthen you in his service.
May the joy of the risen Lord fill your spirit.
May the life of the risen Lord raise you to new life this day.
Amen.

15

Joy in the morning

Those who sow in tears will reap with songs of joy. He who goes out weeping, carrying seed to sow, will return with songs of joy, carrying sheaves with him.

. . .Unless an ear of wheat falls to the ground and dies, it remains only a single seed. But if it dies, it produces many seeds.

I tell you the truth, you will weep and mourn while the world rejoices. You will grieve, but your grief will turn to joy. . . now is your time of grief, but I will see you again and you will rejoice, and no-one will take away your joy.

But we have this treasure in jars of clay to show that this all-surpassing power is from God and not from us. We are hard-pressed, but. . . not in despair; persecuted, but not abandoned; struck down, but not destroyed. We always carry around in our body the death of Jesus, so that the life of Jesus may also be revealed in our body.

To this you were called, because Christ suffered for you, leaving you an example, that you should follow in his steps.

. . .They will be his people, and God himself will be with them and be their God. He will wipe every tear from their eyes. There will be no more death or mourning or crying or pain, for the old order of things has passed away.

(Psalm 126: 5-6; John 12: 24: John 16: 20 and 22; 2 Corinthians 4: 7-10; 1 Peter 2: 21; Revelation 21: 3-4 — all NIV)

In the scriptures, as well as in life, the link between the reality of human experience and suffering and the joy of release, restoration and resurrection is unavoidable. The former is sharply and honestly recorded throughout the long history of God's people. The latter is not so easily grasped or understood, but it is the essential corollary to much of that record and brings meaning and hope to desperately needy people of every age.

Some time ago, when reflecting on this theme, I asked myself a number of questions. They emerged in this way:

What is the place of suffering in the life and growth of the believer and of the church? Is suffering for Christ's sake central to the process of human maturity, sanctification and glorification?

If Christ has brought salvation to us through suffering, and suffered as the pioneer of our salvation, how shall we follow his footsteps?

If Christ learned obedience through the things which he suffered, can we learn obedience without suffering?

How can the theme of suffering be introduced into our theology and our understanding of the Christian life?

It seems that since 'the fall' and the development of its tragic consequences that 'the cross' is marked deeply into the very heart of all human experience and endeavour. There have always been signs of mercy and renewal offered to those who face such suffering, pain and sorrow. The dilemma has been in recognising this mercy and interpreting its source and integrity.

The need for authentic messengers and interpreters to explain the goodness and loving-kindness of God remains our greatest need. People are suffering and dying without hope and without any knowledge of God's mercy and compassion. Our task and responsibility is an awesome one.

The apostle Paul in Romans 10: 14 expressed the urgency of this task when he asked, 'How, then, can they call on the one they have not believed in? And how can they believe in the one of whom they have not heard? And how can they hear without someone preaching to them?'

If we are to be messengers of such hope, then we shall need to be prepared. That preparation emerges within our understanding of these principles. That is — life comes through death. Suffering can be the womb from which joy emerges, and powerlessness and weakness can be the basic elements leading to resurrection.

❧❧

The cross is all of life — it is sleeping in the stone, comes to clearer life in the vine, is clearer still in the animal, shines more fully in man and comes to its fruition and perfection in the cross of Christ. And that cross is the revelation of God. In the beautiful lines of E.M. Plunkett:

> I see his blood upon the rose,
> And in the stars the glory of his eyes,
> His body gleams amid the eternal snows,
> His tears drop from the skies.
> All pathways by his feet are worn,
> His strong heart stirs the everbeating sea,
> His crown of thorns is twined with every thorn,
> His cross is every tree.

E. Stanley Jones, *Christ and Human Suffering*

The breakthrough in biblical teaching came when suffering could be seen as redemptive, and not merely wasteful. This teaching was fulfilled in Jesus Christ. He suffered and died for us, overcoming suffering and making available to us the same power. While on earth he did all he could to alleviate want, pain and anguish, yet he knew he had to suffer. It is of the essence of Christianity, because he said, 'Unless you take up your cross and follow me, you cannot be my disciple.' An affluent, comfortable church cannot be the church of Christ — an affluent church which uses its wealth for itself.

Archbishop Desmond Tutu, *Crying in the Wilderness*

Where we were blind was that when we were weak and dying life was in the offing. When winter is half spent, can spring be far away?. . .as some poet asks. Strength is found in weakness, as life in dying. As Paul put it, what you sow does not come to life unless it dies. What is sown is perishable, what is raised is imperishable; it is sown in dishonour, it is raised in glory; it is sown in weakness, it is raised in power. After having lost much, we find there are more Christians in China than ever before, and more dedicated too. After every church having been closed, we find that for three years now one or two churches are being opened or re-opened every two or three days, and with much greater enthusiasm and vigour. And because we have been a part of the suffering fate of the Chinese people, we today are no longer so dissociated from them, but are in much better conversational relations with them than in the past.

Bishop Ting in a personal letter

The stone suffers
because all speak
of its hardness. . .
And yet
You used to look for a stone
as a pillow for your head,
for you knew and you know
that the hope of stones
is to serve. . .
When they serve
they become as soft
as clouds. . .

Have you ever seen a dry sponge full of chalk dust? Have you ever held in your hand a dry sponge stiff with chalk? If you dip it in water, all the hardness disappears, all the stiffness vanishes.

When I meet hearts that are like sponges stiff with chalk, how I would like to plunge them into the water of God's infinite goodness! One day a lady, a dear friend of mine, said to me: 'I'd be quite happy if my heart were like a sponge stiff with chalk. My case is worse. My heart has turned to stone. What good is a petrified heart?' There are moments when words come to us that we did not know we had, unforeseen words, breathed directly into us by the Spirit of God. I repeated her words and commented on them: 'What good is your heart that has turned to stone? It's marvellous! Magnificent! Christ says he does

not have even a stone on which to lay his head. Offer
him your "stone".'

The next day my friend said to me: 'Yesterday evening
your words about Jesus not having even a stone on which
to lay his head made me say to him: "I find this a bit
awkward. But if it's true that you are looking for a stone
on which to lay your head, well, I have my stone here.
It's a real joy for me to serve you, even in such a poor
way".' And she continued: ' I had an utterly deep sleep
— something very rare for me. And the next day my
heart no longer felt like a stone. I could look at everyone
— even those who hated me and do me evil and are paid
back with even stronger hate from me — I could look at
everyone and almost sing for joy and peace.'

Dom Helder Camara, Hoping Against All Hope

A father's prayer upon the murder of his son:

O God:
We remember not only Bahram but also his murderers;
Not because they killed him in the prime of his youth
and made our hearts bleed and our tears flow.
Not because with this savage act they have brought further
disgrace on the name of our country among the civilised
nations of the world;
But because through their crime we now follow thy
footsteps more closely in the way of sacrifice.
The terrible fire of this calamity burns up all selfishness
and possessiveness in us;
Its flame reveals the depth of depravity and meanness and
suspicion, the dimension of hatred and the measure of
sinfulness in human nature;
It makes obvious as never before our need to trust in
God's love as shown in the cross of Jesus and his resurrection;
Love which makes us free from hate towards our per-
secutors;
Love which brings patience, forebearance, courage, loyalty,
humility, generosity, greatnesss of heart;
Love which more than ever deepens our trust in God's

final victory and his eternal designs for the church and
for the world;
Love which teaches us how to prepare ourselves to face
our own day of death.
O God,
Bahram's blood has multiplied the fruit of the Spirit in
the soil of our souls;
So when his murderers stand before thee on the day of
judgment
Remember the fruit of the Spirit by which they have
enriched our lives,
And forgive.

Hassan Dehquani-Tafti (Bishop of Iran)
written on the death of his son, in 1980

Christians here are like cane-sugar;
they need to be crushed for the sweetness to be released.

A Pakistani Christian to a missionary friend

We know death and resurrection in our closest loves. In
marriage perhaps in particular, we know what it is to
struggle on when there are no rewarding emotions. And
after, there comes a point where the relationship glowers
gloriously beyond our imagination or expectation. . . and
it is impossible afterwards to escape the knowledge that
joy and happiness sprang out of the darkness of the pain.

Archbishop Robert Runcie, *Windows onto God*

Sometimes a light surprises
the Christian while he sings;
it is the Lord who rises
with healing in his wings;
when comforts are declining
he grants the soul again
a season of clear shining
to cheer it after rain.

In holy contemplation
we joyfully pursue
the theme of God's salvation,
and find it ever new.

Set free from present sorrow
we cheerfully can say,
'Now let the unknown morrow
bring with it what it may:

'It can bring with it nothing
but he will bear us through;
who gives the lilies clothing
will clothe his people too;
beneath the spreading heavens
no creature but is fed,
and he who feeds the ravens
will give his children bread.'

Though vine nor fig-tree neither
their wonted fruit should bear,
though all the fields should wither,
nor flocks nor herds be there,
yet, God the same abiding,
his praise shall tune my voice;
for while in him confiding
I cannot but rejoice.

William Cowper, 'Sometimes a Light Surprises'

With Christ, it is impossible to lose the hope.

Don Helder Camara, in Melbourne, 1985

Lord Jesus,
I marvel at your healing, self-giving love.
When I am hurt
Or neglected
Or when friends fail to respond to my love,
I withdraw,
Cold,
Silent,
Prickly,
Bruised.
But your love never gives up.
You see the one you love

And think, not of your own needs,
But of their need to be restored
And loved.
Teach me to give as you give;
To love as you love.
Produce in me a qualitative love -
which is always in season.

Lord, grant that I may seek rather to comfort than to be comforted; to understand than to be understood; to love than to be loved; for it is by forgetting self that one finds; it is by dying that one awakens to eternal life.

St Francis of Assisi

Lord Jesus, your power and your strength are my hope. Your mercy and forgiveness my daily joy. May my life and that of your people be a sign to every person in need and a light to the nations on every side.

Holy Spirit, in the demands and pain of every day, may your comfort and presence prepare me for the joy of renewal and the wonder of the resurrection as I continue to walk in the steps of Jesus.

Father, my heart is overflowing with adoration and praise, that you should restore me to your family, fill me with your Spirit and make me an heir, with Jesus, of all the wonders of heaven.

Eternal God, Father, Son and Holy Spirit,
you alone I worship
you alone are my Saviour
you alone my hope and joy
To you be praise and glory, for ever.

A Benediction

. . .the God of all grace, who has called us to his eternal glory by Jesus Christ, whom God has given to us, will strengthen us to endure these little afflictions that we may be made steadfast and remain in him for ever.

To him be glory and dominion and honour for ever and ever.

Amen.

16

Pain the plow

(Eberhard Arnold)

Blessed are those who mourn, for they will be comforted
. . . Blessed are those who are persecuted because of
righteousness, for theirs is the kingdom of heaven.

Now I rejoice in what was suffered for you, and I fill
up in my flesh what is still lacking in regard to Christ's
afflictions, for the sake of his body, which is the church.
. . I want you to know how much I am struggling for
you and for those at Laodicea, and for all who have not
met me personally.

As servants of God we commend ourselves in every
way: in great endurance; in troubles, hardships and dis-
tresses;. . . sorrowful, yet always rejoicing; poor, yet
making many rich; having nothing, and yet possessing
everything.

Dear friends, do not be surprised at the painful trial
you are suffering, as though something strange were happening to you. But rejoice that you participate in the
sufferings of Christ, so that you may be overjoyed when
his glory is revealed. If you are insulted because of the
name of Christ, you are blessed, for the Spirit of glory
and of God rests on you. . . So then, those who suffer
according to God's will should commit themselves to their
faithful Creator and continue to do good.

For just as the sufferings of Christ flow over into our
lives, so also through Christ our comfort overflows. If we
are distressed, it is for your comfort and salvation; if we
are comforted, it is for your comfort, which produces in
you patient endurance of the same sufferings we suffer.
And our hope for you is firm, because we know that just
as you share in our sufferings, so also you share in our

comfort.

(Matthew 5: 4 and 10; Colossians 1: 24, 2: 1; 2 Corinthians 6: 4 and 10; 1 Peter 4: 12-14,19; 2 Corinthians 1: 5-7 — all NIV)

We live at a strange time, a time when the saints of God are involved simultaneously in the deep embrace and the deep denial of suffering.

In the *favelas* of Rio de Janeiro and the squatter settlements of Manila, God's people are weeping with the world. In the nightclubs of Amsterdam riddled with drugs, the dust of Ethiopia haunted by starvation and the empty suburbs of Sydney soaked with despair, they are meeting people in their cries of pain. In the cluttered streets of Kathmandu and the Muslim villages of the Middle East, they are suffering, even to death, for the name of Christ.

At the same time, from the world-influencing popular religion of North America comes the Prosperity Doctrine. Pentecostals, charismatics, plain old evangelicals: you name it, everyone is naming and claiming it. We're children of the king! We have the right to possess our inheritance in health and wealth!

There are two dangers in this bifurcation of Christian devotion. One is that a growing Spirit-inspired adventurousness in trusting God will be highjacked by a trite triumphalism that profoundly denies pain. The other is that important manifestations of God's mighty grace will be barricaded out by a Spirit-inspired immersion in suffering.

We are truly caught between heaven and earth. We live between the embrace and the denial of suffering. We are called to deny it, for it has no ultimate power to defeat the triumph of Christ's kingdom, and already that eternal rule is turning back its effects. We are called to embrace it because, here and now, it is the only context in which Christ's kingdom can come to his broken world.

Christ himself lived this paradox. His ripped flesh was the deepest embrace and the deepest denial of pain in the history of creation.

This means, for those who follow him, that pain cannot be avoided. The pain that is 'inseparable from this mortal life' (Bonhoeffer); the pain that comes in the course of being reshaped in the image of Christ; the pain of the servant ministering in sacrificial love; the savage pain of persecution.

The seventeenth century American theologian Jonathan Edwards taught that trials have 'a threefold benefit for true religion': they separate true faith from false, they purify faith and increase it, and they 'enhance its genuine beauty and attractiveness'.

Moreover, as we pour ourselves out as an offering for the people we serve, pain softens our hearts so that they are ruled by compassion.

But pain also lifts our sights. 'Persecution,' says Nepalese pastor Nicanor Tamang, 'helps us see the world beyond this world.' And when we see the contours of the glorious kingdom, we are emboldened to pray, 'Your kingdom come, your will be done on earth as it is in heaven' — and to expect that it will.

Anyone genuinely close to the world will find it impossible to avoid pain, and anyone genuinely close to God will find it impossible to avoid joy.

❧

When we try to grasp the nature of suffering, we will feel that suffering is necessary in our search for fellowship with God. . . The more we suffer and become aware of our own wretchedness, the more we realise that Jesus is our only foothold. . . Pain is the plow that tears up our hearts to make us open to truth.

Eberhard Arnold, *God's Revolution*

. . .in the early church the experiences of suffering and healing were woven together in a strange paradox. Both Peter and Paul healed the sick, but both of them eventually came to a martyr's death in Rome. What happened to them mattered little. Their priority was to serve Jesus Christ as their lord and to proclaim the gospel of the kingdom. Imprisonments and trials were just as much occasions for manifestations of the Holy Spirit as were miraculous healings.

John Gunstone, *The Lord is Our Healer*

If we believe suffering is the touch of God's grace, we will avoid resentment, arrogance and above all pride, the primal and satanic sin. . .

It is an easily verified fact, both from observation of others and from experiment yourself, that an attitude of humility and gratitude in suffering brings deep joy, while an attitude of pride and ingratitude, even without suffering, brings joylessness. Proud people simply are not happy.

Peter Kreeft, *Making Sense Out of Suffering*

When I am walking round the exercise yard, I like to go over all the mercies for which I must thank the Lord: for my sorrow, my difficulties, for the work which he has entrusted to me, for service which I have been given to accomplish in these difficult times for the church. I haven't enough fingers to count them all on. In life eternal, the value of suffering for Christ will be even more clearly revealed to me, and I will give thanks to the Lord again and again.

Mikail Khorev, imprisoned Soviet Baptist

I'm deeply convinced that people of action and of light can do nothing unless they rely on those who accept their suffering, immobility and prayer and offer these to make life possible. People who are old or sick and offer themselves to God can become the most precious members of a community — lightning conductors of grace. There is a mystery in the secret strength of those whose bodies are broken, who seem to do nothing all day, but who remain in the presence of God. Their immobility obliges them to keep their minds and hearts fixed on the essential, on the source of life itself. Their suffering and agony bears fruit; they give life.

Jean Vanier, *Community and Growth*

But just as listening to God can elicit paeans of praise so

it can plunge the person at prayer into a deep and terrible pain. . .

When we stand before God and tune into him, we pick up some of the heartbreak he feels for a needy world. In this way God gives us the privilege of 'knowing him' and entering into the 'fellowship of his sufferings'. . .

I do not understand why one tragedy can affect me in this way while another can leave me cold. What I do know is that in prayer I must hold this pain into the healing hands of Christ so that his compassion and our heartache can meet and be matched. This is the solemn responsibility of the person of prayer.

Joyce Huggett, *Listening to God*

I take it as a law of spiritual growth that as we are enabled to enter into the depth of love that the Songs of the Suffering Servant portray, we are gently drawn (*never driven: if it feels like being driven, it is false — ignore it*) to a situation in life where we can choose to accept redemptive suffering for ourselves.

Charles Elliott, *Praying the Kingdom*

The pattern of the messianic life is one of suffering and glory. To share the suffering is therefore an assurance that we shall also share the glory.

L.S. Thornton, *The Common Life in the Body of Christ*

Lord, it's a tightrope walker's journey along the thin rope strung between pain and joy. And I'm no acrobat! I'm so easily caught off balance.

Sometimes all I can sense is the platform behind, the suffering of the world yanking on the rope, swaying it, and then I'm sick with fear. Other times I yearn so desperately for the platform ahead and I allow your eternal music to drown out the cacophonies of pain.

I can speak fine words acknowledging the need for both suffering and grace, but when it comes to the crunch, I want the second without the first. Is that so strange Lord? You didn't make me suffer, but to enjoy you forever; suffering is alien to my deepest being. But I rebelled against you, forfeiting my native glory; and now, like all people, I only receive it back on the other side of death.

It's easy to forget, Lord, that by definition, resurrection only comes after dying.

Help me to face the many deaths I must die, the many pains I must embrace. Much in my past makes it hard to accept suffering; many hurts already experienced make it hard to face hurt in the future. Heal me and strengthen me so that I can walk the tightrope, balanced by you.

A Benediction

Weep for the old world lost in Satan's night,
Laugh for the new world bound in God's light,
Sigh for the call to turn old into new,
God's grace within you, bridging the two.

17

Dear Adam. . . A letter to South Africa

'My God, my God, why have you forsaken me?. . . O, my God, I cry out by day, but you do not answer, by night, and am not silent.'

'I have been allotted months of futility, and nights of misery have been assigned to me. When I lie down I think, "How long before I get up?" The night drags on, and I toss till dawn.'

'Your words have supported those who stumbled; you have strengthened faltering knees. But now trouble comes to you, and you are discouraged. . . Should not your piety be your confidence and your blameless ways your hope?'

Although the Lord gives you the bread of adversity and the water of affliction, your teachers will be hidden no more; with your own eyes you will see them. . . when the Lord binds up the bruises of his people and heals the wounds he inflicted.

Now if we are children, then we are heirs. . . if indeed we share in his sufferings in order that we may also share in his glory.

(Psalm 22: 1 and 2; Job 7: 3 and 4; Job 4: 4-6; Isaiah 30: 20 and 26; Romans 8: 17 — all NIV)

This letter is a reflection on the struggles that both the writer and reader share in being people-helpers:

Dear Adam,
I feel so strange writing this letter to you, a person I don't

know in a situation I know so little about, thousands of miles away. All we have is a mutual caring friend, who asked me to write to you, a mutual profession and a mutual dark night of the soul.

I don't really know what to say as the same words at different times by well-meaning friends have injured or uplifted me, as I have dragged myself through the blackness of depression.

All I can do is sit in the 'dust and ashes' with you, and place my shaking hand on your boil-infested body and quietly share your pain and cry for justice. Words are so inadequate, those around us are threatened by our cries and God seems deaf to our pleas.

In my own room I have cursed the night as once more, like clockwork, my troubled spirit awakens at 2.00 am. I have lain there tossing, turning, shaking and sweating as wave after wave of fear and despair rolled over me like the fever of malaria. My God, what had I done to deserve this, night after night?

The texts on the wall mocked me as they became readable in the growing light:

'Be joyful always. . .'

'they are new every morning. . .'

I just want to turn my face to the wall and die.

Yet I am still here, and have found out that I am not the only one like this. In some strange way I can begin to understand a little of what Paul means when he talks about sharing some of the sufferings and comfort of Christ so we can, in turn, comfort those experiencing similar valleys of shadows as we are.

I also gain some strange comfort in knowing that some of the great men and women of the past and of this century have gone through similar experiences. These include Elijah, David, Job, John of the Cross, Martin Luther, John Wesley, Spurgeon, J.B. Phillips. . . to name a few.

But apart from this growing insight, I have few other answers, Adam, to your (our?) many questions. I don't know why, to quote you, God 'has brought together two people on different continents. . . two people sharing most of the inner distress of walking through a desert blindfolded. . .'

However, I do draw strength from the progress I can read in your letters, faltering as it may be. In your August letter, your feelings of anxiety and depression, the lethargy and lack of energy, your critical spirit were to the fore, while your November letter seemed to indicate some slow but positive re-integration and ability to face others.

Your January letter seems even to have some sense of excitement about 'the learnings that we are to discover and share with each other.' I hope I can catch that beginning sense of excitement. My feelings still fluctuate so much, yet I feel a little of the vision and energy returning, but for how long? I'm so afraid of being hurt further or of hurting those I love with my black moods and critical spirit.

Perhaps you are right in thinking that part of the problem lies in our being 'driven people' rather than 'called', to quote Gordon MacDonald. Like you, I have tried to control my goals and direction and have been disappointed and angered by those who didn't live up to my expectations or 'vision'.

I haven't been 'success-oriented' but, perhaps I have channelled such desires into my Christian life and ministry. Oh, how do I become called rather than driven? I suspect that the 'solutions' lie not only with me, but with the Christian Church as well.

Personally I'm sure I need to learn how to wait and abide more in Christ; to listen to what he is calling me to. Perhaps this is why I have been forced to slow down. In the meantime, I need to forgive and let go those who have unknowingly hurt me and not close off completely to others. I need to spend more time with people that energise me and less with those who drain me. Gordon MacDonald's book *Restoring Your Spiritual Passion* has some good things to say about this.

Also I think the Church has a lot to account for in the way it hasn't enabled the laity to recognise and follow God's calling for them. Because of this, much of the work is left to the very busy few who, in turn, are resentful of the lack of participation by the majority. This often leads eventually to apathy, depression and 'burnout' in these few workers.

Finally, thankyou for sharing your thoughts with me; my attempting to reply has helped some things fall into place. Perhaps some of our questions will never be answered this side of heaven.

Keep the faith,

Shalom. . .

🐟🐟

Tragically, when people who are accustomed to their role as helpers get depressed, they experience more difficulty than the average person in seeking professional help and in making good use of it when they find it.

John White, *Masks of Melancholy*

Spurgeon himself was quick to admit that he was not immune to periodic bouts of depression. He said that he knew 'by most painful experience what deep depression means, being visited there-with at seasons by no means few or far between'. He then went on to cite from the biographies of Martin Luther and John Wesley, which are full of reports about their own experiences of depression.

Arch Hart, *Coping With Depression*

'This evil will come upon us, we know not why, and then it is all the more difficult to drive away. Causeless depression is not to be reasoned with. . . If those who laugh at such melancholy did but feel the grief of it for one hour, their laughter would be sobered into compassion.' (Charles Spurgeon)

H. Norman Wright, *Now I Know Why I Am Depressed*

I have always been plagued by depression, which has often been so excessive that I could neither work nor relate to people. . . This was so extreme, that I wished to die.

Robert Girard, *My Weakness: His Strength*

Walter Trobisch, a Christian counsellor, notes that the word for depression in German is *schwermut*. . . It means the courage to be heavyhearted, the courage to live with what is difficult. Strange as it may seem, courage is part of depression. . .

Once I heard an experienced psychiatrist say, 'All people of worth and value have depressions.' Indeed, superficial people seldom have depressions. It requires a certain inner substance and depth of mind to be depressed.

H. Norman Wright, *Now I Know Why I Am Depressed*

Depression is a symptom which warns us that we're getting into deep water. It is, I believe, designed by God as an emotional reaction to slow us down, to remove us from the race, to pull us back so we can take stock. . . It is a protective device which removes us from further stress and gives us time to recover.

Arch Hart, *Coping with Depression*

There are many Christians — true believers in the Lord Jesus, who are genuinely seeking to follow him — who, like me, have, for too many years, been desperately lonely, and in great emotional distress, each thinking that he or she is the 'only one' who, as a believer, still struggles and fails so miserably against sin. Baffled by repeated defeat in areas where other Christians seem 'to have the victory', these miserable strugglers are on the point of giving up.

Robert Girard, *My Weakness: His Strength*

Friendship is born at the moment when one person says to another, 'What! You too! I thought I was the only one!' (C.S. Lewis)

Robert Girard, *My Weakness: His Strength*

. . .Being fairly suddenly deprived of the ability to 'perform', my sense of security and of being useful deserted me and all kinds of nameless terrors swept over me, usually at night.

Vera Phillips & Edwina Robertson

. . .then we also should have an address book of our special friends. . . special friends are committed to helping each other discover and maintain spiritual passion.

Gordon MacDonald, *Restoring Your Spiritual Passion*

Dear Lord, at times I feel so tired and weary; I have so many questions to ask you, but I don't even have the strength to ask them now.

Please let me rest a while in your arms and be carried close to your heart. Let me cry and drain out all the pain I carry deep inside me for myself and others.

Lord, break me if you will, but do not crush me.

. . .Your Kingdom come, your will be done. . .!Amen.

A Benediction

Here I am, Lord.
Here is my body, Here is my heart, Here is my soul.
Grant that I may be big enough to reach the world,
Strong enough to carry it,
Pure enough to embrace it without wanting to keep it.
Grant that I may be a meeting place, but a temporary one;
A road that does not end in itself, because everything to
be gathered there, everything human, leads towards you.

Michel Quoist, *Prayers of Life*

18

This slight momentary affliction. . .

(2 Corinthians 4: 17)

They strengthened the believers and encouraged them to remain true to the faith. 'We must pass through many troubles to enter the kingdom of God,' they taught.

My dear friends, do not be surprised at the painful test you are suffering, as though something unusual were happening to you. Rather be glad that you are sharing Christ's sufferings, so that you may be full of joy when his glory is revealed.

Everyone who wants to live a godly life in union with Christ Jesus will be persecuted.

Now those who were scattered because of the persecution that arose over Stephen travelled. . . preaching the Lord Jesus. And the hand of the Lord was with them, and a great number that believed turned to the Lord.

Now I rejoice in my sufferings for your sake, and in my flesh I complete what is lacking in Christ's afflictions for the sake of his body, that is, the church. . .

Let us give thanks to the God and Father of our Lord Jesus Christ, the merciful Father, the God from whom all help comes! He helps us in all our troubles, so that we are able to help others who have all kinds of troubles, using the same help that we ourselves have received from God.

We sent Timothy. . . to strengthen and encourage you in your faith, so that no-one would be unsettled by these trials. You know quite well that we were destined for them. In fact, when we were with you, we kept telling you that we would be persecuted. And it turned out that way, as you well know.

When we cry, 'Abba, Father!' it is the Spirit himself bearing witness with our spirit that we are children of God, and if children, then heirs, heirs of God and fellow heirs with Christ, provided we suffer with him in order that we may also be glorified with him.

I have told you these things, so that in me you may have peace. In this world you will have trouble. But take heart! I have overcome the world.

I consider that the sufferings of this present time are not worth comparing with the glory that is to be revealed to us.

So we do not lose heart. . . For this slight momentary affliction is preparing for us an eternal weight of glory beyond all comparison. . .

It was only right that God, who creates and preserves all things, should make Jesus perfect through suffering, in order to bring many children to share his glory.

(Acts 14: 22, GNB; 1 Peter 4: 12-13, GNB; 2 Timothy 3: 12, GNB; Acts 11: 19-21, RSV; Colossians 1: 24, RSV; 2 Corinthians 1: 3 and 4, GNB; 1 Thessalonians 3: 2-4, NIV; Romans 8: 15b-17, RSV; John 16: 33, NIV; Romans 8: 18, RSV; 2 Corinthians 4: 16 and 17, RSV; Hebrews 2: 10, GNB)

The ultimate question for anyone attempting to minister in the name of a loving God is the age-old one: Why would a loving God allow good people to suffer? Related to this basic question are a whole host of similar inquiries that range as far and wide as the whole spectrum of human suffering: Why do people starve? Why do tragic accidents happen to infants, children and young people cut off in the prime of their lives? Why is a good spouse the subject of abuse? Why did God allow the existence of mind-altering chemicals and drugs? The list is endless.

Just when one thinks one has a reasonably good explanation that is intellectually respectable, along comes a tragedy that has no rhyme or reason. Imagine explaining to a young widow that her children's father died meaningfully when his car was struck from above by a five hundred pound beef carcass that ripped through the side of an overturned semi-truck on the bridge above his vehicle. Of all our human experiences, pain and suffering seem the most irrational.

Many writers have made valiant attempts at marshalling their intellectual powers to give this irrationality a rational basis. Some have come closer than others. All fail to a lesser or greater degree. As C.S. Lewis has suggested, pain and suffering can never be made 'palatable'.

This is just the point. What we want in the midst of our pain is not intellectual brilliance, but emotional satisfaction. This is why most explanations fail to comfort. They really do not address the emotional distress. They fail to satisfy.

The value of the incarnation is often overlooked at just this point. In our suffering we want to know that, like little children who run to their parents when hurt, we still have someone *we* can run to – someone who understands and can hold us and comfort us until the pain goes away. Intuitively, as children, we know that our parents understand – they share the same human experience of pain and suffering. *And* so does God! As Hebrews 2: 10 and 11 says, 'In bringing many children to glory, it was fitting that God. . . should make the author of their salvation perfect through suffering. Both the one who makes people holy, and those who are made holy are of the same family.'

Most often, in the midst of our pain, we want comfort, not explanations. This is where our presence as 'little Christs' in the lives of those who hurt is crucial. We are the conveyors of Christ's comfort, which comfort we ourselves have received.

And what of the value of the explanations? They are of great value indeed. They help shape the spirit before and after the suffering. They are the stones upon which our spirit is sharpened. In the midst of the battle no-one takes time to sharpen his blade. The time for sharpening is before we enter the valley of the enemy. . .

❦

The problem of reconciling human suffering with the existence of a God who loves, is only insoluble as long as we attach a trivial meaning to the word 'love', and look on things as if man were the centre of them. Man is not the centre. God does not exist for the sake of man. Man does not exist for his own sake. 'Thou hast created all things, and for thy pleasure they are and were created.' We were not made primarily that we may love God (though we were made for that too), but that God may love us, that we may become objects in which the Divine love may rest 'well pleased'.

To ask that God's love should be content with us as we are is to ask that God should cease to be God: because he is what he is, his love must, in the nature of things, be impeded and repelled by certain stains in our present character, and because he already loves us he must labour to make us lovable. We cannot even wish, in our better moments, that he could reconcile himself to our present impurities. . . What we would here and now call our 'happiness' is not the end God chiefly has in view: but when we are such as he can love without impediment, we shall in fact be happy.

C.S. Lewis, *The Problem of Pain*

In words which can still bring tears to the eyes, St Augustine describes the desolation in which the death of his friend Nebridius plunged him. Then he draws a moral. This is what comes, he says, of giving one's heart to anything but God. All human beings pass away. Do not let your happiness depend on something you may lose. If love is to be a blessing, not a misery, it must be for the only Beloved who will never pass away.

Of course this makes excellent sense. Don't put your goods in a leaky vessel. Don't spend too much on a house you may be turned out of. . . Of all arguments against love none makes so strong an appeal to my nature as 'Careful! This might lead you to suffering. . .'

Even if it were granted that insurances against heartbreak were our highest wisdom, does God himself offer them? Apparently not. Christ comes at last to say, 'Why hast thou forsaken me?'

There is no escape along the lines St Augustine suggests. Nor along any other lines. There is no safe investment. To love at all is to be vulnerable. Love anything, and your heart will certainly be wrung and possibly be broken. If you want to make sure of keeping it intact, you must give your heart to no-one, not even to an animal. Wrap it carefully round with hobbies and little luxuries; avoid all entanglements; lock it up safe in the casket or coffin of your selfishness. But in that casket – safe, dark, motionless, airless – it will change. It will not be broken; it will become unbreakable, impenetrable, irredeemable. The alternative to tragedy, or at least to the risk of tragedy, is damnation. The only place outside heaven where you can be perfectly safe from all the dangers and perturbations of love is hell.

C.S. Lewis, *The Four Loves*

It often seems to those in earnest about the right as if all things conspired to prevent their progress. This, of course, is but an appearance, arising in part from this, that the pilgrim must be headed back from the side paths into which he is constantly wandering.

George MacDonald, *Anthology*

The Son of God suffered unto the death, not that we might not suffer, but that our sufferings might be like his.

George MacDonald, *Unspoken Sermons*

Now God, who made us, knows what we are and that our happiness lies in him. Yet we will not seek it in him as long as he leaves us any other resort where it can even plausibly be looked for. While what we call 'our own life' remains agreeable, we will not surrender it to him. What then can God do in our interests but make 'our own life' less agreeable to us, and take away the plausible sources of false happiness?

It is just here, where God's providence seems at first to be most cruel, that the divine humility, the stooping down of the highest, most deserves praise. We are perplexed to see misfortune falling upon decent, inoffensive, worthy people – on capable, hard-working mothers of families or diligent, thrifty little trades-people, on those who have worked so hard, and so honestly, for their modest stock of happiness and now seem to be entering on the enjoyment of it with the fullest right.

How can I say with sufficient tenderness what here needs to be said? It does not matter that I know I must become, in the eyes of every hostile reader, as it were, personally responsible for all that suffering I try to explain – just as, to this day, everyone talks as if St Augustine *wanted* unbaptised infants to go to hell. But it matters enormously if I alienate anyone from the truth. Let me implore the reader to try to believe, if only for the moment, that God, who made these deserving people, may really be right when he thinks that their modest prosperity and the happiness of their children are not enough to make them blessed: That all this must fall from them in the end, and that if they have not learned to know him they will be wretched. And therefore he troubles them, warning them in advance of an insufficiency that one day they will have to discover. The life to themselves and their families stands between them and the recognition of their need; he makes that life less sweet to them.

I call this a divine humility because it is a poor thing to strike our colours to God when the ship is going down under us; a poor thing to come to him as a last resort, to offer up 'our own' when it is no longer worth keeping. If God were proud he would hardly have us on such terms: but he is not proud, he stoops to conquer, he will have us even though we have shown that we prefer everything else to him, and come to him because there is 'nothing better' now to be had.

C.S. Lewis, *The Problem of Pain*

Even such as ask amiss may sometimes have their prayers answered. The Father will never give the child a stone that asks for bread; but I am not sure that he will never give the child a stone that asks for a stone. If the Father says, 'My child, that is a stone; it is not bread,' and the child answer, 'I am sure it is bread; I want it,' may it not

be well that he should try his bread?
George MacDonald, *Anthology*

One thing is clear in regard to every trouble – that the natural way with it is straight to the Father's knee. The Father is father *for* his children, else why did he make himself their father?

The Lord had come to wipe away our tears. He is doing it; he will have it done as soon as he can; and until he can, he would have them flow without bitterness; to which end he tells us it is a blessed thing to mourn, because of the comfort on its way. Accept his comfort now, and so prepare for the comfort at hand. He is getting you ready for it, but you must be a fellow-worker with him, or he will never have done. He *must* have you pure in heart, eager after righteousness, a very child of his Father in heaven.
George MacDonald, *Life Essential*

The working out of this our salvation must be pain, and the handing of it down to them that are below must ever be in pain; but the eternal form of the will of God in and for us, is intensity of bliss.
George MacDonald, *Anthology*

Father, I hurt. Sometimes I hurt physically. Sometimes I hurt emotionally. But hardly an hour passes that I do not hurt. O Lord Jesus, grant that I should not become focussed on and absorbed in my pain, but instead that my pain might cause me to remember your pain and the pain of the other five billion persons on this planet. Help me to see that not even one of those five billion can live in avoidance of pain.

Grant me compassion, Lord, as I see these others who seem so separate from me and yet share in this same pain and suffering in which I live. Help me to see the pain in their lives. Help me to look beyond the inappropriate behaviour, past the striking out and the anger and let me see the pain that lies at the bottom of it all. Help me, as I experience pain, to remember those others who are also in pain and let me feel compassion towards them. And Lord, grant that my compassion might grow wings that I might fly to their side and minister to their needs in some way that will display to them your love for them, your solidarity with them. O Father, let not my own pain separate me either from you or from these others. Grant that I might know your comforting arms around me as I struggle with my suffering. Let my arms become your arms for some other one who suffers, whether in sickness or in loneliness or in desperation or in hunger or in anger. And until I see more clearly, let me rest in your arms and commit myself wholly to you.

A Benediction

Be still, my soul: the Lord is on thy side;
Bear patiently the cross of grief or pain;
Leave to thy God to order and provide;
In every change he faithful will remain.
Be still my soul: thy best, thy heavenly friend
Through thorny ways leads to a joyful end.

Katharina von Schlegel

God grant me this day to live trusting you, my Father, Lord and Saviour. In Christ's holy name I ask it, Amen.

The only way is up

Out of the depth I cry to thee, O Lord! Lord, hear my voice!

My grief is beyond healing, my heart is sick within me. . . I mourn, and dismay has taken hold on me. Is there no balm in Gilead?

[Elijah] went a day's journey into the wilderness, and came and sat down under a broom tree; and he asked that he might die, saying, 'It is enough; now, O Lord, take away my life; for I am no better than my fathers.' . . And the angel of the Lord came. . . and said, 'Arise and eat, else the journey will be too great for you.'

I will lift up my eyes to the hills. From whence does my help come? My help comes from the Lord, who made heaven and earth.

For the Lord is a great God, and a great King above all gods. In his hand are the depths of the earth; the heights of the mountains are his also.

[Jesus said] 'Let not your hearts be troubled; believe in God, believe also in me. . . I will not leave you desolate; I will come to you'.

I am sure that neither death, nor life, nor angels, nor principalities, nor things present, nor things to come, nor powers, nor height, nor depth, nor anything else in all creation, will be able to separate us from the love of God in Christ Jesus our Lord.

If then you have been raised with Christ, seek the things that are above. . . Set your minds on things that are above, not on things that are on earth.

(Psalm 130: 1; Jeremiah 8: 18, 21-22; 1 Kings 19: 4 and 7; Psalm 121: 1-2; Psalm 95: 3-4; John 14: 1 and 18; Romans 8: 38-39; Colossians 3: 1-2 — all RSV)

There are times for all of us when 'the only way is up', when life itself seems a valley experience, with no redeeming peaks or vistas, and when no light at all appears to penetrate the gloom of the present moment. Well-meaning friends urge us to 'look on the bright side' when, like the blind person, we no longer have a concept of 'bright' at all. Whatever the explanation may be for such times, the feelings of helplessness and oppression are typical. Passivity seems the only response to our inability to control our circumstances and environment. We stop trying to *do* anything, because it seems there is nothing we *can* do — we simply give up, overwhelmed by the towering peaks above and the gloom below.

Some personalities are perhaps more prone to depression, and some of life's experiences, patterns of coping learned in childhood, predispose others to capitulate too quickly to valley experiences. But God wants to break through our faulty perceptions and assure us of his help in our helplessness, his strength in our weakness, his upward call in even our lowest moments. We need to allow Paul to speak to us 'in the pit': 'I can do *all things* in [Christ] who strengthens me' and God will *never* fail us nor forsake us.

So it is right to 'have a go' even when we feel least like it, because we're far from alone; it is important to move into some *active response* to restore the knowledge that, in however small a way, we can challenge our own helplessness. Somehow this mobilises our God-given resources, or frees God to work in new ways in us, and we know again that the Helper, the Comforter, has been with us in the valley, and the valley walls and passes no longer look so daunting. We didn't need to feel helpless after all.

A woman, in depression after her husband's sudden death, went on a Quaker retreat for several weeks. There she had time to be alone or to be with others, to sit or to walk, to read or talk or meditate. The time and space for quiet communion with God, and the caring, understanding community, cracked the husk of helplessness that surrounded her; it encouraged her not only to *look* up, but to begin herself to *strive* upward from the 'slough named Despond' that had bound her.

Even in valley times, it is possible to begin to affirm and appropriate with Julian of Norwich that 'All shall be well. . . and all manner of things shall be well'.

❧

That awful and sickening endless sinking, sinking
    through the slow, corruptive levels of disintegrative
    knowledge
when the self has fallen from the hands of God
and sinks, seething and sinking, corrupt
and sinking still, in depth after depth of disintegrative
    consciousness
sinking in the endless undoing, the awful katabolism
    into the abyss.

D.H. Lawrence, 'The hands of God'

Pride, so Christian theology teaches, is the deadliest of the seven sins since it prevents us from recognising our sins and repenting and reforming. Sin or not, it is pride that keeps you locked in the prison of depression. It is pride that prevents you from changing and finding your way out of the prison.

Dorothy Rowe, *Depression*

Not, I'll not, carrion comfort, Despair, not feast on thee;
Not untwist — slack they may be — these last strands
    of man
In me or, most weary, cry *I can no more*. I can;
can something, hope, wish day come, not choose not
    to be.

Gerard Manley Hopkins, 'Carrion Comfort'

The rough small hills fold back,
The rivers twist their valleys
This way and that way
Beneath smiling sky;
But where shall I begin
To find the piece of ground

On which a man can act
If every footstep falls
Among the vapours of neutrality?

Chris Wallace-Crabbe, 'Stanzas written in Connecticut'

Depression is a complex emotion, not always recognisable by the depressed individual. It may express itself in many guises and may or may not be a consequence of what is happening in the environment. . . the committed Christian has tremendous *resources* for dealing with the *causes* of depression [but there is] no evidence in scripture to support the idea that. . . we are given a 'go to heaven and bypass all human suffering' card. . . The key to coping with depression. . . lies in removing the *cause* of the depression, but not in fighting the *experience* of the depression itself. . . In the final analysis, grieving is what most psychological depressions are all about, and Christians ought to know how to grieve. . . Building resistance to depression takes discipline and, if a person has developed the habit of deriving satisfaction from being depressed, it also takes a sacrificing of those benefits.

Archibald D. Hart,
Coping with Depression in the Ministry and Other Helping Professions

When, for one reason or another, we begin to wake up a little bit, to lift the nose from the ground and notice that spiritual light and that spiritual atmosphere are real constituents of our human world; then the whole situation is changed. Our horizon is widened, our experience is enormously enriched, and. . . our responsibilities enlarged. For now we get an entirely new idea of what human beings are for, and what they can achieve.

Evelyn Underhill, *The Spiritual Life*

In a sentence it comes to this, that the sufferings of men and women are the sufferings of God. . . If we are the children of God and are suffering, he not only puts everlasting arms around us and draws us very close, he is also immanent. We are, in a real sense, part of himself. . .

Leslie D. Weatherhead, *Why Do Men Suffer?*

He who dwells constantly in his own suffering does not

know how to conquer. But he who bears suffering for the sake of God makes of suffering an art. This attitude is the starting point for transfiguring suffering into beauty . . . The sanctification of suffering is the ultimate art of God.

Toyohiko Kagawa, *The Practising Christian*

My friends, have we made our moods into an idol?
    shall we obey our feelings rather than God?
Hey, everyone! Make a stand with me!
    Defy your feelings and trust the Lord!
Call the bluff of cloudy chaos,
    and make room for some life and shape;
In the midst of the gloom, God speaks,
    Saying, 'Let there be light'.

Bruce Prewer, 'When we are feeling down'

Who am I? This or the Other?
Am I one person today and tomorrow another?
Am I both at once? A hypocrite before others,
and before myself a contemptible woebegone weakling?
Or is something within me still like a beaten army
fleeing in disorder from victory already achieved?

Who am I? They mock me, these lonely questions of mine.
Whoever I am, Thou knowest, O God, I am thine!

Dietrich Bonhoeffer, *Letters and Papers from Prison*

The only final healing for [depression], which causes a slowdown or shutdown of many bodily processes, is being touched by a centre of meaning and concern that is transcendental. Jung put it well when he wrote, 'the approach to the numinous is the real therapy'.

Morton T. Kelsey, *Companions on the Inner Way*

This is the glimmering verge of Heaven, and these
The columns of the heavenly palaces!
And, in the sweeping of the wind, your ear
The passage of the Angel's wings will hear,
And on the lichen-crusted leaves above
The rustle of the eternal rain of love.

Matthew Arnold, 'A Tomb Among the Mountains'

When we become depressed by our human failure
   and sin,
give us the wisdom to find divine compassion and mercy,
the forgiveness which Jesus came to bring,
enabling us to name him Saviour from personal
   experience.   Bruce Prewer, 'Searching and finding'

You and I must be valleys. . . valleys are not curious, are
not puffed up, are not climbing constantly to peep over
to see how things are turning out in the great beyond.
They do not stand apart, as mountains, in lonely glory.
Valleys attend to their own humble business of carrying
God's living waters down to the lowlands. They do not
concern themselves with results. They know their only
importance is in their willingness to be channels. We want
to be channels — deep and unobstructed — through which
God's torrential love may flow.

Glenn Clark, *Windows of Heaven*

Everest has become a symbol. Everest stands for all that
is highest, purest and most difficult of attainment. As the
climbers struggle gasping towards the summit they will
be putting heart into all who are striving upward in
whatever field. This knowledge will do most to put heart
into themselves. . . 'The fight is worth it — worth it every
time.'

Amy Carmichael, *Rose from Brier*

Though Christ a thousand times
In Bethlehem be born,
If he's not born in thee,
Thou art still forlorn.
The cross on Golgotha
Will never save thy soul,
The cross in thine own heart
Alone can make thee whole.

Angelus Silesius

Lord, life seems heavy sometimes, the loads impossible to carry, people impossible to change; there are times when I don't know what to do or where to turn. I confess that my reserves are too easily used up, and I'm too easily obsessed with the weight of my own problems. Helper of the helpless, release me from this valley of preoccupation with my own troubles; restore my soul; spark my spirit again. I would share my load with you, and allow you entry to my darkness. With your help, I choose to look up again, I decide to put one foot forward on your way, I see that there is a track leading from the valley, I know that you are bringing healing and strength to my whole being. I receive again your gift of life. Thankyou, Lord.

A Benediction

The Lord sends forth springs into your valleys, they rise in his mountains and bring sustenance for your soul. The world is filled with the fruit of his works, and he is the one who brings strength and joy. Know that his is the way and his the light. Go in peace, one foot at a time, on the upward way. May the Lord keep your going out and your coming in, from this time forth and for ever more. Amen.

20

The flipside

But Jesus often withdrew to lonely places and prayed.

Turn to me and be gracious to me, for I am lonely and afflicted.

All night long on my bed I looked for the one my heart loves; I looked for him but did not find him. I will get up now and go about the city, through its streets and squares; I will search for the one my heart loves. So I looked for him but did not find him.

Alexander the coppersmith did me a great deal of harm. . . At the first hearing of my case no-one came into court to support me: they all left me in the lurch . . . But the Lord stood by me and lent me strength. . . And the Lord did rescue me from every attempt to do me harm, and keep me safe until his heavenly reign begins. Glory to him, for ever and ever! Amen.

(Luke 5: 16, NIV; Psalm 25: 16, NIV; Song of Songs 3: 1-2, NIV; 2 Timothy 4: 14, 16-18, NEB)

Loneliness is a normal experience for most of us. It invades our lives in a variety of forms. In grief, as well as separation from loved ones, we encounter emotional loneliness. In frictions at work, at church, with family and with peers we find we are temporarily socially alone. Through such despair comes spiritual desolation as pain and shock replaces the presence of God.

The loneliness that produces a lasting hurt is not usually that which flows as a natural consequence of our age of mobility, nor is it the desertedness that surfaces because of the spirits of independence and competitiveness that surround us. It is the aloneness that results from human frailty as people, through their words and actions or lack of them, wound themselves and each other.

Loneliness can produce aggression, hatred or low self-esteem. However, it need not be altogether negative; it may be an opportunity to assess our lives and to address the origin of our anguish. It is also a time to draw close to Jesus; to rediscover him as a friend, not just in programmed religious activity, but in everyday life; to take him into the mundane, the workplace, sport, the car, chores and our inactivity.

In loneliness we are reminded that Jesus is Immanuel, God-with-us. It can have a touch of the sacred.

❄❄❄

Yes, a good life, alone but not lonely. Not with Christ near. And sometimes the sacred seems all around me.

Sheldon Vanauken, *Under the Mercy*

The priest looked at her sharply. 'You can offer idleness to God,' he said. 'Unemployment, idleness, whatever. To do nothing in someone's presence is a greater compliment than being busy and preoccupied.'

Gail Morgan, *Promise of Rain*

If I had my life to live over, I would start barefooted earlier in the spring and stay that way later in the fall. I would play more. I would ride on more merry-go-rounds. I'd pick more daisies.

Brother Jeremiah

He lays no great burden upon us — a little remembrance of him from time to time, a little adoration; sometimes to pray for his grace, sometimes to offer him your sorrows, sometimes to return him thanks for the benefits he has bestowed upon you and is still bestowing in the midst of your troubles. He asks you to console yourself with him the oftenest you can. Lift up your heart to him even at your meals, or when you are in company — the least little remembrance will always be acceptable to him. You need not cry very loud: he is nearer to us than we think. To be with God, there is no need to be continually in church.

Brother Lawrence, *The Practice of the Presence of God*

Fellowship with Christ is a table only for two — set in the wilderness. Inwardness is not a gaudy party, but the meeting of lovers in the lonely desert of the human heart. There, where all life and fellowship can hold no more than two, we sit together and he speaks as much as we, and even when both of us say nothing there is our welded oneness. And suddenly we see we cannot be complete until his perfect presence joins with ours.

Calvin Miller, *The Table of Inwardness*

When Jesus is present, all is well, and nothing seems difficult; but when Jesus is absent, everything is hard.

Thomas à Kempis, *The Imitation of Christ*

Consider this question: In view of God's infinite power and wisdom and beauty, what would his love to a human being involve? Or to put it another way: What could God give us to enjoy that would prove him most loving? There is only one possible answer: *himself!* If he withholds himself from our contemplation and companionship, no matter what else he gives us, he is not loving.

John Piper, *Desiring God: Meditations of a Christian Hedonist*

But of course the only perfect answer to the problem (loneliness) is a spiritual one, and consists in the presence of God himself, known and enjoyed by faith. There was an ancient Latin motto which said, 'Solvitus ambulando' ('It is solved by walking'). The Christian would add two words, 'Cum Deo' ('with God').

John Eddisdon, *The Troubled Mind*

To live a spiritual life we must first find the courage to enter into the desert of our loneliness and to change it by gentle and persistent efforts into a garden of solitude. This requires not only courage but also a strong faith. As hard as it is to believe that the dry desolate desert can yield endless varieties of flowers, it is equally hard to imagine that our loneliness is hiding unknown beauty. The movement from loneliness to solitude, however, is the beginning of any spiritual life because it is the movement from the restless sense to the restful spirit, from the outward-reaching cravings to the inward-reaching search, from the fearful clinging to the fearless play.

Henri Nouwen, *Reaching Out*

Father, Son and Holy Spirit, with some difficulty I thank you for my experiences of loneliness. Lord, in them I learn so much about myself, others and your eternal friendship. Help me in such times to forgive those, including myself, who may have caused my sense of aloneness. Allow me in these moments to know you in the basic areas of my life. May your peace touch all who are alone today and may I have a ministry to them through prayer, presence and deed.

I don't need to climb another mountain
Set my sail across the seven seas
The paradise that I was always looking for
Was found when you loved me.
And now my greatest joy is loving you
The hope that I lost was found and made anew
Now my lonely days are fin'ly through
I have found my life in loving you.

Scott Wesley Brown in the song, *My Treasure*

A Benediction
To you, O Lord, I lift up my soul; in you I trust, O my God.
Psalm 25: 1-2a, NIV

21

Halfway through life

I was living in peace, but God took me by the throat and battered me and crushed me. God uses me for target practice and shoots arrows at me from every side – arrows that pierce and wound me; and even then he shows no pity. He wounds me again and again; he attacks like a soldier gone mad with hate. I mourn and wear clothes made of sackcloth, and I sit here in the dust defeated. I have cried until my face is red, and my eyes are swollen and circled with shadows, but I am not guilty of any violence, and my prayer to God is sincere.

You like your ancestors before you, have turned away from my laws and have not kept them. Turn back to me, and I will turn to you. But you ask, 'What must we do to turn back to you?'

The people of Judah had a song they sang: 'We grow weak carrying burdens; there's so much rubble to take away. How can we build the wall today?'

(Job 16: 12-17; Malachi 3: 7; Nehemiah 4: 10 — all GNB)

For the first twenty years or so of personal Christian pilgrimage, the 'high mountains' of experience keep us going: the weekend conference; the spiritual retreat; the inspiring preacher; the encouraging response to witness; the growth of the congregation. These high points give us sufficient stimulus to keep going through the boring and monotonous phases of life and of ministry.

But my observation is that, as the years go past, and as one's own mortality creeps up, the high points are less frequent and the deep valleys predominate. When one turns fifty (and it happens at different ages for different people!), it is possible for a Christian to enter a deep valley of experience which seems to have no end – a kind of spiritual desert.

It's hard even to remember the high points of experience of a few years back; external circumstances seem to press harder than ever; and one's own life-cycle catches up on one. Teenage children grow into adults and move away. The familiar worlds seem hostile instead of comforting; the secular environment seems hard against the gospel; and it is difficult to find something new about the Christian faith which gives stimulus and excitement any more.

What do you do if you get into this situation – especially if you are in a position of Christian leadership in a congregation? It's very hard to keep pretending that all is well, but there must be some clues in the scriptures and Christian experience to lead us out of this valley.

❧❧❧

I look at Jesus in agony
on the night before he died. . .
I stand quite close to him
and watch him reaching out for human help. . .
but no-one now can reach him
— he is entirely on his own before he dies. . .
As I watch I realise
that man will ultimately come to terms
with God, with destiny and with himself
only when he dares to seek aloneness.
I give myself a taste
of what it means to be alone:
I am living in a desert:
no books. . . no occupation. . .
no sound of human voice. . .
— for a whole day. . . a week. . . for months. . .
I see how I react
when I am thrown back on my own resources. . .
when I am stripped of what I mostly use
to run away from looking at myself:

work and human company. . .
Then I see myself in a solitary prison cell:
sound-proof walls, a narrow room,
the dim light of a bulb all day. . .
never the glimpse of a human face. . .
or of any living thing. . .
or sun or sky. . .
never a sound of human voice or Nature. . .
for weeks. . . for months on end. . .
not knowing when it will end. . .

Finally — I have lapsed into a coma:
I can hear the words of people
and feel their touch. . .
but cannot reach them. . .
Now I return to life:
to my worries and my work. . .
my comforts and attachments. . .
the world of human beings. . .
but I realise that I am not the same
from having been exposed
to the rigours of aloneness. . .

Every now and then my heart returns
to Jesus in his agony. . .
I watch him as he grapples with God
and with his destiny. . .
and the sight gives me a wisdom
that thinking never could.
So I linger there and look. . .

Anthony de Mello, 'The Desert'

Middle age — that difficult period between juvenile delin-
quency and senior citizenship when you have to take care
of yourself.

Anonymous

'I recently turned fifty,' America's most famous father, Bill
Cosby, writes at the outset of his book *Time Flies*, 'which
is young for a tree, midlife for an elephant, and ancient
for a quarter-miler, whose son now says, "Dad, I just can't

run the quarter with you any more unless I bring something to read'".

Time magazine

It is said by Anthony Power that we date ourselves by
the standards against which we rebel. . . The themes of
great literature — love, disappointment, the texture of time
— are the themes of ordinary life. Indeed, the older I get,
the more I see the inexhaustible interestingness of the
ordinary.

It is said that God gave us memory so we could have
roses in winter. But it is also true that without memory
we cannot have a self in any season. The more memories
you have, the more 'you' you have. That is why, as Swift
said, no wise person ever wished to be younger.

George F. Will, 'On Turning 40'

The midlife crisis might be best understood as the 'crisis
of limits'. . . the awareness of physical decline. . . the sense
of one's own mortality. There is the sense of loss and limits
in terms of one's role and relationships in the family, and
in one's career. . .

People can remain locked in the experience of brokenness or they can reject these feelings, deny them and
pretend they are not there. Alternatively, the negative experience may become the purgatorial environment through
which people can confront and own their brokenness and
their resistance to the sense of threat that the experience
of physical decline precipitates. . . To understand that there
is fellowship in human existence as well as in human
achievement, that developing and maintaining a relationship may be as important as being a success requires one
to rework one's dream and vision even more radically
than before.

Maryanne Confoy, 'Challenges to Faith in Life's Journey'

When everything takes on the taste of death and destruction then in actual fact it is the Holy Spirit who is at work
in us. This then is the hour of his grace. Then the seemingly uncanny, bottomless depth of our existence as
experienced by us is the bottomless depth of his com-

municating himself to us, the dawning of his approaching infinity. . . which is tasted like nothing because it is infinity.

Karl Rahner, 'Reflections on the Experience of Grace'

Where my bitterness overflowed all bounds was at the sight of the rifts developing in the Order and the intestinal strife now raging between the innovators and those who wished to remain strictly faithful to the rule.

The disputes over the rule paralysed me. Unity was everything to me. Above all it was the sign of God's grace and loving response to our efforts to be faithful to him.

The sight of the divisions among us, the sound of gospel texts being mouthed without meaning and twisted from their original simplicity, left me helpless.

I really felt as though darkness had fallen on what I held most dear in the world — my family.

At the Pentecost Chapter, held in May 1221, the very triumph of numbers increased my uneasiness. There were more than five thousand of us.

I no longer felt capable of guiding the Order. At the same time I wanted to keep a hand in everything.

Fortunately, I was thrust aside, and Fre Elias was nominated General.

Suddenly I felt better, relieved of a responsibility which had been weighing on me. But my peace did not last long.

The most intransigent, those who claimed to be loyalest to me, returned to the assault, and the divisions became more acute than ever.

'Francis, you must come back. You must take up the reins again. You must make your weight felt.'

'Father, you must expel the most dangerous brothers. . .'

And on the other hand, those who thought themselves the pure, the spiritual ones, and who, making fidelity to the original rule their excuse, were becoming eccentric and unbalanced, living in such a way as to attract rebuke from the bishops by their inhuman penances and their wild and repulsive appearance.

No, I had certainly ruined everything.

Carlo Carretto, I, Francis

Bernie was staying for a while at Martha's, an Anglican shelter for homeless women. The age of the twelve women at Martha's averaged about thirty years. Some women had fled marriages or relationships involving physical abuse, some had been put out of the family home, some had children being cared for elsewhere. One young woman of nineteen had come from hospital where she had undergone brief psychiatric treatment and then had been sent to a place for care where ninety per cent of patients were well over seventy years. For two weeks no-one spoke to her.

Bernie's life fell apart when her husband went off with someone else. Without children and under thirty years of age she was entitled to CAN$164 per month from welfare for her expenses. Even with an extra housing subsidy allowance, she could not make ends meet on her own. She seemed appalled at her homeless state:

> This is the second time that I have ended up living on the street and going to the women's shelter and staying there for a while. This time I ended up at Martha's. I never thought that I would ever end up on the street and I don't think any of us think that. We all think that we will get through our hardships and we'll never be this way and I don't think anyone plans being on the street, just somehow that's the way circumstances go — you know, bad timing, not being prepared.'

Joan Clarke,
Motherhood Principles and Labour Pains: Women and Families

Lord, I move in a twilight zone between the harsh reality of life around me, personal dilemmas, relationship difficulties, anxiety about children, feeling overwhelmed at how secular the world is. I used to be in a black-and-white world, where you could identify the Christians, where we had the right attitudes about everything, and we knew where evil resided. Now, Lord, I know that life has become so much more complex than that: Christian people do bad things, even manipulate others; and there are good people right outside the Christian fold who sometimes act better than the Christians in caring for one another and for me.

In this twilight world, Lord, bring your light to bear on my life. Help my judgments to be clearer, my conscience to be forgiven, and my Christianity to be realistic. I ask this in the name of the greatest realist of all, Jesus Christ. Amen.

Lord Jesus, you went into the desert and survived. Help me to live through this desert experience, to learn new things, to find God afresh without the normal props and supports that comfort me, and get me through to the other side of the desert so that I can enjoy life again. Amen.

God, Father and Mother of us all, help me within the family and in my friendships to find a new vitality, a new energy, a greater capacity to forgive, new grace to face the next set of trials and difficulties. Lord, you lived on this earth in the context of an ordinary family which contained an extraordinary secret of divinity. Help me to live within my ordinary family with the extraordinary secret that God is with us, even though it may not be apparent to us or to others. Help us to know and experience your presence in the ordinary life-cycle that we are going through. In Jesus' name, Amen.

A Benediction

Let us pray that the Spirit of God will renew our lives:
Lord, increase our eagerness to do your will
and help us to know the saving power of your love.
Grant this through our Lord Jesus Christ, your Son, who lives and reigns with you and the Holy Spirit, one God, for ever and ever. Amen.

Collect for Ordinary Sunday 34

22

The alchemy of years
(Eugene Bianchi)

Lord, I put my hope in you; I have trusted in you since I was young. I have relied on you all my life; you have protected me since the day I was born. I will always praise you. My life has been an example to many, because you have been my strong defender. All day long I praise you and proclaim your glory. Do not reject me now that I am old, do not abandon me now that I am feeble. . . You have taught me ever since I was young, and I still tell of your wonderful acts. Now that I am old and my hair is grey, do not abandon me, O God! Be with me while I proclaim your power and might to all generations to come.

There was a very old prophetess, a widow named Anna, daughter of Phanuel of the tribe of Asher. She had been married for only seven years and was now eighty-four years old. She never left the temple; day and night she worshipped God, fasting and praying.

We who have this spiritual treasure are like common clay pots, in order to show that the supreme power belongs to God, not to us. We are often troubled, but not crushed; sometimes in doubt, but never in despair; there are many enemies, but we are never without a friend; and though badly hurt at times, we are not destroyed. At all times we carry in our mortal bodies the death of Jesus, so that his life also may be seen in our bodies.

For this reason we never become discouraged. Even though our physical being is gradually decaying, yet our spiritual being is renewed day after day. And this small temporary trouble we suffer will bring us a tremendous and eternal glory, much greater than the trouble. For we fix our attention, not on things that are seen, but on things that are unseen. What can be seen lasts only for a time, but what cannot be seen lasts for ever.

(Psalm 71: 5-9, 17-18; Luke 2: 36-38; 2 Corinthians 4: 7-10; 2 Corinthians 4: 16-18 — all GNB)

What is old age and when does it start? Some persons seem to be old at forty in that they resist personal growth and change. Others are still youthful at seventy, filled with enthusiasm.

At every age or stage of life, dignity and meaningfulness in life are essential. This is especially so for aging people in a society that tends to devalue them as persons.

In his outline of the stages of life, Erik Erikson suggests two key questions for those in later life: 'Can I make peace with my finitude, accept my brief place in life with gratitude and serenity? Can I experience and prize the transcendent?'

Theologian and author, Eugene Bianchi, sees aging as a spiritual journey that continues until the day we die. The hazards and rewards are part of an ongoing pilgrimage that can take us deeper into God.

The challenge for the older person in the face of decreasing mobility and power and often declining health is to find acceptance and meaning in the phase of life he or she is in at the present time. This involves getting in touch with feelings of fear and loss rather than evading them. Death constitutes the ultimate loss challenging the older person.

The recent film, *Cocoon*, depicts the plight of a group of senior citizens in Florida (even this patronising description tends to dodge the issue of aging!). Having bathed in rejuvenating waters and recaptured some of the vigour of youth, they succumb to the temptation of leaving family and friends to fly off with a bunch of aliens to a place of eternal youth where they will never age, sicken or die!

I found the film a sad reflection on our Western society's attitude to old age. I saw their flight as a two-way loss, for young and old have much to give to each other. Older people with their long view of their rich life experience can lend spiritual weight to any family or group by their involved presence. Each one of us is on a continuum of aging and needs loving interaction with others at all stages.

Those of us who learn in midlife to 'experience and prize the transcendent' will find that in old age — as at any age — God's grace is sufficient and that our spirits may bloom even as our bodies decay.

❦

Take kindly the counsel of the years, gracefully surrendering the things of youth. Nurture strength of spirit to shield you in sudden misfortune. But do not distress yourself with imaginings. Many fears are born of fatigue and loneliness. Beyond a wholesome discipline, be gentle with youself. You are a child of the universe no less than the trees and the stars. You have a right to be here and whether or not it is clear to you, no doubt the universe is unfolding as it should. Therefore be at peace with God. . .

Desiderata: found in Old
St Paul's Church, Baltimore, 1692

He will grow old and you will grow old,
He will love you and you love him.
May your sun set in a blaze of gold
And the night creep in.

Author unknown

He who lives with a sense for the (divine) presence knows that to get older does not mean to lose time but rather to gain time. And he also knows that in all his deeds, the chief task of man is to sanctify time. All it takes to sanctify time is God, a soul and a moment. And the three are always here.

Abraham J. Heschel,
The Older Person and the Family in the Perspective of Jewish Tradition

An aged man is but a paltry thing,
A tattered coat upon a stick, unless

> Soul clap its hands and sing, and louder sing
> For every tatter in its mortal dress. . .
>
> W.B. Yeats, *Sailing to Byzantium*

The word 'experience' is too abstract for telling young people about old age. Rather, tell how it feels to weather through hard times and somehow be aware that you've been helped to come through. And the young people can sense that maybe they can, too. It's an affirmation at the other end of the dark valley that older people can make. Young people don't appreciate the warnings we give them. . . I think they need older people who have suffered and who are not glib.

> Clarice Bowman

> Upon an airy upland,
> Within me and far away,
> A child that's ageless dances
> All delicately gay;
> A dance that is like sunshine
> When I am old and grey.
>
> Author unknown

At their best, aging artists manifest an amazing energy. This is not the strenuous energy of youth, full of activity, hedged about by social expectation and fearful of failure. Rather the old artist possesses a more subtle dynamism that combines truth-speaking, playfulness and a degree of liberating insight that pierces into the mystery of life. . . The old artist seems better able to unite with the world in an accepting way. The alchemy of years produces a gentle but profound union with the joys and sorrows of existence.

> Eugene C. Bianchi, *Aging as a Spiritual Journey*

> And now in age I bud again;
> After so many deaths I live. . .
>
> George Herbert, *The Flower*

Max is an old Aboriginal man and he lives in a pensioners' hostel just down the street from us in Chippendale. Every day he is standing outside the door of the hostel as I walk past on my way to Redfern station. We always greet each other and exchange a few words. This day I was feeling rather tired and when Max said to me, 'How are you, mate?', I said, 'I'm OK thanks Max, but it's a bit wet today, isn't it?' He smiled a beautiful smile, standing there in his bare feet and old clothes and he said, 'Ah, but what about when the sun comes out?' I marvelled at the depth of his hope and his ministry to me.

Dorothy McMahon, *Called to be Human*

Creative aging is not an abrupt thing. It comes on day by day in a gradual evolution, and the state of mind in which aging leaves people is conditioned by their past and their native endowment. Some have been resourceful and imaginative persons from their youth, and these, I think, are better able to face old age with serenity.

John Tracey Ellis

If older people view life with its limitations and with its heartaches, within a spiritual context and with enthusiasm, then they are giving a kind of witness to the validity of religious thought that no young person can ever give. . .

Charles J. Fahey

When it comes to aging, I have my things all laid out. If I am physically able to do it, I intend to stay alive my whole life. . . When and if I retire I have three things I want to do. One, I plan to finish the book that I have on my desk in its first draft. . . Secondly, I am going to the nearest nursery school and I am going to say, 'You have just acquired a resident grandfather. I am going to be here a couple of days each week. I just want to love the children.' A third thing is that I am going to go to some church, probably here in Washington, and say to the pastor, 'Now I am an experienced counsellor. I just want to join your staff for a couple of afternoons a week. . .'

I have the feeling that I ought to touch people's lives for good. . . I believe that it was God's intention that people actualise the possibility with which they were born, so that it can come to full flower.

Lawrence Jones

In heavenly love abiding,
No change my heart shall fear;
And safe in such confiding,
For nothing changes here.
The storm may roar without me,
My heart may low be laid,
But God is round about me,
And can I be dismayed?

Anna Letitia Waring

Night is drawing nigh;
for all that has been, thanks;
for all that shall be, yes.

Dag Hammarskjold, *Markings*

Thank you, Lord, for all that has been.
As I look back I see that my whole life-journey has been charted
by you — your strong presence has never left me.
Remember how I beseeched you, Lord, to take away that 'thorn',
the affliction that gave me such pain;
but you left it there and revealed instead your marvellous grace!
Thank you, Lord, for your faithfulness;
Thank you for weaving all my life experiences — both dark and
radiant — into a rich tapestry of life.
All power and praise to you!
  Thank you, Lord, for all that is now. . .
Autumn is smouldering in the trees, but the colours are rich
and beautiful;
Leaves are beginning to fall: my eyesight, hearing and memory
are not as sharp, my energy and independence are diminishing,
yet compensations are many —
loving relationships that have stood the test of time,
grandchildren laughing in the garden,
creative interests and time to pursue them,
so many precious things. . .
Above all, thankyou for your unfailing love.
I celebrate the life that is now.

For all that shall be, yes!
I affirm that the best is yet to come.
Although the future is mist-shrouded I am quietly confident that
all will be well.
You who have led me so surely will lead me safely to my desired
haven.
You are both with me and within me;
you are both the way and the end, what have I to fear?
I am the resurrection and the life, you said, the firstfruits of
those who will never die;
Eternal life is to know God and Jesus Christ whom he has sent
— this means eternal life has begun!
All praise to Father, Son and Holy Spirit.

A Benediction
May the God who gives us peace make you holy in every way
and keep your whole being — spirit, soul and body — from
every fault at the coming of our Lord Jesus.
  And God's peace, which is far beyond human understanding,
will keep your hearts and minds safe in union with Christ Jesus.
(1 Thessalonians 5: 23; Philippians 3: 7 — both GNB)

23

Make friends with your shadow

I have complete confidence, O God! I will sing and praise you! Wake up, my soul! Wake up, my harp and lyre! I will wake up the sun. I will thank you, O Lord, among the nations. I will praise you among the peoples. Your constant love reaches above the heavens; your faithfulness touches the skies. Show your greatness in the sky, O God, and your glory over all the earth. Save us by your might; answer my prayer, so that the people you love may be rescued.

Who, O God, will take me into the fortified city? Who will lead me to Edom? Have you really rejected us? Aren't you going to march out with our armies? Help us against the enemy; human help is worthless. With God on our side we will win; he will defeat our enemies.

I ask that your minds may be opened to see his light, so that you will know what is the hope to which he has called you, how rich are the wonderful blessings he promises his people, and how very great is his power at work in us who believe.

But God's mercy is so abundant, and his love for us is so great, that while we were spiritually dead in our disobedience he brought us to life with Christ. It is by God's grace that you have been saved. In our union with Christ Jesus he raised us up with him to rule with him in the heavenly world. He did this to demonstrate for all time to come the extraordinary greatness of his grace in the love he showed us in Christ Jesus.

He did this to prepare all God's people for the work of Christian service, in order to build up the body of Christ. And so shall all come together to that oneness in our faith and in our knowledge of the Son of God;

we shall become mature people reaching to the very height of Christ's full stature.

(Psalm 108:1-6; Psalm 108:10-13; Ephesians 1:18-19; Ephesians 2:4-7; Ephesians 4:12-13 — all GNB)

Gentle, reflective listening to the unfolding of God's Word in our daily lives has been a practice recommended by spiritual leaders over many centuries. To become aware of God's action in our lives we must stop and quietly reflect on where we have been and what has happened in our lives, to bring to our consciousness the beautiful ways in which God has called us into being and to acknowledge before him our frailty and our brokenness.

It is a process of discerning each day our movements towards and away from God to acknowledge the gifts with which he has showered us and to ask his help to become ever more aware of the darker side of our personalities which if unattended may harm or cripple us. If we are prepared to enter into our inner sanctum or the fortified city (Psalm 108: 10), we will be in touch with the deeper forces that are beyond our ordinary consciousness and which have the power to exert enormous influence on our actions.

This process of silent listening in God's presence will enable us gradually to experience a greater appreciation of the inner meaning and relationship of those disparate parts of ourselves and of the world around us. As this understanding takes place so will our transformation or personal integration be enhanced.

The liberating spark of the 'light that shines in the darkness' (John 1: 5) will bring new life and light to our hearts and minds and our every action will become a vehicle for God's presence to us and our presence to him in love.

❧❧

In actual life it requires the greatest discipline to be simple, and the acceptance of oneself is the essence of the moral problem and the epitome of a whole outlook upon life.

That I feed the hungry, that I forgive an insult, that I love my enemy in the name of Christ — all these are undoubtedly great virtues. What I do unto the least of my brethren, that I do unto Christ. But what if I should discover that the least amongst them all, the poorest of all the beggars, the most impudent of all offenders, the very enemy himself — that these are within me, and I myself stand in need of the alms of my own kindness — that I myself am the enemy who must be loved — what then?

As a rule, the Christian's attitude is [to hide this] from the world; we refuse to admit ever having met this least among the lowly in ourselves. . . We therefore do not hesitate, but lightheartedly choose the complicated course of remaining in ignorance about ourselves while busying ourselves with other people and their troubles and sins. This activity lends us an air of virtue, and we thus deceive ourselves and those around us. In this way, thank God, we can escape from ourselves. There are countless people who can do this with impunity, but not everyone can, and these few break down on the road to Damascus and succumb to a neurosis. How can I help these persons if I am myself a fugitive?

C.G. Jung, *Modern Man in Search of a Soul*

The tremendous compulsion towards goodness and the immense moral force of Christianity are not merely an argument in the latter's favour, they are also a proof of the strength of its suppressed and repressed counterpart — the antichristian, barbarian element. The existence within us of something that can turn against us, that can become a serious matter for us, I regard not merely as a dangerous peculiarity, but as a valuable and congenial asset as well. It is a still untouched fortune, an uncorrupted treasure, a sign of youthfulness, an earnest of rebirth. . .

The shadow is a tight passage, a narrow door, whose painful constriction no-one is spared who goes down to the deep well. But one must learn to know oneself in order to know who one is. For what comes after the door

is, surprisingly enough, a boundless expanse full of un-
precedented uncertainty, with apparently no inside and no
outside, no above and no below, no here or there, no mine
and no thine, no good and no bad.   It is the world of
water, where all life floats in suspension; where the realm
of the sympathetic system, the soul of everything living,
begins; where I am indivisibly this *and* that; where I
experience the other in myself and the other-than-myself
experiences.

C.G. Jung, *Psychological Reflections*

The teachings of Jesus suggest. . . that we should not
wait until we know all about suffering to find our need.
We need to be delivered from the source of our in-
humanity, Jesus taught, and he told us first of all to pray,
'Deliver us from the evil one.' Then in various ways he
showed that the task is to look within and to know what
is causing the trouble and whether we are nursing anger
or harmful desires in our hearts. Our job is not just to
wait for evil to happen in the outer world and then try
to do something about the pain and the agony it causes.
Instead, Christians are to recognise the source of evil
within themselves so that they can seek help in order to
stand outwardly against it.

Morton T. Kelsey, *The Other Side of Silence*

True knowledge of God always goes hand in hand with
a painful self-knowledge. John of the Cross expresses it
beautifully by means of the famous metaphor of the log
of wood being transformed into fire. As the wood burns,
it becomes blackened, it cracks and steams and all the
knotholes and flaws are exposed. If the log could speak
it would cry out: 'My seeking to become a fire was a
mistake! I am now worse than when I started — black,
ugly and flawed. I was better off before.' The log is the
soul and the fire is God.

And the truth, of course, is that the log is not worse
off then it was before. All the ugliness and defects were
present before but they were concealed. The only way
the log can become fire is to be revealed honestly and

openly as what it is in itself. The process is painful but, contrary to appearances, it is the mark of real growth in union with God. That is why good souls who are making real progress often feel they are regressing and getting further from God.

Thomas H. Green, *Opening to God*

O, to vex me contraries meet in one;
Inconstancy unnaturally hath begot
A constant habit, that when I would not
I change in vows and in devotion.
As humorous is my contrition
As my profane love, and as soon forgot,
As riddlingly distempered, cold and hot;
I durst not view heaven yesterday, and today
In prayers and flattering speeches I court God;
Tomorrow I quake with true fear of his rod.
So my devout fits come and go away
Like a fantastic ague, save that here
Those are my best days when I shake with fear.

John Donne, *Holy Sonnets VI*

One reason why most of us experience alternating consolation and desolation is because our minds have layers upon layers of consciousness. At one level of consciousness I may be full of faith that all power belongs to God and that without him I can do nothing. Then my security is threatened in some way and I reach a deeper level of consciousness to which my faith has not penetrated and where I have been living in a state of unconscious atheism. This moment of crisis is an invitation to grow in faith. I may accept the invitation and for a few years I live in this deeper level. Then another crisis occurs and I become aware of an even deeper level of atheism within me. In our journey towards God we proceed like those small birds whose flight is in loops. They always seem to be about to drop, but the drop in their flight seems to urge them forwards. . .

'The answer is in the pain.' We fear whatever causes us pain and try to escape, but in escaping we are running away from the answer, and so another useful guideline in learning to read our moods is:

Face the fears that haunt you

In Jungian language, 'Face your shadow'. Fear, like guilt, is a healthy human reaction to danger, but if we refuse to face the fear, we cannot discover the danger which is threatening. If we refuse to face the fear, the fear may become a ruthless tyrant pervading and poisoning every aspect of our lives. Once faced, the fears often turn out to be illusory.

Gerard W. Hughes, *God of Surprises*

The act of love — extending oneself — requires a moving out against the inertia of laziness (work) or the resistance engendered by fear (courage). Let us turn now from the work of love to the courage of love. When we extend ourselves, our self enters new and unfamiliar territory, so to speak. Our self becomes a new and different self. We do things we are not accustomed to do. We change. The experience of change, of unaccustomed activity, of being on unfamiliar ground, of doing things differently is frightening. It always was and always will be. People handle their fear of change in different ways, but the fear is inescapable if they are in fact to change. Courage is not the absence of fear; it is the making of action in spite of fear, the moving out against the resistance engendered by fear into the unknown and into the future. On some level spiritual growth, and therefore love, always requires courage and involves risk.

M. Scott Peck, *The Road Less Travelled*

Lord, I do love the darkness
The hours folk call the night
Where others see but blackness
I know a lordly light.
The light that burns within
Each breathing hopeful heart
And gives all living kin
Of godliness some part.
Lord I do love the sunlight

Reflected by the moon,
I move by it at midnight
But hide from it at noon.
Your daylight dawning blinds me,
Reveals me from above,
Ungainly and unkindly
Unworthy of your love.
Lord, I do love the darkness
The hours folk call the night
Where others see but starkness
I know a lordly light.
I dance between the trees
Of this cathedral wood.
I scent the gentlest breeze
And know your will is good.

George Scott Moncrieff, *Prayer of the Badger*

Lord Jesus,
may you yourself prepare
in the wilderness of our hearts
the path of your return.

The hills of our pride —
tear them down with your humility.
The valleys of our despair —
fill them with your hope.
The winding roads of our lives —
straighten them with your truth,
and let bloom in our desert
    the daffodils of your joy.

Then will we be able to see your glory
    and adore your presence
in the face of each of our brothers and sisters.

Lucien Deiss, *Biblical Prayers*

A Benediction
May the Lord bless you and take care of you;
May the Lord be kind and gracious to you;

*May the Lord look on you with favour and give
you peace.*

(Numbers 6: 24-26)

'We are doomed, sir! What shall we do?'. . . Then Elisha prayed 'O Lord, open his eyes and let him see!' The Lord answered his prayer, and Elisha's servant looked up and saw the hillside covered with horses and chariots of fire all around Elisha.

And the Lord said to [Moses], 'Take off the shoes from your feet, for the place where you are standing is holy ground.'

If I ascend to heaven, thou art there! If I make my bed in Sheol, thou art there!

Blessed are the pure in heart, for they shall see God.

And he was transfigured before them, and his face shone like the sun, and his garments became white as light.

He who loves me will be loved by my father, and I will love him and manifest myself to him.

Strive for peace with all, and for the holiness without which no-one will see the Lord.

I am telling you the truth: no-one can see the kingdom of God unless he is born again.

Then the righteous will answer him, 'Lord, when did we see you hungry and feed you or thirsty and give you drink?'. . .as you did it to one of the least of these my brethren, you did it to me.

The king's heart is a stream of water in the hand of the Lord; he turns it wherever he will.

(2 Kings 6: 15 and 17, GNB; Acts 7: 33, RSV; Psalm 139: 8, RSV; Matthew 5: 8, RSV; Matthew 17: 2, RSV; John 14: 21b, RSV; Hebrews 12: 14, RSV; John 3: 3, GNB; Matthew 25: 37 and 40, RSV; Proverbs 21: 1, RSV)

I was having a dream and in it we were packing to move. There were some perishables left, so I bottled the peaches and put them in a basket with passionfruit and other things and set the container adrift — on the water or in the air. We left, and were travelling, were still on the move. I was watching out for something yellow in the sky and seeking to listen to God subconsciously to be in the right place at the right time.

We drove around a big bend and down onto the beach, where I spied this bottle of peaches in the sand. At first I didn't recognise it as mine, wondering whose it was and amazed that it was intact in the flotsam cast up by the tide. Then it dawned on me — it was mine, and I found a passionfruit, too! The wonder of the coincidence hit me and I stopped looking for other things, to tell those I was with how amazing it was that we had been there to find it. But no-one was interested. They gave me only the briefest acknowledgement. I had no-one with whom to share the wonder and amazement, except God. But that was okay.

The dream spoke to me of the wonder of God's provision and protection. What I had given out returned to bless when I needed it, as I sought for it in faith. The touch of God on the whole plan gave the mundane events of my life a deeper purpose than I had ever imagined. I felt the security of it enfold me. To see God in and through and behind each event of my life, even the devastations, the unlikely places, the unlovely people, is a constant growth in trust that doesn't come easily. But I see it as one of the marks of a saint and therefore strive towards that height, of living continuously in an awareness of the active presence of God in my life. To become more and more aware of what God is doing around me is so exciting that it is worth the climb many times over.

The new vision is starting to make all the difference to the way I see myself. I am just an earthen vessel, but filled with what Jesus has to offer, despite imperfections. Therefore I am trusting him to be everything that is needful through me, in spite of the critics. And that's so relaxing. I am trusting the people around me to be God's people for the job, even the ones needing help. And that trust helps them to grow into all that God desires them to be. I am seeing that my resources of time and money and other practical needs will all be more than adequate for each task. And that is the key to anxiety elimination. I can't wait to experience that higher vision, continuously.

Such a vision of God doesn't make me a pantheist. The way in which the Shepherd is in and through and behind all my life is a mystery to me, in dimensions beyond time and space. It doesn't limit God to the things he has created, nor do I feel I am worshipping the creature, but the Creator who is beyond, while he is also through all he has made. His active participation in my life needs my will, my assent. Yet he is also behind my assent, calling it into being. But enough of mysteries. They can wait for final answers. The practicalities, meanwhile, are life-changing.

৵◌৶

The Search
Watching through the windows of my life,
from out of my cocoon of comfortableness,
I search for God.
The weary world goes by on my TV screen.
My attention is distracted but
my heart's not involved, for God is not there.
The doorbell interrupts my search,
I smile politely, get done with the business,
my heart's not involved, for God is not there.
The round of routine keeps my hands busy, but
my heart's not involved, for God is not there.
Memories meander into my mind,
super-sensitive sore spots.
I hug my wounds to me
My heart is involved, but God is not there.
So I gaze at the rain running down my window
and retreat into wishes, 'If onlys' and cares.

'I am here!' cries the Master
'don't doubt and despair, I'm nearer than breathing

or the touch of your hair. You're special and lovely,
but blind as a bat. Your vision is clouded
but I can fix that. You missed me today in the face of
your friend,
didn't come to my aid and help me to mend
the world's weary heartaches
but thought that your own was enough of a burden to
bear all alone.
To the call of your conscience,
you turned a deaf ear,
and missed the love-letter I planned you to hear.

'You called out my name,
but your glance skittered by and onto the screen or the
mark of a fly.
I gave you a prod to minister to me
but you managed to stay within your routine.
I pour out my peace through the trees as you pass,
but you miss the message and head for the bus.
The brittle-bright lights that beckon you on,
to lust after lingerie, lounges and fun
have warped and distorted the plan that I
had for your happiness, and I sigh
at contentment thus missed, and joy thrown away,
while you wish and whine for a better day.

'My call says, "Come!" Oh, will you not hear?
Let me wash away the grime of the years.
A pure heart sees clearly through all the sham,
to the heart of the world which is where I am.
As you love me, obey and the grime falls away
to reveal my glory in life, Word and day.
Take time to gaze, not a mere fleeting glance;
concentrate in wonder, expect in advance
to behold me in glory; take off your shoes
in reverent awe. You have nothing to lose
but your blindness to me as you sit in your chair,
thinking there's no-one but you in your lair.

'You cannot love me, as much as you should?

Then gaze at my love for you and you could
be overwhelmed in the wink of an eye
as my love pours through you, unselfish and high.
Relax to my Spirit, while letting the flow
wash away grudges; resentment will go.
All unforgiveness will eventually yield
To the pressure of love pouring through you to heal.
The smog and the grime that has clouded your vision
gives way to a brightness, a new sense of mission.'

My Lord and My God!

I want this mountain-top experience to stay,
As I behold your love, your power, your way.
To worship and love is my heart's deep desire,
to live in this love, not have it expire.
Yet your promptings, I know, tell me that I must go
to the thirsty and hurting in the lowlands below.
Your love must be poured out, or else it can't flow,
through a life of love to the valley so low.
A miracle Lord, yet it is quite simple
Why didn't I see it? Your plan is so ample
Just hold out my vessel for a filling from you
— takes time, I know, but I must renew,
then pouring it out, your telling me where —
why, Lord! You're receiving it! You're even *there*?

Bronwyn Pryor

The very first step is to try to forget about the self altogether. Your real, new self will not come as long as you
are looking for it. It will come when you are looking for
him. . . if we let him, for we can prevent him if we choose
— he will make the feeblest and filthiest of us into a god
or goddess, a dazzling, radiant, immortal creature, pulsating all through with such energy and joy and wisdom and
love as we cannot now imagine, a bright stainless mirror
which reflects back to God perfectly (though of course, on
a smaller scale) his own boundless power and delight and
goodness. The process will be long and in parts very
painful, but that is what we are in for. Nothing less. . .

though Christianity seems at first to be all about morality. . . one has a glimpse of a country where they do not talk of those things, except perhaps as a joke. Everyone there is filled full with what we should call goodness as a mirror is filled with light. But. . . they are not thinking of it. They are too busy looking at the source from which it comes. But this is near the stage where the road passes over the rim of our world.

C.S. Lewis, *Mere Christianity*

I concentrate on what God is telling me to do, not on the patient's condition. Just the sight of a very ill person — the physical deterioration, machines, needles and hospital personnel — can damage my faith. When I concentrate on the patient, I become overwhelmed by the impossibility of healing. But when my attention is given to God, I am confident that he can heal.

John Wimber, *Power Healing*

A subtle change occurred in Nita that day. Her prayer life experienced a fundamental change. 'I'm not asking for healing any more,' she told the Lord each day. 'I'm not asking to be taken home to heaven. Just tell me what you created me for, and do anything you like with me. . .' Gradually, prayerfully, Nita's eyes closed for longer stretches, as she began to be enveloped in the awesome presence of God. . . She was longing to see Jesus. Just at 3.30 he came into the room with blinding glory. Nita gazed into his face, and everything within her struggled to reach out to him, to draw even a bit closer to him.

Her healing was no more a factor. . . she only longed to touch him. . . to connect somehow with that fabulous source of light and love. . . the chains of paralysis exploded away as Nita rocketed out over the end of the bed. She landed on her knees with a thud, and her first sensation was the cold, hard tile floor beneath her. . . In the days to come she would realise that God had touched her so warmly only to thrust her into a ministry of fervent intercessory prayer in the cold real world.

Mark Buntain, *Miracle in the Mirror*

The faith that is imparted to the individual for the healing of his physical body is only the result of God's mercy; the overflow of his great compassion and grace. It is a gift. You do not pray for faith; you seek the Lord and faith will come.

Kathryn Kuhlman, *I Believe in Miracles*

We need less 'praying through' and more 'seeing through'. See through the distressing circumstances to the redemptive purposes that we know are there. The object of prayer is not to change God's mind. We are to pray 'thy will be done' not 'thy will be changed'. Prayer should not be a way out of our present circumstances, but an opportunity to confess — agree with God — in every circumstance. To pray for change is to say, 'No, God. You've done things wrong and need to straighten them out.' That's not prayer, that's unbelief. . . an immediate visible change in circumstances is not our main objective.

The primary objective of prayer is to bring ourselves to the point of release. We must know a release within that allows us to see God as love-in-action in the circumstances just as they are at that moment. . . Our only 'need', if we want to label it that way, is a clearer revelation and consciousness of who we are in Christ. The infinite supply is always within, but the level of our awareness increases as we 'grow up' spiritually.

Bill Volkman, *The Wink of Faith*

Father, you are here, saturating everything you have made, filling me with your Spirit. Your shepherding love is caring so completely for me, and those I love, that nothing is forgotten for my good. Even the painful times, I trust, are being rightfully used by you, for ultimate blessings I can still barely conceive. I give you permission to strip my eyes of their cataracts, my heart of its dross.

Thank you, Jesus, that as I look within, and learn to see only you, I am trusting your love to melt away all that is unlovely within me: your strength to cover all my powerlessness and your faith to meet every need as I trust your faithfulness. In the quietness of this time, I know that you have all I will ever need for the circumstances of this day, and you are within me. All your resources are there as I need them — boundless, freely heaped upon me to enable me to do your will without undue strain or effort. The Kingdom of Heaven is truly available to me this day, whether I know it or not. I just have to learn to see where you are working. Give me sharpness of vision to find you, Lord, and thus worship all day long as I dwell in this heavenly kingdom.

A Benediction
Christ is with you, Christ within you,
Christ behind you, Christ before you,
Christ beside you, Christ to win you,
Christ to comfort and restore you.
Christ beneath you, Christ above you,
Christ in quiet, Christ in danger.
Christ in hearts of all that love you
Christ in mouth of friend and stranger.

St Patrick

Choose life

For this commandment which I command you this day
is not too hard for you, neither is it far off. It is not in
heaven, that you should say, 'Who will go up for us to
heaven, and bring it to us, that we may hear it and do
it?' Neither is it beyond the sea, that you should say,
'Who will go over the sea for us, and bring it to us, that
we may hear and do it?' But the word is very near you;
it is in your mouth and in your heart, so that you can
do it. . . I have set before you this day life and good,
death and evil. . . therefore choose life, that you and
your descendants may live. . .

'Have I not commanded you? Be strong and of good
courage; be not frightened, neither be dismayed; for the
Lord your God is with you wherever you go.'

Why are you cast down, O my soul, and why are you
disquieted within me? Hope in God; for I shall again
praise him, my help and my God.

In the shadow of thy wings I will take refuge, till the
storms of destruction pass by.

O my enemies, do not exult over me;
I have fallen, but shall rise again;
though I dwell in darkness, the Lord is my light.
Although the fig-tree does not burgeon,
the vines bear no fruit,
the olive crop fails,
the orchards yield no food,
the fold is bereft of its flock
and there are no cattle in the stalls,
yet I will exult in the Lord
and rejoice in the God of my deliverance
I have forgotten what happiness is. . .

But this I call to mind,
and therefore I have hope:
The steadfast love of the Lord never ceases,
his mercies never come to an end;
they are new every morning;
great is thy faithfulness.
For we should like you to realise. . . that the things
we had to undergo in Asia were more of a burden than
we could carry, so that we despaired of coming through
alive. . . we were carrying our own death warrant with
us, and it has taught us not to rely on ourselves but
only on God, who raises the dead to life.
So we do not lose heart.
If anyone is in Christ, he is a new creation; the old
has passed away, behold the new has come.

(Deuteronomy 30: 11-15, 19, RSV; Joshua 1: 9, RSV; Psalm 42: 11,
RSV; Psalm 57: 1, RSV; Micah 7: 8, NEB; Habakkuk 3: 17-18, NEB;
Lamentations 3: 17, 21-23, RSV: 2 Corinthians 1: 8-9, JB; 2 Corin-
thians 4: 16, RSV; 2 Corinthians 5: 17, RSV)

The image of the valley evokes different pictures. It may
be a beautiful place, full of tranquillity and fruitfulness, a
haven of safety and satisfaction. But it may at times be
a dark and difficult area where a sense of vulnerability
and exposure fill us with fear and terrible insecurity. It
is gloomy and dangerous and we are conscious of being
enclosed by the hills with no way out. Escape seems
impossible and we are unable to conceive of any
worthwhile future. No far horizons beckon us to new and
exciting possibilities. The long wide view so easily seen
from the summit of the mountains is painfully absent here.
Everywhere we are surrounded by the barrier of impenetrable hills and there is no apparent way of moving
beyond them. Hope fails, courage melts, dreams topple
and we are reduced to an enervating and sorrowful existence with the spectre of self-pity constantly dogging our
disheartened steps.

We cannot live on this planet without sometimes finding
ourselves in such a valley. Perhaps we blunder there by

our own foolishness and the bitter remorse of this does nothing to alleviate our despair at finding ourselves in such a situation. More often, we are plunged into the valley by circumstances which hurtle in upon us — unexpected, unwanted, unasked. Without consultation with us, we are thrown from the higher ground of the mountains, over the precipice and into the deep valley below with a frightening rapidity for which we are unprepared. Failure, illness, betrayal, bereavement and a host of other related calamities can pitch us without warning into the dark valley experience.

What we do when we find ourselves so unwillingly there is of tremendous importance. It is usual to feel overwhelmed with fear, despair, exhaustion and sometimes deep bitterness and anger. Such emotions are characteristic of the valley. All hope seems gone. The laughter and happiness of other places flees. We want most of all to curl up and sleep in a small safe hole where we can avoid the overhwelming weariness and pain of the place. But such luxuries are seldom permitted and we find ourselves plodding along day after weary day wondering when it will all end.

In utter defiance of the terrifying misery and hopelessness of the valley, God speaks. What he says is in such blatant contradiction of the circumstances that it leaves the listener stunned: ' My presence is sufficient to sustain the most feeble traveller on the arduous valley trek. There are no dead ends. There is definitely a way out into the more invigorating and beautiful heights of the mountains and you will find yourself further along the range than you were previously. More than this, there is even a rare beauty to be found in the valley, a different, but wonderful music, and where you have felt so isolated and alone there are many travelling companions to share the journey and enrich you.'

Whilst the valley experience may underline the fact that our control over our own destiny is more limited than we had thought, and our freedom to choose more hedged about by restrictions than we had believed, it is nevertheless true that we retain the freedom to choose our basic mind-set. To believe or not to believe, to choose life or to choose death, to open our minds to the transforming power of the Christ who promises to bring resurrection, or to remain buried in our disaster — these things we may decide. Not that choosing life is easy or painless — it, alas, involves the agony of a death also. A very real and very hard death. But it issues in a birth into new life and full of promise and unimagined possibilities.'Behold, I have set before you life and death. . . Choose life.'

We who lived in concentration camps can remember the men who walked through the huts comforting others, giving away their last piece of bread. They may have been few in number, but they offer sufficient proof that everything can be taken from us but one thing: the last of the human freedoms — to choose one's attitude to any given set of circumstances, to choose one's way.

Victor Frankl, *Man's Search for Meaning*

What if I cannot recognise the given as blessing? What if it is not sunshine that pours down on us, but hailstones like hammer-blows? What if it is acid rain? Here again, the gift within the gift is opportunity. I have the opportunity, for example, to do something about that acid rain, face the facts, inform myself about the causes, go to their roots, alert others, band together with them for self-help, for protest. By taking each opportunity as it is offered, I show myself grateful. . . Why not drop the complications we put in our own way? What brings fulfillment is gratefulness, the simple response of our heart to this given life in all its fulness.

David Steindl-Rast, *Gratefulness, the Heart of Prayer*

We require a perspective that reaches beyond the particularity of events and encompasses our life as a whole. Since all the events that we experience are part of the moving process of our life, they reflect something of our past and they also carry the possibilities of our future. Those events that we perceive as adversities may be experienced as painful, and we may wish that they had been avoided; but they may also be the vehicles by which an expanded awareness of the meaning of our life is being opened up to us.

The choice we have before us. . . is whether we shall react directly to the event itself, or whether we shall place it in the context of the movement of our life and let it speak to us. In general, it is more usual for setbacks or other painful occurrences to serve as the events that have a message for us.

Ira Progoff, At a Journal Workshop

In every life there are a few special moments that count for more than all the rest because they meant the taking of a stand, a self-commitment, a decisive choice. . . The turning points in life are generally few in number. They are always an encounter. . . before which the subject cannot remain neutral. One has to take sides, commit oneself.

Paul Tournier, The Seasons of Life

. . .There is so much pain in the world. What does it mean to suffer so much if our lives are nothing more than the blink of an eye?. . . I learned a long time ago, Reuven, that the blink of an eye in itself is nothing. But the eye that blinks, *that* is something. A span of life is nothing. But the man who lives that span, *he* is something. He can fill that tiny span with meaning, so its quality is immeasurable though its quantity may be insignificant. Do you understand what I am saying? A man must fill his life with meaning; meaning is not automatically given to life. It is hard work to fill one's life with meaning.

Chaim Potok, The Chosen

If we do not believe, the waves engulf us,
the winds blow, nourishment fails,
sickness lays us low or kills us,
the divine power is impotent or remote.
If, on the other hand, we believe,
the waters are welcoming and sweet,

the bread is multiplied, our eyes are open,
the dead rise again,
the power of God is as it were
drawn from him by force
and spreads throughout all nature.

Pierre Teilhard de Chardin

In any lifetime. . . there are innumerable little deaths —
always painful and frightening (that can't be avoided): the
break-up of a love affair; the loss of a childish faith; seeing
one's child leave home for the first time; moving house;
the loss of a job; retirement. Cling to what you have at
that moment, and you're lost. Unclench your hands and
let it slip away, and you are ready to receive the
unimagined new life. If we learn that habit from all the
small occasions for dying which may come to us, then
when the last letting-go is called for, it will be familiar
and confident. Our formation of that habit will be immeasurably strengthened as we keep our eyes on the truth
about God and life revealed in Jesus, whose attitude was:
'I lay down my life to receive it again. No-one has robbed
me of it. I am laying it down of my own free will. I
have the inner authority to lay it down and to receive it
back again. This charge I received from my Father' (John
10: 17-18).

So the choice for every human being is between death
or death — the death of a letting go that hurts like hell
but leads to resurrection, or the death of slow extinction
as all the energies are spent on getting and keeping instead
of living and giving.

John V. Taylor, *A Matter of Life and Death*

If there are any among us who are at their wit's end, they
ought to try for once to put aside all their grievances and
perhaps even all their petitions and simply praise God. . .
Nothing so changes us — precisely in the darkest moments of life — as the praise of God. We can praise
human persons only when we have seen what they accomplish. But we must praise God in order to see what
he accomplishes. And therefore we should praise him at

the very moments in life when there seems to be no way out. Then we shall learn to see the way out for our own lives, simply because God is there at the end of every way and every blind alley.

Helmut Thielicke, *The Prayer that Spans the World*

Father, when the way is hard and I am overwhelmed and shattered by my situation, help me to choose life. By the mysterious working of your Spirit in my mind, rekindle in me the courage I need. Strengthen my feeble resolve to allow you to perform your healing work deep within me. Help me to co-operate with you in the mending of my brokenness and increase my faith that you will keep your word and out of this death experience you will bring new and vital life.

By your help and grace I choose not to remain in bitterness and despair, but to allow you to lead me beyond it. I choose not to indulge in self-pity, but to cultivate the spirit of gratitude for all the good things which have come to me. I choose to follow your leading along the valley in the hope that you will bring me safely through it and up into the clear air of the mountains where you will give me views I have not yet glimpsed.

For your mercy and compassion, I thank you.

For your faithfulness which is new every morning, I praise you.

For your life which overcomes all deaths and swallows them up in abundant life, I worship you.

A Benediction
Rise up with Christ into a new day, a new life; because for anyone who is in Christ, there is a new creation. The old has gone and the new is here. Therefore, go forth in joy. Amen.

26

Morning has broken

And there was evening and there was morning — the first day.

Awake, my soul! Awake, harp and lyre! I will awaken the dawn.

But I will sing of your strength, in the morning I will sing of your love.

Morning by morning, O Lord, you hear my voice, morning by morning I lay my requests before you and wait in expectation. As morning breaks, I look to you O God, to be my strength this day.

His anger lasts only a moment, but his favour lasts a lifetime; weeping may remain for a night, but rejoicing comes in the morning.

The steadfast love of the Lord never ceases, his mercies never come to an end; they are new every morning; great is thy faithfulness.

But for you who revere my name, the sun of righteousness will rise with healing in its wings. And you will go out and leap like calves released from the stall.

And the day shall dawn upon us from on high to give light to those who sit in darkness and in the shadow of death, to guide our feet into the way of peace.

Very early in the morning, while it was still dark, Jesus got up, left the house and went off to a solitary place, where he prayed.

Early on the first day of the week, while it was still dark, Mary of Magdala went to the tomb and saw the stone had been removed from the entrance.

Early in the morning, Jesus stood on the shore, but the disciples did not realise that it was Jesus. He called out to them, 'Friends, haven't you any fish?' 'No,' they answered. He said, 'Throw your net on the right side of the boat and you will find some.' When they did, they were unable to haul the net in because of the large number of fish. . . Jesus said to them, 'Come and have breakfast.'

(Genesis 1: 5, NIV; Psalm 57: 8, NIV; Psalm 59: 16, NIV; Psalm 5: 3, NIV; Psalm 30: 5, NIV; Lamentations 3: 22-23, RSV; Malachi 4: 2, NIV; Luke 1: 78-79, RSV; Mark 1: 35, NIV; John 20: 1, NIV; John 21: 4-6,12, NIV)

A friend in the midst of a black-as-night depression once sent me a Christmas card from a psychiatric hospital. It was inscribed with the words, 'the sun of righteousness shall dawn upon you with healing in his wings.' It was these words, she said, that had kept her going. We need to know that tears will run their course, even when etched deep into our cheeks, and that each morning is another chance, an opportunity to get up and dance or at least take one hesitant step forward. The resurrection is the assurance that there will be a morning of rejoicing and healing.

Morning is the time to greet the day, to receive our lives afresh again, direct from God's hand. It is the time to arise and pray, not as a way of earning our way into God's good books, or because evangelical tradition decrees so, but as a way of receiving the day as sheer grace, and not taking it for granted. It is to recognise the wonder of it all, that we are alive and awake, not still asleep, dead or non-existent as we could quite easily be. From the womb of the morning, of the resurrection morning, we are brought to birth and new birth, day after day.

We can then face each day as an act of daring, of defying death and depression, of rising to new life with Christ. We can face it even when worn out after a night of heavy and fruitless fishing, worn out by the work of the kingdom. We can face it utterly dependent on the risen Jesus, standing on the shore, giving us courage to lower our nets once more, listening for a word to show us the way to abundant and fruitful ministry and mission. But

above all, any considerations of ministry or mission
productivity aside, he is the one who invites us to breakfast with him. Let's join him.

❧

Morning has broken
like the first morning
blackbird has spoken
like the first bird.
Praise for the singing,
praise for the morning,
praise for them, springing
fresh from the word. . .
Mine is the sunlight;
mine is the morning
born of the one light
Eden saw play
Praise with elation
praise every morning
God's recreation
of the new day.

Eleanor Farjeon, 'Morning Has Broken'

Beloved, it is morn!
A redder berry on the thorn,
A deeper yellow on the corn,
For this good day new-born:
Pray, Sweet, for me
That I may be
Faithful to God and thee

Emily Henrietta Hickey, 'Beloved, it is Morn'

The day does now dark night dispel;
Dear Christians, wake and rouse you well,
Give glory to our God and Lord
Once more the daylight shines abroad,
O brethren let us praise the Lord,
Whose grace and mercy thus have kept
The nightly watch while we have slept
We offer up ourselves to thee,

That heart and word and deed may be
In all things guided by thy mind
And in thine eyes acceptance find.
Bohemian Brethren
'Ere yet the dawn hath filled the skies
Behold my Saviour Christ arise.
He chaseth from us sin and night,
And brings us joy and life and light.

Hallelujah!

Reformation hymn

What do we today, who no longer have any fear or awe of night, know of the great joy that our forefathers and the early Christians felt every morning at the return of light? If we were to learn again something of the praise and adoration that is due the triune God at break of day, God the Father and Creator, who has preserved our life through the dark night and wakened us to a new day, God the Son and Saviour, who conquered death and hell for us, and dwells in our midst as Victor, God the Holy Spirit, who pours the bright gleam of God's Word into our hearts at the dawn of day, driving away all darkness and sin and teaching us to pray aright — then we would also begin to sense something of the joy that comes when night is past and brethren who dwell together in unity come together early in the morning for common praise of their God, common hearing of the Word and common prayer. Morning does not belong to the individual, it belongs to the Church, to the Christian family, to the brotherhood. . .

For Christians, the beginning of the day should not be burdened and oppressed with besetting concerns for the day's work. At the threshold of the new day stands the Lord who made it. All the darkness and distraction of the dreams of night retreat before the clear light of Jesus Christ and his wakening Word. All unrest, all impurity, all care and anxiety flee before him.

Therefore, at the beginning of the day let all distraction and empty talk be silenced and let the first thought and the first word belong to him to whom our life belongs.

'Awake thou that sleepest, and arise from the dead, and Christ shall give thee light' (Eph 5: 14).

Dietrich Bonhoeffer, *Life Together*

I wake up, rested, jump out of bed, grab a cup of coffee, and rush out the door to get things started. The first thing I discover (a great blow to the ego) is that everything was started hours ago. All the important things got underway while I was fast asleep. When I dash into the workday, I walk into an operation that is half over already. I enter into work in which the basic plan is already established, the assignments given, the operations in motion.

Sometimes, still in a stupor, I blunder into the middle of something that is nearly done and go to work thinking I am starting it. But when I do, I interfere with what has already been accomplished. My sincere intentions and cheerful whistle while I work make it no less a blunder and an aggravation. The sensible thing is to ask, 'Where do I fit? Where do you need an extra hand? What still needs to be done?'

The Hebrew evening/morning sequence conditions us to the rhythms of grace. We go to sleep, and God begins his work. . . We wake and are called out to participate in God's creative action. We respond in faith, in work. We wake into a world we didn't make, into a salvation we didn't earn.

Eugene H. Peterson, 'The Pastor's Sabbath'

. . .As earth waits patiently
for sun's warmth, so must
my soul, expectant, wait
in silent, unseeing trust.
Only if Love wills
shall his finger find me
and piercing darkness, bind me.

Merle Davis, 'Morning Prayer'

Lord, you have already passed this way,
And laid in wait the coming day.

The tassels of your robe have brushed
The dust away.
And though the storms you have not hushed
Nor spared the troubles,
Yours is a wondrous strategy.

Help me to see
The people placed in awkward corners
By your grace,
The kindly loan, The warmth of voice on the telephone,
The love in each new smiling face.

Help me then to throw to you beyond the wall,
The ball of each new day;
For only then can I unfettered, child-like play,
As through time I go.

Pauline Young, 'A Prayer'

Creating God,
  as the curtain of night is drawn back,
  and the golden robes of the day
  arrive over sea and mountain,
expel from our minds all sour thoughts,
that we may greet this new day as a gift
  fresh from the hands of creation,
  and filled with hope, and bright with gladness,
and glorify the One who makes all things new:
Through Jesus Christ our Lord.

As the fieldlark
rises at daybreak
to offer its praise
high above wheatfields,
trees and farmhouses:
So may we,
in this hour of awakening,
let our gratitude ascend to you
O Lord Most High.

God of the inner light,

come to us
   on the golden rays of the morning,
   warming moods that are frosty;
   enlightening minds that are gloomy;
and, as the sun swings higher,
so may our lives rise to you
   in the active praise of this day's duties:
through Jesus, our risen Light.

Spirit of new life,
grant unto us this day
   the grace to recognise new life
   breaking through
   in unlikely events;
and, in so recognising it,
   to be ready to trust it
   and delight in it:
through Jesus Christ our Lord.
Bruce Prewer, Australian Prayers

A Benediction
May the God who makes each morning like creation's first morning, give us grace to greet every day in the light of the Resurrection morning, to grasp its unique opportunity with eager hands, to experience it as gift and calling before demand, and so to pass it on as a gift to others. Amen.

Theme: Provision

. . .for time and eternity

Lord, you have been our refuge
   from age to age.
Before the mountains were born,
   before the earth and the world came to birth,
from eternity to eternity you are God. . .

You respond to us with the marvels of your saving
   justice,
   God our Saviour,
hope of the whole wide world,
   even the distant islands.

By your strength you hold the mountains steady;
   being clothed in power,
you calm the turmoil of the seas,
   the turmoil of their waves. . .

You crown the year with your generosity,
   richness seeps from your tracks,
the pastures of the desert grow moist,
 the hillsides are wrapped in joy,
the meadows are covered with flocks,
   the valleys clothed with wheat;
they shout and sing for joy.

Psalms 90: 1-2; 65: 5-7 and 11-13, NJB

27

Gratefulness,
the heart of prayer

(David Steindl-Rast)

One of them, when he saw he was healed, came back, praising God in a loud voice. He threw himself at Jesus' feet and thanked him — and he was a Samaritan. Jesus asked, 'Were not all ten cleansed? Where are the other nine? Was no-one found to return and give praise to God except this foreigner?'

Praise the Lord, O my soul; all my inmost being, praise his holy name. Praise the Lord, O my soul, and forget not all his benefits. He forgives all my sins and heals all my diseases; he redeems my life from the pit and crowns me with love and compassion. He satisfies my desir es with good things, so that my youth is renewed like the eagle's.

I will praise you, O Lord my God, with all my heart; I will glorify your name forever.

It is good to praise the Lord and make music to your name, O Most High, to proclaim your love in the morning and your faithfulness at night. . .

Always giving thanks to God the Father for everything, in the name of our Lord Jesus Christ.

Worthy is the Lamb, who was slain, to receive power and wealth and wisdom and strength and honour and glory and praise!

(Luke 17: 15-18; Psalm 103: 1-5; Psalm 86: 12; Psalm 92: 1-2; Ephesians 5: 20; Revelation 5: 12 — all NIV)

It is not enough to merely speak about the spiritual life — we must also live it. Gratefulness is the theme of such a life. Quiet joy and solid peace reward those who truly search with grateful hearts after God.

It's usually easy to be thankful for what others do or say, but deep gratefulness recognises the many gifts that most people take for granted. . . the surprising colour and profusion of flowers in a suburban garden, with perhaps a white-throated honey-eater dining on nectar. . . the wonder and splendour of a blue sky slashed through with brilliant white clouds. . . the work of a master painter. Music, poetry and handmade craftwork all evoke admiration and praise. God keeps on showering us with new gifts, giving us endless new occasions to say thanks and offer praise.

When so much of our lives is affected by strife, hatred, violence and war we can still gratefully look beyond all that and see that joy and peace are much closer at hand than we realise. Gratefulness allows us to do that.

Gratefulness sets us free to love wholeheartedly, give thanks and praise, be surprised by the unexpected and to discover fullness of life. Fullness follows gratefulness. And there's no reversing the order.

❦

There was a time when I screamed, 'Good Lord, where are you?' Then you touched my despairing soul with healing, and delivered me from my private little hell. Thus I shout God's praises, and exhort all who know him to do the same.

And my nights of despair resolve into the dawn of new joy.

And you turned my griping into gratitude, my screams of despair into proclamations of joy.

Leslie F. Brandt, *Psalms Now*

In our innermost heart we know that wholeness is more basic, more primordial than alienation, and so we never quite lose an inborn trust that in the end we shall be whole and together.

The German poet Rainer Maria Rilke celebrates both our longing for healing and wholeness and our primordial conviction that God's healing power wells up in our own innermost heart. He finds God in 'the spot that is healing', while we, like children picking on a scar, keep ripping it open with the sharp edges of our thoughts. If only we could quiet all that agitation within and around us, the din that distracts us.

Rilke's answer is thanksgiving.

Oh, if for once all were completely still!
If all mere happenstance and chance
were silenced, and the laughter next door, too;
if all that droning of my senses
did not prevent my being wide awake -
Then, with one thousandfold thought,
I would reach your horizon
and, for the span of a smile, hold you
to give you away to all life
as thanksgiving.

David Steindl-Rast, *Gratefulness, the Heart of Prayer*

On your birthday you get something special in the mail, a gift from a friend. You want to sit right down and write a thankyou note. Or someone brings you flowers. Your eyes light up; you reach out and embrace your friend. The embrace is as much a gift as the flowers. The note or the embrace continue the spiral of joy.

The gesture of thanks moves both the giver and receiver to another level. It expresses a unity; it solidifies a relationship. We start out with a giver, a gift and a receiver, and we arrive at the embrace of thanks. Thanks is expressed and then accepted by the giver. And in the final kiss of gratitude it's impossible to distinguish the giver from the receiver.

Don Postema, *Space for God*

The heart is the pulsating core of our aliveness in more than merely the physical sense. To say 'I will give you my heart' is to say, 'I will give you my life.' Gratefulness is full aliveness, and that very aliveness is summed up in the symbol of the heart. All of my past history, all of my future possibilities, this heartbeat in the present moment holds all of it together.

David Steindl-Rast, *Gratefulness, the Heart of Prayer*

It will perhaps be clear by now that the heart, in the ancient sense of the word, is not the discursive intelligence with which we reason, nor the 'feelings' with which we respond to another person, nor yet the superficial emotion we call sentimentality. The heart is something that lies much deeper within us, the innermost core of our being, the root of our existence or, conversely, our summit, what the French mystics call 'the very peak of the soul'.

Andre Louf, *Teach Us to Pray*

Everything I see, every noise I hear, every dawn that returns, every encounter I achieve, are signs of something or someone who has gone before me and questions me: God.

Carlo Carretto, *The Desert in the City*

God makes space for us in the covenant family. We are embraced as children. We belong.

We respond by making space for God, by being open to God in our lives, by living thankfully. Gratitude is an attitude of receptivity. We are there with open hands ready to receive. Gratitude is an expression of appreciation. We are eager to show our gratitude.

Our heart is the personal 'place' of such receptivity and response. . . The heart is a person, the whole person, the spiritual centre where we are always available to God.

Don Postema, *Space for God*

I thank you, Lord, with all my heart,
    you have heard the words of my mouth.
Before the angels I will bless you.
    I will adore you before your holy temple.

I thank you for your faithfulness and love
    which excel all we ever knew of you.
On the day I called, you answered;
    you increased the strength of my soul.
Though I walk in the midst of affliction

you give me life and frustrate my foes.
You stretch out your hand and save me,
   your hand will do all things for me.
Your love, O Lord, is eternal. . .

Psalm 138: 1-3, 7-8
A New Translation

Thank you, Lord, for this moment.
Thank you, Lord, that I am together here with you in the place
where my intellect and will and feelings, my mind and body,
my past and future come together.
Thank you that you are here in that spot where my life holds
together, deep within my heart.

With a grateful and thankful heart, I dare to believe that you
are making me whole within myself so that I am able to live
intimately with myself, with others, and with God. In the depth
of my heart I find that 'God is closer to me than I am to myself.'

Accept I pray this humble offering from my deeply grateful
heart.

A Benediction

Go into each moment of this day, remembering you are God's
servant. Let gratefulness surprise you often. Allow God's gifts
galore to urge you into a fully alive, frequently grateful response
so that in the final kiss of gratitude, it's impossible to distinguish
the giver from the receiver. Go in his name. Amen.

28

Lilies in hard ground

But Hezekiah was too proud to show gratitude for what the Lord had done for him, and Judah and Jerusalem suffered for it.

Give thanks to him, bless his name! For the Lord is good.

Sing psalms and hymns and spiritual songs with thankfulness in your hearts to God. And whatever you do, in word or deed, do everything in the name of the Lord Jesus, giving thanks to God the Father through him.

The evil you planned to do me has by God's design been turned to good, that he might bring about, as indeed he has, the deliverance of a numerous people.

Have no anxiety about anything, but in everything by prayer and supplication with thanksgiving let your requests be made known to God.

My brothers, consider yourselves fortunate when all kinds of trials come your way, for you know that when your faith succeeds in facing such trials, the result is the ability to endure.

Rejoice always, pray constantly, give thanks in all circumstances; for this is the will of God in Christ Jesus for you.

Do not be worried and upset; do not be afraid.

I have told you this so that my joy may be in you and that your joy may be complete.

And they returned to Jerusalem with great joy, and were continually in the temple blessing God.

But about midnight Paul and Silas were praying and singing hymns to God, and the prisoners were listening to them.

For you had compassion on the prisoners, and you joyfully accepted the plundering of your property, since you knew that you yourselves had a better possession and an abiding one.

(2 Chronicles 32: 25, GNB; Psalm 100: 4-5, RSV; Colossians 3: 16-17, RSV; Genesis 50: 20, JB; Philippians 4: 6, RSV; James 1: 2, GNB; 1 Thessalonians 5: 16-18, RSV; John 14: 27, GNB; John 15: 11, GNB; Luke 24: 52-53, RSV; Acts 16: 25, RSV; Hebrews 10: 34, RSV)

I was amazed to see how many references there are in the Bible to the word 'praise'. Together with accompanying words like 'bless', 'exalt', 'thank', 'glorify', 'honour', 'magnify' and 'extol', there are over five hundred verses, the majority of which are encouraging us to praise our God. The sheer magnitude of the messages should be overpowering, but I knew my own gratitude to God fell sadly short. The high peaks of my life, yes, they were Spirit-drenched, I knew, but the valleys and the plains? These 'Godless' cloud-heavy plains weren't anything to be grateful about, were they? My mind traced down from the peaks of my life to the specific valleys joining them. I peered through the fog with the eye of faith. They were a unified whole of opposites and contrasts, all revealing the mighty touch of God to the eye of faith, no matter what my senses felt about it.

So where was my gratitude? My life held fulfilment, growth and much joy. Even my senses told me I was mostly very happy with it. But my gratitude to God for it, even the peaks, seemed to have become mislaid, diverted, related in some way to my satisfaction with myself and my life. A suspicion lurked just below the edge of my consciousness, but gradually I drew it out. I had been siphoning off, for myself, the gratitude that should have been given to God. Failing to acknowledge the source of those strengths within me — the abilities, the care, the thoughts that came, was indeed folly beyond folly. By failing to point out to others the source of my strength, inspiration and love, I had been, maybe, encouraging them to admire the flowerpot instead of the flower within. And they suffered because of it, unable to see that the strength within me was just as available to them also. The fragrance of humble, unselfish trust hadn't been getting to me, through me, to those God wanted to bless. So, praise on the plains and in the valleys, as well as on the peaks, is the outward expression of inner trust that keeps our eyes on the Father.

❧❧❧

Oh wind! Blow upon my garden,
let its fragrance be wafted abroad.
You are a tree 'neath the breath of God,
well-watered, and firm beneath the sod.
Strong and healthy your spirit grows,
each one different, in highs and lows:
each one different, but in the plan
I've planted you in my garden of man.

The breath of my Spirit blows around you each day,
strongly or still, but come what may you've only to bend,
and joyfully sway.
Bend your proud back and happily nod,
as my Spirit brings over you rain, sun or cloud.
The way to survive is to bend, not to break,
to go with my wind and allow it to shake
you loose from your pride, and your other endeavours
by which you had thought to weather all weathers,
right all wrongs, and bring people to me;
mend broken hearts, save the drowning at sea.

A truly proud streak, and I love your straight back,
your stretching ambitions, but see where you lack?
I alone can do my work, but through vessels sound.
The way to help me, is only found
in flexible trust of all that I bring,
with praise in your heart that helps you to sing.

As you bend and sway 'neath my Spirit this day,
I am making you into a wonderful way
by which men may shelter, gather food and find peace.

You're my inspiration of fragrant increase.
I love your deep yearnings to do things for me,
but all I want is for you to be
a thing of beauty right where you belong,
breathing my air and growing strong.

Trust me to make of you all you could dream,
because you and I are a part of a team.
I do the work as you thankfully see
that the rain, cold and clouds are as useful to thee
as the summer and sunshine, the heat and the bees;
all help you to grow to be one of my trees.

Don't take any credit for your beauty of leaf,
but give it to me, your climate and chief.
Be thankful and grateful, and glorify me.
Let others be glad to encounter a tree.

Bronwyn Pryor

It was that night in the quiet of my [cell] that I made the total surrender, completing what had begun. . . eighteen long months before: 'Lord, if this is what it is all about,' I said, 'then I thank you. I praise you for leaving me in prison, for letting them take away my licence to practise law, yes — even for my son being arrested. I praise you for giving me your love through these four men, for being God, for just letting me walk with Jesus!

With those words came the greatest joy of all — the final release, turning it all over to God as my brother Harold had told me to do. And in the hours that followed I discovered more strength than I'd ever known before. This was the real mountaintop experience. Above and around me the world was filled with joy and love and beauty. For the first time, I felt truly free, even as the fortunes of my life seemed at their lowest ebb. [Forty-eight hours later. . . an order was being prepared to release Charles Colson from prison immediately. . .] Jack said, 'I kind of knew [the Lord] would set you free today.' 'Thank you, brother,' I said, 'but he did it two nights ago.'

Charles Colson, *Born Again*

That is why we must not be surprised if we are in for a rough time. When a man turns to Christ and seems to be getting on pretty well (in the sense that some of his bad habits are now corrected), he often feels that it would now be natural if things went fairly smoothly. When troubles come along — illnesses, money troubles, new kinds of temptations — he is disappointed. These things, he feels, might have been necessary to rouse him and make him repent in his bad old days; but why now? Because God is forcing him on, or up, to a higher level: putting him into situations where he will have to be very much braver, or more patient, or more loving, than he ever dreamed of being before. It seems to us all unnecessary: but that is because we have not yet had the slightest notion of the tremendous thing he means to make of us.

C.S. Lewis, *Mere Christianity*

'Your formula works, Marion.' 'What formula?' 'The restoration formula from your book, "The Nevertheless Principle"'. . . Oh, yes! Yes, it did work. I could remember the formula almost word for word. When I was slowly watching my husband die from a brain tumor, I carefully examined my restoration formula: 'No matter what is taken away from you, if you keep your eyes on Jesus and praise him, he will restore it to you. You will be joyful to the exact same degree you have hurt. What you have lost will be replaced. . . joy for mourning. . . beauty for ashes. . .' God, I don't see how it could work now. . . But I won't limit you, so I'm going to remember this moment for the rest of my life. And if and when you restore the years that the locusts have eaten, I will tell people about it and write about it.

Marion Bond West, *Marion's Marriage*

Many of the 'praise' perspectives of the more successful churches seem to mask an inability to develop a theology of suffering and an unwillingness to embrace the cross of Christ and its consequences. Western culture-Christianity views success, good feelings, comfort, material excellence, health and overall joyous prosperity as the mark of God's approval, and therefore the mark of God's friendship and presence. If things go well, we *feel* close to the Lord. If successive failure or disaster accompanies our efforts, we wonder what rebuking word God has for us. He seems so far away. . . It is a far cry from biblical reality.

John Smith, 'Praise or Pain?'

Roll the burden of cares of thy life's way upon the Lord. *Cause it to go*, the Hebrew says; a push will do it. Cast thy care, *hurl* it — so the word is there. Hurl it with a forceful act of will: it is not enough to think of doing it. Do it. . . The burden has not come of itself. It is a gift, a trust. If we deal with it as we are told we may, we shall find rest unto our souls. . .

These words touch more than illness of the body. If only we allow them to sink deep into our being, if only we refuse forbidding feelings and believe that even to us this grace is given, we shall indeed find rest. In that rest we shall climb. The unrestful cannot climb. They are too busy adjusting and readjusting their burdens to have breath or strength to spare for such ascents. . . The joy of the Lord is your strength. The saints are full of it, even when cast down and oppressed by circumstances. Love and joy breathed from them, and everybody felt they had a blessed secret to impart. . . 'Joy is not gush: joy is not jolliness. Joy is simply perfect acquiescence in God's will, because the soul delights itself in God himself. . . rejoice in the will of God, and in nothing else. Bow down your heads and your hearts before God, and let the will, the blessed will of God, be done.'

Amy Carmichael, *Gold by Moonlight*

Paul said: 'But if we are afflicted, it is for your comfort and salvation; or if we are comforted, it is for your comfort'. . . Paul saw the ultimate secret of Being — the truth that because of who we are in Christ we can be totally content, irrespective of outer circumstances. . . All the *things* of the world, whether we call them good or bad, merely serve as vehicles of God's grace and truth. These vehicles are wearing out, as God has promised they would, so we should not be too concerned about their good and evil appearances. What is important is that they get us to God's Life, not in the hereafter, but in each moment of our daily lives.

Bill Volkman, *The Wink of Faith*

When Christmas came, both of us felt sadness about being locked up, separated from our families. Late Christmas Eve, Willie shared the doubts he had gathered in his heart. . . 'I don't understand how God could allow this to happen.' 'Big Willie, I know your thoughts, I'm depressed too. But. . . Paul was in a dungeon with his ankles in stocks. He couldn't walk around as you and I can in this cell. . . We have much for which to be thankful. . . We don't have anything materially, but we have the greatest possession on the face of the earth — Jesus Christ. And one day we're going to be joint heirs with him!'. . . 'We are lucky, aren't we?' he said. Like the Apostle Paul we prayed and praised God with our voices while tears washed our faces. It was a very special time as the depression gave way to joy.

Harold Morris, *Twice Pardoned*

As Kathy grew increasingly discontented with herself, I prayed for God to show us a way to keep her from the negative thoughts that seemed to be growing inside her. One day she was doing what we call 'counting the empties' — talking about the things she could *not* do, rather than emphasising those things that she *could* do. I stopped her right on the spot, and we bowed our heads and prayed for God to teach us how to maintain a better attitude, to show us an alternative. . . I felt, as I prayed, that God wanted us to set a goal, something specific to work towards, which would keep our minds on 'can do' rather than 'can't do'. So I asked Kathy, 'What single thing would you like to be able to do again that you could do before the accident?' Kathy answered. . . 'run'.

Barbara Miller, *Kathy*

During the time of prayers for healing I encourage people

to 'dial down', that is, to relax and resist becoming emotionally worked up. Stirred up emotions rarely aid the healing process, and usually impede learning about how to pray for the sick. So I try to create an atmosphere that is clinical and rational while at the same time it is powerful and spiritually sensitive. . .

When we are out in the marketplace we cannot worship aloud; nevertheless, God hears praise and thanksgiving in our hearts and sends his Spirit. Back in 1982 a friend. . . wrote me a note in which he described his experience of the relationship between worship and effective healing prayer. . . 'It's happening, John! Six out of the seven things I've prayed for in the past five days for my family in the way of healing have occurred within two minutes!. . . I now realise what my mistake was: by just jumping in and praying for healing without worshipping God first, I was actually taking him for granted.'

John Wimber, *Power Healing*

'I am learning never to be disappointed, but to praise,' Arnot of Central Africa wrote in his journal long ago. . . I think it must hurt the tender love of our Father when we press for reasons for his dealings with us, as though he were not Love, as though not he but another chose our inheritance for us, and as though what he chose to allow could be less than the very best and dearest that Love Eternal had to give. . . But I do not find that this position, that of unbroken peacefulness and inward song, is one which we can hope to hold unassailed. It is no soft arrangement of pillows, no easy-chair. It is a fort in an enemy's country, and the foe is wise in assault and especially in surprise. And yet there can be nothing to fear, for it is not a place that we must keep, but a stronghold in which we are kept, if only, in the moment we are conscious of attack, we look. . . unto. . . Jesus.

Amy Carmichael, *Rose from Brier*

Suffering is all too real at the level of our senses. Our emotional responses to all human suffering — be it our pain, loss, separation or limitation — are valid, and need not be suppressed. These responses are God's way to remind us that we are earthen vessels with his treasure in our inner being. At that inner level we can rejoice in faith, even though we are hurting and crying on the outside. But as we operate at this faith level, we recognise the outer appearances as illusion, for they have no effect on our true inner selves in union with Christ. . .

God turned the adversity and evil of the next five years into adventure and good for our entire family. The nightmare of rebellion which manifested itself in [our son] Scott's life in riotous living, drugs, run-ins with the police and verbal abuse of the family seemed like it would never end. But we ultimately saw that the low road Scott had chosen was a major part of God's redemptive plan for opening the eyes of the whole family to true reality. . . his rebellion was no more of a tragedy than Christ's crucifixion — both were wonderful blessings in disguise . . . the resulting revelations of truth were well worth the temporary pain.

Bill Bolkman, *The Wink of Faith*

Father, sometimes I know you're so close and it is easy to praise you for the evidence that you are working within me and through me. Thank you. I know I'm in your will. And often I am amazed at the evidence of your work in the lives of those around me, for whom I pray. I bask in the sunshine of your blessings. My growth is easy and natural, centred in you. I praise you and thank you for doing this within me.

But now life is a struggle again, and there seem so many burdens to weigh me down. My heart is sore. I am tired. I don't know which way to turn first. Yet I praise you, my Lord, for the experiences of these past days. I trust that they are all part of your plan to use me to bless others. I trust you, Lord, that they are necessary — in fact, vital — for your purpose to be accomplished within me and through me. I give you the problems, the temptations, the festering hurts. I lift them up and throw them down at your feet. My hands are free, free to bless you. In my imagination, I lift them high in joy and wonder and praise, for I would become a praise-filled person, trusting you to use even these overcast days for your glory. All is well. I am yours. The sunshine of your love still lies behind the clouds. And your care for me is beyond my wildest imaginations. I bless you, my God.

A Benediction
Enter the day ahead with joy, determined to be available for Jesus to live his life through you. Relax to its hardships working on you, trusting God to mould you and carry you through them. The climb can be tough, but take each event as from the hand of God and praise him, leaving the results in his hands. Then watch for the signs of the lilies in the hard ground. Amen.

Water in dry places

O God you are my God: eagerly will I seek you. My soul thirsts for you; my flesh longs for you: as a dry and thirsty land where no water is.

My soul is thirsty for God, thirsty for the living God.

Blessed are those whose strength is in you: in whose heart are the highways to Zion; who going through the valley of dryness find there a spring from which to drink.

I will make the wilderness a pool of water, and the dry land springs of water.

Behold, water was issuing from below the threshold of the temple. . . this water flows towards the eastern region and goes down into the Arabah; and when it enters the stagnant waters of the sea, the water will become fresh.

On the last day of the feast, the great day, Jesus stood up and proclaimed, 'If any one thirst, let him come to me and drink. He who believes in me, as the scripture has said, 'Out of his heart shall flow rivers of living water.'

All my fresh springs are in you.

(Psalm 63: 1-2; Psalm 42: 2; Psalm 84: 5-6 — all *The Psalms, A New Translation for Worship*; Isaiah 41: 18; Ezekiel 47: 1 and 8; John 7: 37-38; Psalm 87: 7 — all RSV)

The predominantly arid nature of Australia and the prevalence of drought mean that many Australians know what it is to be in a dry and parched place. The very ground cries out in its desolate need for water.

The Psalmist can see in his dry surroundings a vivid

image of his own thirst for God. The farmer longs for the sound of the drops of rain on the roof: otherwise he faces ruin.

The flow of God's spirit seems at times to be withheld from me. The memory of other times of refreshment and comfort only serve to increase my feelings of dryness. My sins, committed in moments of angry despair and impatient self-centredness, only serve to aggravate my sense of desolation. 'Where is your God now?'

Do not withhold your mercy from me, my God. Refresh and water me in my dry state. Penetrate the hard layers; soak me with the waters of your Spirit. May I not be satisfied with anything less, any temporary respite.

Jesus thirsted to do your will. In the scroll of the book it is written of me that I should do your will: O my God, I long to do it; your law delights my heart.

Give me that heart that longs to do your will. There is no other way for me.

> What amazes me about you, Lord
> is that the source of your love
> doesn't dry up.
> There is always more.
> 'Inexhaustible, incomprehensible, incalculable'
> — big words those.
> We use them as we use you;
> but still there is more.

❧

> Our needy souls sustain
> with fresh supplies of love
>
> Charles Wesley

'My soul thirsts for God, for the living God: when shall I come and appear before God?' (Psalm 42: 2). The thirst of this poet is not unique. It is universal. Just as these bodies of ours are not self-sustaining, but must be watered and fed from resources external to themselves, even so it is with our souls. If our bodies do not have physical food and water, they will hunger and thirst and die. Just so, if our souls do not have God, the Bread of Life and the Water of Life, they, too, will hunger and thirst and die.

Clovis Chappell, 'The Great Thirst'

Fr Dimitri Dudko, a Moscow priest, asked the young people of his congregation to write to him to tell of their experiences in coming to faith. The following is a letter which he received and subsequently read to the congregation:

Dear Father Dimitri,

You asked your young parishioners to describe their path to faith. So I'm writing to you about myself.

The people in my family are deeply atheistic by disposition. Even my grandmother and grandfather were non-believers. From childhood I learned my lesson well that God is just a fable invented by ignorant people.

The more I thought about what lay around me, the more clearly I saw and understood that everything is gibberish, not worth a brass farthing. So I came to the point of rejecting everything and everyone. Concepts such as conscience, truth and morality were empty to me. . .

Nothing made me really happy. Nothing was pleasant. I started to drink. You get drunk and things get a little easier. The longer it went on, the longer it took me to get really smashed. On my days off I'd drink myself unconscious.

I got away with everything for a while, but you always reach the end of your rope. It all came very simply and very quickly. I got drunk, got into a fight and found myself in jail.

There was this guy in my cell, a Baptist who prayed a lot and would always cross himself before meals. Many people — including me — mocked him for this. Out of boredom I dragged him into a dispute over religion. At first, I just let my words run away with me, interspersing facetious comments about how old women just thought God up. He answered every one of my flippant arguments seriously. His unshakable conviction that he was correct began to irritate me. Soon — just for the fun of it — I began defending atheism seriously, proving by whatever means necessary that God could not exist.

I really couldn't have cared less either about God or atheism. I just wanted to break his confidence — that was the main thing. Arrogance pushed me on. And I achieved what I wanted. My cell-mate stopped talking. He fell silent, and then began to cry. He began praying that his faith would be strengthened.

I felt no satisfaction in my victory. A horrible weight fell upon me. I felt sick, like I'd done something mean to someone. And he just kept on praying, but more calmly now. Suddenly he looked at me and smiled. I was amazed at his face — there was something joyful about it, pure, like it had been washed. The weight immediately fell from my soul, I understood that he had forgiven me. And then a light of some sort penetrated me, and I understood that God exists. It wasn't even so much that I understood, but that I sensed it with my whole being. He exists! He alone has always been and will always be. He is everywhere. He is our Father! We are his children, brothers one to another. I forgot that I was in prison and felt only one thing — a great joy and thankfulness to the Lord who revealed himself to me who am unworthy.

After this a strange and radiant thing happened to me. As a non-believer, I had read the Bible but had always hit on the 'dark and incomprehensible'. For me, the scriptures were 'woven of contradictions'. After I came to believe, each word of the Gospel was filled with meaning for me, close to my mind and heart.

From *Light through the Curtain*

Love bade me welcome; yet my soul drew back,
    Guilty of dust and sin.
But quick-ey'd Love, observing me grow slack
    From my first entrance in,
Drew nearer to me, sweetly questioning
    If I lack'd any thing.

'A guest,' I answer'd, 'worthy to be here':
   Love said, 'You shall be he.'
'I, the unkind, ungrateful? Ah, my dear,
   I cannot look on Thee.'
Love took my hand, and smiling did reply,
   'Who made the eyes but I?'

'Truth, Lord; but I have marr'd them; let my shame
   Go where it doth deserve.'
'And know you not,' says Love, 'Who bore the
   blame?'
   'My dear, then I will serve.'
'You must sit down,' says Love, 'and taste my meat.'
   So I did sit and eat.

George Herbert, 'Love'

I heard the voice of Jesus say, 'Behold I freely give.
The living water; thirsty one, stoop down and drink
and live.'
I came to Jesus, and I drank of that live-giving stream;
My thirst was quenched, my soul revived, and now I
live in him.

God is as near as our burning thirst. We do not have to
wait for some far-off tomorrow to find him. He is ready
to meet our needs in the here and now. And nobody can
rob us of our finding him but ourselves. This is Jesus'
amazing claim. Shall we take him seriously and drink
and live, or shall we go on our feverish way feeling that
his promise is altogether too good to be true?

Clovis Chappell, 'The Great Thirst'

The residual essence of religious devotion is that the object
of one's dedication is the All. The poet wrote, 'O God,
thou art my God, I seek thee, my soul thirsts for thee, as
in a dry and weary land where no water is.' (Psalm 63:
1). The saintly Fenelon said, 'We must be God's without
any reservation. When we have found God, there is nothing more to look for in others. We must sacrifice our best

friends. The good friend is within our heart. He is the bridegroom who is jealous and who does away with all the rest.' Fenelon was archbishop of Cambrai and tutor to the Duke of Burgundy, but the profligacy of the court of Louis XIV in which he lived was spiritually as weary and waterless as the Babylon — real or fancied — of our poet.

Edwin McNeill Poteat, *Interpreter's Bible*

Tu nos fecisti ad te, Domine,
et cor nostrum inquietum est,
donec requiescat in te.

You have made us for yourself, Lord,
and our heart is restless
until it rests in you.

St Augustine of Hippo

Lord, you have often refreshed me in dry places. I had gone along with little sense of your presence, then found an unexpected experience of grace. I cannot deny that you have worked through me — I've seen the results, but all quite out of proportion to my state of preparation and the shallowness of my prayer. Time and time again, I've seen good things happen even under my own hand. Thank you for including me in your purpose, when I've done little to deserve it, and much to spoil and frustrate it.

Give me fresh springs of joy in the dry places of my being; then I shall be able to minister grace to others in all kinds of circumstances.

A Benediction
May God in the plenitude of his love pour upon you the torrents of his grace, bless you and keep you in his holy fear, prepare you for a happy eternity, and receive you at last into immortal glory.

Blessing at the Consecration of Coventry Cathedral

He gives his beloved sleep

And there was evening and there was morning — the first day.

So the Lord God caused the man to fall into a deep sleep; and while he was sleeping, he took one of the man's ribs and closed up the place with flesh. Then the Lord God made a woman from the rib he had taken out of the man, and he brought her to the man.

I remember thee upon my bed, and meditate on thee in the night watches.

At midnight I will rise to give thanks unto thee because of thy righteous judgments.

My eyes are awake before the watches of the night, that I may meditate on your promises.

Unless the Lord builds the house, those who build it labour in vain. Unless the Lord watches over the city, the watchman stays awake in vain. It is in vain that you rise up early and go late to rest, eating the bread of anxious toil; for he gives to his beloved sleep.

He who watches over Israel will neither slumber nor sleep. The Lord watches over you — the Lord is your shade at your right hand; the sun will not harm you by day, nor the moon by night. The Lord will keep you from all harm — he will watch over your life; the Lord will watch over your coming and going both now and for evermore.

The day is yours, and yours also the night; you established the sun and moon.

When you lie down, you will not be afraid; when you lie down, your sleep will be sweet.

The sleep of a labourer is sweet, whether he eats little or much, but the abundance of a rich man permits him no sleep.

This is what the kingdom of God is like. A man scatters seed on the ground. Night and day, whether he sleeps or gets up, the seed sprouts and grows, though he does not know how. All by itself the soil produces corn.

Jesus was in the stern, sleeping on a cushion. The disciples woke him and said to him, 'Teacher, don't you care if we drown?' He got up, rebuked the wind and said to the waves, 'Quiet! be still!' Then the wind died down and it was completely calm.

They urged him strongly, 'Stay with us, for it is nearly evening; the day is almost over.' So he went in to stay with them. When he was at the table with them, he took bread, gave thanks, broke it and began to give it to them. Then their eyes were opened and they recognised him, and he disappeared from their sight.

Do not let the sun go down while you are still angry, and do not give the devil a foothold.

(Genesis 1: 5, NIV; Genesis 2: 21-22, NIV; Psalm 63: 6, KJV; Psalm 119: 62, KJV; Psalm 119: 148, RSV; Psalm 127: 1-2, RSV; Psalm 121: 4-8, NIV; Psalm 74: 16, NIV; Proverbs 3: 24, NIV; Ecclesiastes 5: 12, NIV; Mark 4: 26-28, 38-39, NIV; Luke 24: 29-31, NIV; Ephesians 4: 26-27, NIV)

There is no more innocent, peaceful sight than that of a young child blissfully asleep. There is no more refreshing feeling than crisp, cool sheets on a hot summer's night after a hard day's work. There is nothing more tortuous than the inability to sleep. It is a premonition of hell, almost endless duration, endless frustration.

The secret of good sleep is to be able to leave all that is undone and unsaid, and all that has been done and said that we wish could be undone, in the Lord's hands. When the storm is raging around us, when pastoral and work problems beset us, when the little boat of the church is buffeted by great waves, we can let our heads hit the pillow and sleep soundly just as Jesus did. For our sleeping can be, like his, not a sign of lack of care and concern for those who are perishing, but of trust in the totally competent care of the Father. It was a truly faithful woman who, during the bombing of London, was heard to excuse herself for having laid quietly in bed, with the words, 'Well, I reflected that God does not sleep, and there seemed no reason why *both* of us should stay awake.'

It is in vain that we allow anxiety to strangle good sleep. Burning the midnight oil has its place occasionally as some Psalms remind us, though not for the purpose of worrying or feverish working. When it becomes a regular practice it can be a sign of lack of faith in the One who keeps watch, and grows the grain of the kingdom while we sleep. It can also represent a refusal to respect the inbuilt rhythms of the Creator, like the beach mission team I once was on, which expected the teenage team to survive on six hours sleep a night and then wondered why everyone was tired and irritable towards the end of the mission, and why the team's witness was slipping.

We can kid ourselves that we are somehow infinite and immortal, forgetting that we are mere dust, and we need our sleep. Bonhoeffer once asked, 'Who is there among us who can give himself with an easy conscience to the cultivation of music, friendship, games or happiness? Surely not ethical man, but only the Christian.' One might well add sleep to that list. The person who sleeps too little or doesn't sleep well may be taking life too seriously. It is good to simply let the Lord lavish his love upon us, while we sleep.

❧

My subject is the theology of sleep. It is an unusual subject, but I make no apology for it. I think we hear too few sermons about sleep. After all, we spend a very large share of our lives sleeping. I suppose that on an average I've slept for eight hours out of twenty-four during the whole of my life, and that means that I've slept for well over twenty years. What an old Rip van Winkle I am! But then, what Rip van Winkles you all are, or will one day become! Don't you agree then that the Christian gospel should have something to say about the sleeping third of our lives as well as about the waking two-thirds of it?

John Baillie, 'The Theology of Sleep'

As we re-enter that sequence of days when God spoke energy and matter into existence, we repeatedly come upon the refrain, 'And there was evening and there was morning' one day. . . a second day. . . on and on six times.

This is the Hebrew way of understanding day, but it is not ours. Our day begins with an alarm clock ripping the predawn darkness and closes, not with evening but several hours past that, when we turn off the electric lights. In our conventional references today, we do not include the night except for the two or three hours we steal from either end to give us more time to work. Because our definition of day is so different, we have to make an imaginative effort to understand the Hebrew phrase *evening and morning, one day.* More than idiomatic speech is involved here; there is a sense of rhythm.

Day is the basic unit of God's creative work; evening is the beginning of that day. It is the onset of God speaking light, stars, earth, vegetation, animals, man, woman into being. But it is also the time when we quit our activity and go to sleep. When it is evening, 'I lay me down to sleep and pray the Lord my soul to keep' and drift off into semiconciousness. . . a state in which I am absolutely nonproductive and have no cash value.

Evening: God begins, without our help, his creative day. Morning: God calls us to enjoy and share and develop the work he initiated.

Creation and covenant are sheer grace and there to greet us every morning. George MacDonald once wrote that sleep is God's contrivance for giving us the help he cannot get into us when we are awake.

We read and reread the opening pages of Genesis, along with certain sequences of Psalms, and recover these deep, elemental rhythms, internalising the reality in which the strong, initial pulse is God's creating/saving Word, God's providential/sustaining presence, God's grace.

As this biblical rhythm works in me, I also discover something else: when I quit my day's work, nothing essential stops. I prepare for sleep not with a feeling of exhausted frustration because there is much yet undone and unfinished, but with expectancy. The day is about to begin! God's genesis words are about to be spoken again. During the hours of my sleep, how will he prepare to use my obedience, service and speech when morning breaks? I go to sleep to get out of the way for a while. I get into the rhythm of salvation.

While we sleep, great and marvellous things, far beyond our capacities to invent or engineer, are in process — the moon marking the seasons, the lion roaring for its prey, the earthworms aerating the earth, the stars turning in their courses, the proteins repairing our muscles, our dreaming brains restoring a deeper sanity beneath the gossip and scheming of our waking hours. Our work settles into the context of God's work. Human effort is honoured and respected not as a thing in itself but by its integration into the rhythms of grace and blessing.

Eugene H. Peterson, *The Pastor's Sabbath*

It is a decisive rule of every Christian fellowship that every dissension that the day has brought must be healed in the evening. It is perilous for the Christian to lie down to sleep with an unreconciled heart. Therefore, it is well that there be a special place for the prayer of brotherly forgiveness in every evening's devotion, that reconciliation be made and fellowship established anew.

In all the ancient evening prayers, we are struck by the frequency with which we encounter the prayer for preservation during the night from the devil, from terror and from an evil, sudden death. The ancient had a persistent sense of their helplessness while sleeping, of the kinship of sleep with death, of the devil's cunning in making them fall when defenceless. So they prayed for the protection of the holy angels and their golden weapons, for the heavenly hosts, at the time when Satan would gain power over them.

Most remarkable and profound is the ancient church's

prayer that when our eyes are closed in sleep, God may nevertheless keep our hearts awake. It is the prayer that God may dwell with us and in us even when we are unconscious of his presence, that he may keep our hearts pure and holy in spite of all the cares and temptations of the night, to make our hearts ever alert to his call and, like the boy Samuel, answer him even in the night with: 'Speak, Lord; for your servant is listening' (1 Samuel 3: 9). Even in sleep God can perform his wonders upon us or evil bring us to destruction. So we pray at evening:

> When our eyes with sleep are girt,
> Be our hearts to thee alert;
> Shield us, Lord, with thy right arm,
> Save us from sin's dreadful harm.   (Luther)
>
> Dietrich Bonhoeffer, *Life Together*

If a psychologist wants to understand the sort of person I am, he will not listen to the conversation I make, or read what I write on paper; he will rather try to penetrate beneath this official selfhood to my most secret thoughts. He is not hidden in the public show-places of my mind, but in its hidden nooks and crannies. He would like to know what visions I see in the clouds of my tobacco smoke as I lie back in my easy chair. He would like to know what I think of as I lie awake in bed, and he will question me in particular about the dreams that come to me when at last I drop off to sleep. It is the inner life that counts . . . What do I remember on my bed, and on what do I meditate in the night watches?. . .

These old worthies went to the centre at once. When they laid their heads upon their rude pillows, they remembered God. When they composed themselves to sleep, they were thinking upon his Word. And if they woke up in the middle of the night it was to meditate on his precepts. . . I think some of these Psalmists were dwellers in tents [awake and on guard] perhaps in the course of a pilgrimage to Jerusalem, and others were Levites on night-duty at the Temple; and what they are telling here is how they spent these hours of enforced wakefulness. But one of them at least tells us more than that — he tells us that he gets up a little sooner than he has to, in order to have time to think about God.

John Baillie, 'Night Thoughts'

If we have surrendered our hearts to God in the sunlight, he will be with us no less during the hours of darkness. Nor can the devil get at us by night, if we have not allowed him *some* entry by day. It is certain that if there were no evil in our waking souls, there would be no evil in our dreams. But, of course, evil is always at our doors, at least in the form of temptation. . . There is, after all, one way in which we can exercise some control over our dreams, and that is by the proper direction of our thoughts before we retire. . . Everyone who calls himself a Christian should go to sleep thinking about the love of God as it has visited us in the person of his Son, Jesus Christ our Lord.

John Baillie, 'The Theology of Sleep'

Those whose spirits are stirred by the breath of the Holy Spirit of God go forwards even in sleep.

Brother Laurence, *The Practice of the Presence of God*

God is my portion and joy,
His counsels are my light;
He gives me sweet advice by day
And gentle hints by night.

Isaac Watts

Of all the thoughts of God that are
Born inward into souls afar,
Along the Psalmist's music deep,
Now tell me if that any is,
For gift or grace, surpassing this —
'He giveth his beloved sleep'?

Elizabeth Barrett Browning

My head and hands and feet
Their rest with gladness greet,
And know their work is o'er;

My heart, thou too shalt be
From sinful works set free,
Nor pine in weary sorrow more.

Paul Gerhardt

Nature has ended another day,
struck down another life!
Someone has music in the evening,
others the fruit of strife,
Yet in the balance:
Love draws the curtains
and makes her entrance, embracing the suffering to
her side.

Kenneth T. Crotty, 'Nature had Ended Another Day'

All is still and gentle
as if all creation shares
with tender empathy
the last whisper of this dying day.
The lights are low now,
and everything is suspended
as if waiting
for some final word.

Bruce Prewer, 'Vespers by the Murray River'

Now that dusk is near —
with parrots in the gum trees
lessening their chatter,
with the distant roar of cars
fading to a mere murmur —
may I hear
the voice of the One
who walks in the garden
in the cool of the evening
and, in hearing that voice,
find a little of the Eden-peace
which some day will be perfected.
This I pray
in the name of him

who was once mistaken for a gardener.

Bruce Prewer, 'God of the Evening'

Lighten our darkness, Lord, we pray: and in your great mercy defend us from all perils and dangers of this night; for the love of your only Son our Saviour Jesus Christ. Amen.

Be present, merciful God, and protect us through the hours of this night: that we, who are wearied by the changes and chances of this fleeting world, may rest on your eternal changelessness; through Jesus Christ our Lord.

Evening Prayer collects, *An Australian Prayer Book*

Lord, be the guest of this house;
keep far from it the deceits of the evil one.
May your holy angels watch over us
as guardians of our peace.
And may your blessing be always upon us, through
Jesus Christ our Lord. Amen.

Lord Jesus Christ, Son of the Living God,
who at this evening hour rested in the sepulchre,
and sanctified the grave to be a bed of hope to
your people:
make us so to abound in sorrow for our sins,
which were the cause of your passion,
that when our bodies lie in the dust
we may live with you, through the saving merits
of your cross;
for you live and reign with the Father and the
Holy Spirit, one God, now and for ever. Amen.

As watchmen look for the morning,
so we wait eagerly for you, O Lord.
Come with the dawning of the day
and make yourself known to us in the breaking of
the bread,
for you are our God, for ever and ever. Amen.

A Benediction

Let us praise the Father, the Son, and the Holy Spirit;
let us praise and magnify him for ever.
The almighty and merciful God preserve us and give us
his blessing. Amen.

Prayer at the End of the Day, *An Australian Prayer Book*

31

A silk purse out of a sow's ear

That night Jacob got up and took his two wives, his two maidservants and his eleven sons and crossed the ford of the Jabbok. After he had sent them across the stream, he sent over all his possessions. So Jacob was left alone, and a man wrestled with him till daybreak. When the man saw that he could not overpower him, he touched the socket of Jacob's hip so that his hip was wrenched as he wrestled with the man. Then the man said, 'Let me go, for it is daybreak.' But Jacob replied, 'I will not let you go unless you bless me.' The man asked him, 'What is your name?' 'Jacob,' he answered. Then the man said, 'Your name will no longer be Jacob, but Israel because you have struggled with God and with men and have overcome.' Jacob said, 'Please tell me your name.' But he replied, 'Why do you ask my name?' Then he blessed him there. So Jacob called the place Peniel, saying, 'It is because I saw God face to face, and yet my life was spared.' The sun rose above him as he passed Peniel, and he was limping because of his hip.

(Genesis 32: 22-31, NIV)

Jacob was a crook. He was mean, unscrupulous and reflected the insecurities of an unhappy childhood and a divided home. Jacob was also a believer and this created a maelstrom in his inner person. What matters in a journey is the end and not the beginning. Jacob finished well despite the poor beginning. On his pilgrimage there were three important events which stand out. In chapter 28 of Genesis he marked a spot as Bethel. Here he saw that he was in God's house and there was a relationship between him and God. In chapter 32 of Genesis, he named a place as Mahanaim. Here he had an overwhelming assurance of the sovereignty of God. His next experience, in chapter 32, was at Peniel. This was where he saw God's face.

In each of these experiences it was God who took the initiative. And yet Jacob is not a passive partner in this process. He had over the years struggled with God and man. The struggle, the unhappiness, the rivalry in the home, form the stuff out of which God's princes are made. There was the struggle, the seeking, the failing and the fresh seeking and in this new and great struggle, all his determination and resourcefulness were directed against the messenger. All the fight drained from him as his hip was dislocated. There were no devices or stratagems left. All he wanted was a blessing.

The other factor in the formation of God's princes is, of course, God's amazing grace. God came in love but was greeted with clenched fists and clever headlocks. But in breathtaking humility, he matched arm and leg against Jacob's; it was in anticipation of his becoming bone of our bone and flesh of our flesh and, entering fully into our humanity and meeting us as a human being, God dealt with Jacob personally and intimately.

Jacob had to name himself. His name really meant a 'trickster'. And so he was. He was a cheat. But his new name spoke of better things. The man who would always limp and never again regained his physical strength and stubbornness would be a prince in God's kingdom. A cripple and a prince — that's our Jacob.

To see God's face — how we long for it. The Psalmist wrote, 'My heart says of you "Seek his face!" Your face, O Lord, I will seek' (Psalm 27: 8, NIV).

Where will our Peniel be? Who can tell when we deal with a God who lovingly takes the initiative and meets us on the way. But this we can certainly say — it will be at a place where we have stopped fighting and it will be a place where the significance of the gospel of our Lord Jesus Christ will be clear. 'For God who said, "Let light shine out of darkness", made his light shine in our hearts to give us the light of the knowledge of the glory of God in the face of Christ' (2 Corinthians 4: 6).

Naked I wait thy love's uplifted stroke!
My harness piece by piece thou hast hewn from me,
  And smitten me to my knee;
I am defenceless utterly.

Francis Thompson, *The Hound of Heaven*

  Halts by me that footfall:
  Is my gloom, after all,
Shade of his hand, outstretched caressingly?
  Ah, fondest, blendest, weakest
  I am he whom thou seekest!
Thou drawest love from thee, who drawest me.

Francis Thompson, *The Hound of Heaven*

No one ever saw God and liv'd; and yet I shall not live till I see God; and when I have seen him I shall never dye.

John Donne, *Sermons*

Yet dearely, I love you, and would be loved faine,
But am betroth'd unto your enemie:
Divorce me, untie, or break that knot again,
Take me to you, imprison mee, for I
Except you enthrall mee, never shall be free,
Nor ever chast, except you ravish mee.

John Donne, *Sonnet 14*

Jacob is here knighted on the field, as it were, and has a title of honour given to him by him that is the fountain of honour which will remain, to his praise, to the end of time.

Matthew Henry, *Commentary*

  In vain thou strugglest to get free
    I never will unloose my hold;
  Art thou the man that died for me?
    The secret of thy love unfold.
  Wrestling I will not let thee go,

Till I thy name, thy nature know.

'Tis love!, 'tis love! thou diedst for me!
I hear thy whisper in my heart!
The morning breaks, the shadows flee;
Pure universal love thou art!

Charles Wesley, 'Come, O Thou Traveller Unknown'

It is painful to read the Gospel record of this blindfolded
Christ, but more of how he has been blindfolded again
and again for nineteen centuries and then mocked. We
cannot leave the Christ alone. His face rivets attention.
Those who look into his eyes need no other light; those
who have seen his face will follow no other leader.

Samuel M. Zwemer, *The Glory of the Cross*

It is an overwhelming experience to fall into the hands of
the living God, to be invaded to the depths of one's being
by his presence, to be, without warning, wholly uprooted
from all earth-born securities and assurances, and to be
blown by a tempest of unbelievable power which leaves
one's old proud self utterly, utterly defenceless, until one
cries, 'All thy waves and thy billows are gone over me'
(Psalm 42: 7). Then is the soul swept into a Loving Centre
of ineffable sweetness, where calm and unspeakable peace
and ravishing joy steal over one. One knows ever after
that the eternal lover of the world, the Hound of Heaven,
is utterly, utterly real and life must henceforth be forever
determined by that Real.

Thomas R. Kelly, *A Testament of Devotion*

I will write on him the name of my God and the name
of the city of my God, the new Jerusalem, which is coming
down out of heaven from my God; and I will also write
on him my new name (Revelation 3: 12).

He will reign over the house of Jacob forever (Luke
1: 33).

I recall with great clarity, settling down in the corner
of my room and following Jacob over the brook Jabbok
in my mind's eye. The struggle of the angel with Jacob,

as a man walking in the flesh, portrayed my state so perfectly. He had touched me in the seat of my natural strength, and now, broken and shattered through solitary confinement, with everything gone — my work, my liberty, my Bible — and now it seemed life itself, I could only cling to him for his blessing. I would, no doubt, never be the same again.

Then like a shaft of light in the mind, the relevance of Jacob's act of faith in the *Epistle to the Hebrews*, where he is seen leaning on his staff in worship, to the conflict with the representative of the camp of God, flashed into my mind. What does it matter if I am never the same again, provided my name is Israel; and then as a prince with God, having no confidence in the flesh, will I lean on my staff for my lameness and worship till the day dawn and the shadows flee away. Let that be my highest and final act of faith towards God, my strength and my Redeemer. And then I remembered that God's word says, that as Jacob passed over Peniel the sun rose upon him. So after this I viewed everything as walking into the dawning, going on into the golden daybreak and the morning without a cloud.

Geoffrey Bull, *When Iron Gates Yield*
(written after a period of extensive brainwashing)

Let us pray
    *for a fresh desire to see God in the face of our Lord
    Jesus Christ,
    for spiritual insight to recognise the graciousness
    of God's purposes in my life during this week,
    for opportunities to be alone and to find strength
    and peace at the centre,
    for ability to order the affairs of work and home so time
    is spent with the one who wants to meet and bless me
    for the discovery of power through powerlessness.*

O Lord our God, grant us grace to desire you with our whole heart; that so desiring you, we may seek and find you; and so finding you may love you, and loving you may hate those sins from which you have redeemed us; through Jesus Christ our Lord.

Anselm

A Benediction
Spirit of the Living Christ,
*   come upon us in the glory of your risen power;*
Spirit of the Living Christ,
*   come upon us in all the humility of your wondrous love;*
Spirit of the Living Christ,
*   come upon us that new life may course within our veins,*
*   new love bind us together in one faith,*
*   and a new vision of the kingdom of God*
*   spur us on to serve you with fearless passion.*

Iona Community

32

Bless me, even me also

The Lord commanded Moses to tell Aaron and his sons to use the following words in blessing the people of Israel: May the Lord bless you and take care of you; May the Lord be kind and gracious to you; May the Lord look on you with favour and give you peace. And the Lord said, 'If they pronounce my name as a blessing upon the people of Israel, I will bless them.'

Blessed is he whose transgression is forgiven, whose sin is covered. Blessed is the man to whom the Lord imputes no iniquity, and in whose spirit is no deceit.

Then he took the children in his arms, placed his hands on each of them, and blessed them.

Love your enemies, do good to those who hate you, bless those who curse you, and pray for those who ill-treat you.

I tell you, then, the great love she has shown proves that her many sins have been forgiven. But whoever has been forgiven little shows only a little love.

Then he led them out of the city as far as Bethany, where he raised his hands and blessed them. As he was blessing them, he departed from them and was taken up into heaven. They worshipped him and went back into Jerusalem, filled with great joy.

And so God chose his Servant and sent him first to you, to bless you by making every one of you turn away from his wicked ways.

And I am sure that when I come, the Lord will give me a great blessing for you!

Let us give thanks to the God and Father of our Lord Jesus Christ! For in our union with Christ he has blessed us by giving us every spiritual blessing in the heavenly world.

God's divine power has given us everything we need to live a truly religious life through our knowledge of the one who called us to share in his own glory and goodness.

(Numbers 6: 22-27, GNB; Psalm 32: 1-2, RSV; Mark 10: 16, GNB; Luke 6: 27-28, GNB; Luke 7: 47, GNB; Luke 24: 50-52, GNB; Acts 3: 26, GNB; Romans 15: 29, LB; Ephesians 1: 3, GNB; 2 Peter 1: 3, GNB)

Tremendous importance in Old Testament times was attached to the giving or withholding of the blessing. High drama unfolded in the early history of the patriarchs. The story is told in the middle chapters of Genesis. Jacob, coached by Rebekah, first stole Esau's birthright, then his blessing. Realising he had been deceived, with mounting alarm Esau pleaded with his father: 'Bless me, even me, my father! Have you not reserved a blessing for me? Have you not one blessing, my father? Bless me, even me also!'

The desire for a blessing is often a cry from the heart.

Martin Buber says, 'We wish to be confirmed in our being by significant others. . . Secretly and bashfully we watch for that "yes" which allows us to be and become.'

Not only the patriarchs, but we also have the capacity to bless others. People live out the blessings we give. They also live out our curses. The challenge to Christian leaders, pastors and parents is to take hold of their opportunities to bless others. The purpose of worship-leadership has been stated this way: so to conduct yourself and the worship and so to preach the good news that people leave the service 'ransomed, healed, restored, forgiven'.

The 'blessing' in the Old Testament period was usually material: land, flocks and other possessions. The one who was 'blessed' was enhanced in specific ways. 'To bless' means to add something to someone. The blessing is our bestowal of favour, our 'yes' to others. The giving of a blessing, in word and/or deed is a signal, Carl Rogers says, that we hold the other in 'unjudging positive regard'. Our blessing others enhances their sense of worth as God's children. Blessing others is a powerful reminder of God's blessing, of the availability of grace, God's free forgiveness and love. Christians bless others by their presence and by their words, and by symbolic gestures and caring behaviour: moving closer, a smile, a touch, a hug, attending and caring behaviour, and focussed listening.

The withholding of blessing will have the opposite effect, the increase of shame and guilt. Deprived of the blessing, Esau wandered the earth, unsure of his identity, without roots, not knowing where he belonged, even in the land of promise.

The one who can give the blessing to others is the one who has first received the blessing. The risen Lord blesses his disciples still and sends them out to bring the blessings of the good news to all.

∽✺∾

Blessings abound where'er he reigns;
The prisoner leaps to loose his chains;
The weary find eternal rest,
And all the sons of want are blest.

Isaac Watts, 'Jesus shall reign where'er the sun'

A very gentle, loving young man. . . arrived unannounced at a lady's house, and she came to the door with her hair 'teased' in six million directions. There was nothing for her to do but comment, so she said, 'How do you like my hair?' Soberly, graciously he replied, 'It looks as if it's just about to become something great.'

Ray and Anne Ortlund, *The Best Half of Life*

One day a boy named Ben discovered some bottles of coloured ink in his home. His mother had gone out leaving him in charge of his little sister Sally. The bottles were a temptation and the boy began to paint Sally's portrait. In doing so he made a terrible mess with ink blots all over. When his mother returned, she saw the mess, but also the drawing with its striking resemblance to her daughter. She said nothing about the blots but exclaimed, 'Why! It's Sally.' Then she stooped and kissed her son. The boy, Benjamin West, went on to become a famous artist who used to say proudly, 'My mother's kiss made me a painter.'

Source unknown

Barnabas. . . is one of the most attractive characters in the New Testament. He possessed the rare gift of discerning merit in others. Probably inferior in ability to Paul, he was his superior in Christian graces. He seems to have been utterly without jealousy, eager to excuse the faults of others, quick to recognise merit, ready to compromise for the sake of peace. Paul's elevation of character makes him scarcely human, whilst the virtues of Barnabas make him singularly lovable. The Paul of history contributes to the progress of the world; Barnabas and those like him make it endurable to live in.

Source unknown

Almost daily I pass the place where she threw herself in front of the train. She was only sixteen. I wonder whether she would have done it had she been in our youth group. . . Church is where we are loved unconditionally, because church is where you find people who know *they* are loved unconditionally. How do they know that? Because they know someone died for them two thousand years ago. It would be ludicrous if it weren't so pragmatic. The idea that Jesus died for them has saved a lot of people from suicide and much else. It is church youth groups that have a unique opportunity to get that idea across early in life.

Robert K. Hudnut, *This People, This Parish*

We are pilgrims on a journey
We are brothers on the road
We are here to help each other
Walk the mile and bear the load.

Richard Gillard, 'The Servant Song'

Results of a questionnaire, seeking responses to statements

about desirable qualities and actions of ministers, revealed that the highest rated of eleven themes was a factor that was titled, 'Open, Affirming Style'. Five thousand persons completed and returned the questionnaire.

The theme that attracts this top rating is only partially communicated by the title given it. It is a dimension of ministry that is more than a 'style', more than 'openness', more than 'affirming', even more than the impact of the three yoked together. This theme weaves into a common fabric ideas about the function of ministry and the qualities and style of approach that transcend the function. It is a theme of ministry in which the priest or minister not only 'works at further development of pastoral skills', but also 'helps others see the best in people'. . . This theme portrays style in the foreground and function in the background. The factor's high rating indicates that, while the expectations of ministry or priesthood in North America includes competence in function, it is also highly sensitive to the character and spirit of the person who carries out these functions.

David S. Schuller et al, *Ministry in America*

If we are faithful in our preaching about sin, righteousness and judgment, we must at the same time be careful to avoid any imbalance. It has to be admitted that some preachers enjoy thundering forth God's judgments. They find a morbid satisfaction in seeing their audience writhe under the lash of their whip. . . Anthony Trollope in *Barchester Towers* very evidently despised his character, the Rev. Obadiah Slope, for this very thing. Although he was 'gifted with a certain kind of pulpit eloquence', yet, Trollope wrote, 'in his sermons he deals greatly in denunciations'. Indeed, 'his looks and tone are extremely severe. . . As he walks through the streets, his very face denotes his horror of the world's wickedness, and there is always an anathema lurking in the corner of his eye. . . To him the mercies of our Saviour speak in vain.' In a neat phrase of Colin Morris, he used the pulpit 'to purvey Good Chidings rather than Good Tidings'.

The more we feel it necessary, especially in days of

moral laxity, to dwell on the judgment of God upon sin, the more we need also to dwell on his mercy towards sinners. Jesus' own woes against the scribes and Pharisees for their hypocrisy are among the fiercest denunciations in the whole Bible, yet he was called 'the friend of sinners'. They flocked around him and listened to him gladly, he invited them to come to him with their burdens and promised to give them rest, he accepted the demonstrative affection of a forgiven prostitute, and he said to the woman caught in adultery, 'neither do I condemn you; go and do not sin again.'

John R.W. Stott, *I Believe in Preaching*

If with pleasure you are viewing, any work a man
is doing,
If you like him, or you love him, tell him *now*;
Don't withhold your approbation till the person
makes oration
And he lies with snowy lilies o'er his brow,
For no matter how you shout it he won't really
care about it,
He won't know how many tear-drops you have shed.
If you think some praise is due him, *now's* the time
to slip it to him
For he cannot read his tombstone when he's dead.

More than fame and more than money, is the comment
kind and sunny
And the hearty warm approval of a friend,
For it gives to life a savour, and it makes you stronger,
braver,
And it give you heart and spirit to the end.
If he earns your praise, bestow it, if you like him, let
him know it
Let the words of true encouragement be said.
Do not wait till life is over, and he's underneath
the clover,
For he cannot read his tombstone when he's dead.

Author unknown

Priestly listening emphasises the need for critical solidarity with the hearers lest the preacher exempt himself or herself from those whom the text addresses and so use the text as a club on the congregation. . . When preaching from the Gospels, it is important to remember that sociologically, and perhaps theologically as well, the preacher is the scribe and the Pharisee — the professional interpreter who is always in danger of using exegetical know-how to protect himself or herself from the impact of the text. . .

Because 'prophetic' is an adjective most preachers cherish for their ministry, including their preaching, it is useful to recall that preaching in the prophetic mode involves love and compassion for those addressed. If prophetic preaching is not motivated by and infused with love it becomes harsh and scolding. When this is the case, what is actually communicated is animosity, or one's own moral superiority, or one's own alienation from 'the system'. . . Truly prophetic preaching, at least as exemplified by biblical prophets, struggles to combine clear insight with deep compassion. . . Whoever wants to preach prophetically must earn the moral right to do so by compassionate critical solidarity with those addressed. It is not enough to be right.

Leander E. Keck, *The Bible in the Pulpit*

Lord, I have received so much, so freely, from you. Help me to be generous to others, all others.

Lord, the blessing in the Old Testament period was frequently selective; the blessing was for the first-born or for other(s) favoured already. I thank you that your covenant of grace places the emphasis elsewhere. In the Sermon on the Mount you pronounced blessings on the most unlikely. Help me to show no partiality, but to show undefeatable good will, unconditional love to others, all others, especially those who are crying out for a blessing. In my family life and in my significant relationships, free me from making excessive demands on those I love. As you accept me as I am, and love me as I am, and bless me, help me to accept, love and bless others. Let it not be that they leave my/our presence/home/church without a blessing, but with the forlorn cry, 'Bless me, even me also.'

> *Out in the highways and by-ways of life,*
> *Many are weary and sad;*
> *Carry the sunshine where darkness is rife,*
> *Making the sorrowing glad.*
> *Make me a blessing, make me a blessing,*
> *Out of my life may Jesus shine.*
> *Make me a blessing, O Saviour I pray,*
> *Make me a blessing to someone today.*

Geo. S. Schuler, Youth Sings

A Benediction

> *I thought to wish that God*
>   *might truly bless you;*
> *But that, I see, he's clearly bound to do:*
> *He is himself the fountain of all blessing,*
> *And loves to bless his children,*
>   *therefore you!*
>
> *I thought to wish that for*
>   *your earthly journey*
> *God would supply your need (could he forget?):*
> *But now I see that he has clearly promised*
> *To meet all need*
>   *and so it shall be met!*
>
> *Then I might ask that God*
>   *himself would guide you;*
> *But this is needless, since he is your guide:*
> *Since he has promised*
>   *constantly to guide us*
> *Until we reach, at last, the other side.*
>
> *What shall I ask then,*
>   *What indeed is left me;*
> *What to say to gladden as you journey here?*
> *How can I help to comfort,*
>   *strengthen, hearten,*
> *As you tread nobly through each passing year?*

How can I, save that, gently,
*   I remind you*
Being his child you are
*   supremely blest;*
And that what'er may come, of joy and sorrow—
All that he gives or sends is aye the best.

J. Danson Smith

33

Touching life. . . allowing life

Deliver me, O God. . . I am sinking. . . You know my reproach, my shame, my disgrace. . .

Sing to the Lord a song of praise. . . who provides rain. . . who gives to the raven's brood what they cry for.

Sing joyously to God, our strength. . . I am the Lord your God who brought you out. . . open your mouth and I will fill it.

We have sinned like our forefathers; we have gone astray, done evil. . . Yet he saved them. . . to make known his might. . . Then they believed his promise, and sang his praises. But they soon forgot his deeds; they would not wait to learn his plan. . . Deliver us, O Lord our God. . .

(Psalm 69: 1 and 19; Psalm 147: 7, 8 and 9; Psalm 81: 1 and 10; Psalm 106: 6, 8, 12, 13 and 47 — all Tanakh)

In Latin dictionaries, in the Latin-English section, one of the entries reads: 'Patior, pati, passus sum — let, allow, suffer.' The same word serves two apparently quite different meanings. For example, the King James Version translates Jesus as saying, 'Suffer the little children to come to me'. More contemporary translations render this as: 'Let [them] come. . .'

If 'suffer' is interchangeable with 'let', then suffering is interchangeable with letting. Does suffering mean our allowing the realities of life to come to us; acknowledging that pain and joy are our common experience; granting that tragedies and delights are the context of life; accepting that there is an ecology about human existence which we cannot avoid?

The passion of Christ, the 'suffering' of Christ, your suffering, mine — whether at baptism-wilderness times, in deaths of Lazaruses, in garden-trial-crucifixion climaxes — is the allowing of human life in all its fullness to come to us; and be met by us; and be transformed by us.

We read the Gospels in order to discover the connections between our situations and Jesus' situations. The scripture still offers us this opportunity to 'connect'; and still undergirds us in our struggles to be genuine disciples in our pilgrimage and in our witness.

❧

Yes, it is finished. Thirty years
of godhead fleshed in words,
Words charged with God,
Raises his head to the clouds,
Their dark violence, their threat
Of thunder. Repeats once more
From another Psalm: *Into thy hands*
O Lord, I commit my spirit.
And the head drops, jarred at the neck.
It is finished. The mob is breaking,
Thinking of shelter. Women in despair
Weeping beyond consolation.
But I, his friend,
Loving no less than they,
Feel only calm — peace
After victory. For these words
Echo in my mind and will always echo:
The ends of the world will remember
And turn to the Lord.

Clive Sanson, 'John'

Glaucous gulls fly over. In the shore lead are phalaropes, with their twiglike legs. In the distance I see flocks of oldsquaw against the sky, and a few cormorants. . . a patch of shadow that could be several thousand crested auklets — too far away to know. Out there are whales — I have seen six or eight grey whales as I walked this evening. And the ice, pale as the dove-coloured sky. The wind raises the surface of the water. Wake of a seal in the shore lead, gone now. I bowed. . .

. . .an expression of allegiance with the mystery of life.

I looked out over the Bering Sea and brought my hands folded to the breast of my parka and bowed from the waist deeply toward the north, the great strait filled with life, the ice and the water. I held the bow to the pale sulphur sky at the northern rim of the earth. I held the bow until my back ached, and my mind was emptied of its categories and designs, its plans and speculations. I bowed before the simple evidence of the moment in my life in a tangible place on the earth that was beautiful.

When I stood I thought I glimpsed my own desire. The landscape and the animals were like something found at the end of a dream.

The edges of the real landscape became one with the edges of something I had dreamed. But what I had dreamed was only a pattern, some beautiful pattern of light. . . the continuous work of the imagination, I thought, to bring what is actual together with what is dreamed is an expression of human evolution. The conscious desire is to achieve a state, even momentarily, that like light is unbounded, nurturing, suffused with wisdom and creation, a state in which one has absorbed that very darkness which before was the perpetual sign of defeat.

Whatever world that is, it lies far ahead. But its outline, its adumbration, is clear in the landscape, and upon this one can actually hope we will find our way.

I bowed again, deeply, toward the north, and turned south to retrace my steps over the dark cobbles to the home where I was staying. I was full of appreciation for all that I had seen.

Barry Lopez, *Arctic Dreams*

Nature's silence is its one remark.

Martin Buber says: 'The crisis of all primitive mankind comes with the discovery of that which is fundamentally not-holy, the a-sacramental.'

Now we are no longer primitive; now the whole world

seems not-holy. We have. . . moved from pantheism to pan-atheism. Silence is not our heritage but our destiny; we live where we want to live.

The soul may ask God for anything, and never fail. You may ask God for his presence, or. . . that he. . . go away. . .

It is difficult to undo our own damage, and to recall to our presence that which we have asked to leave. It is hard to desecrate a grove and change your mind. . .

We doused the burning bush and cannot rekindle it; we are lighting matches in vain under every green tree. Did the wind used to cry, and the hills shout forth praise? Now speech has perished from among the lifeless things of earth, and the living things say very little to very few.

Annie Dillard, *Teaching a Stone to Talk*

The eighteenth century Jesuit, Père de Caussade, speaks of. . . 'Le moment présent est toujours comme un ambassadeur qui déclare l'ordre de Dieu. . . toutes les routes et toutes les manières l'avancent également vers le large et infini. Tour lui est moyen; tour lui est instrument de saintété, sans aucune difference.' I like that idea of each moment being an ambassador accosting us from God with a message how to deal with it.

Rose Macauley, *Letters to a Friend*

If one can realise that there is need for love close at home, growth can begin right there, with the healthiest kind of groundwork to build on. We do not have to worry too much about our own feelings at the time; what matters is doing something that makes the other person feel loved. The test is not just whether we feel loving; it is more whether or not the other person feels loved by us. Christian love is not complete until the other person feels loved through contact with us.

As we turn toward a wider circle, however, a different kind of action is obviously required of us. Is there a way of expressing real love to a neighbour or acquaintance, to one's club or church?

Certainly it is easier to know if one can put an arm

around the person and sense a reaction. But there is definitely another way, as a friend of mine discovered when he was faced with difficulties of administering an industrial plant for which he was responsible.

This man was not afraid of prayer, and so he asked what to do. The answer that he was given offers an unparalleled description of the way of love. Out of the blue he heard the words: 'Create those conditions whereby each individual may develop to the maximum of their potential within the opportunities at hand.' When he tried to follow that instruction explicitly, the reaction among his employees was like the lifting of a cloud. Love is not only feeling; it is action.

Morton Kelsey, *The Other Side of Silence*

Spiritual life is but a mirror of our natural life. Grace does build on nature. Our life in God is incarnate. In the same way in which we seek the security of internal and external mastered patterns in our natural living, we can seek them in our spiritual life, and most probably will. What is our conception of God? Have we categorised the Deity according to our needs and so mastered another element in our world? Have we determined the manner of our relating to God and thus, in our own mind, guaranteed our salvation? And what does all this say about the freedom that is the promise of Christ? What does it say about becoming (like) little children who follow him, who respond to the radical demands of a Way that can only be lived in its fullness if we let go of ourselves completely and give ourselves totally to him — to abandon ourselves?

My thesis is that since grace builds on nature, there is an essential need for each of us, in the natural order, to have a 'basic attitude toward life' which will be the basis for the radical demands of the Christian way of life. I will concede that there are those who go through radical conversions which seem to change both the natural and supernatural ordering of their lives. But for most of us our faith and the living of the Christian life have grown side by side with our natural maturing process and been ultimately affected by it. We need to break out. Not just in prayer and fasting, but through a view, an attitude or stance toward life that will free us in both the natural and supernatural order.

James Grace, 'Spirituality Today'

I was wakened at 6.23 in the morning of April 11, 1969, by a tremendous crash, followed by shouts of 'Help!'. I thought somebody must have driven a car smack into the faculty club at seventy miles per hour. I discovered then that I am, after all, a coward. Instead of running out immediately to the rescue, I dithered for about a minute, trying to pull myself together to face whatever had to be faced. For a minute I was paralysed. And in that minute Dover Sharp burned to death. . .

The faculty club has only six bedrooms. Dover Sharp was caretaker of the building and lived in one of the bedrooms. I had come to the University of California at Santa Barbara as a visiting lecturer and was occupying another bedroom. Nobody else was in the building at the time of the explosion. Dover Sharp had come down in the morning and found a large cardboard box lying in front of the door that opened into the dining room. It was booby-trapped to explode when he opened it. It contained a half-gallon wine jug filled with gasoline, a six-inch piece of pipe packed with high explosive, and a battery-powered fuse to set it off. There was no message to indicate who had put it there or why. . .

The police investigating the murder called me in for questioning. I was not able to tell them anything useful. They did not ask me why I had been dithering in my room during the minute that it took the students to run across to the rescue from the San Rafael dormitory. For the police, that minute of delay had no bearing on the case. Only for Dover Sharp, it might have made the difference between life and death. And for me, it is a fact which I cannot change. I have to live with it as best I can.

The psychologist Robert Lifton has written a book, *Death in Life*, about the survivors of the atomic bombing in

Hiroshima. He describes their feelings as told to him in interviews seventeen years after the bombing. Through all their stories runs the common thread of guilt for having lived when others died. . .

All I have left of Dover Sharp is a name. Dover Sharp. At least I will hang on to that. I forget what he looked like, how his voice sounded, what words of greeting he used when I came down to breakfast at the faculty club. I hardly spoke to him all the time I was there. I never knew him as a person. I treated him as if he were part of the furniture. It is a bad habit that many professors have, to treat caretakers of buildings as if they were part of the furniture. This bad habit was one of the causes of Dover Sharp's death. If I had got to know him as a friend and as a human being, I would not have hesitated to save his life.

Freeman Dyson, *Disturbing the Universe*

O God, grant to us the will to move from 'coming to terms with' to 'coming to grips with'. You know that we talk about engaging with life. . . and we're past-masters at meandering on the peripheries of life.

We ask that you who know our frailties and who sense our disappointed yearning may give to us the wisdom which is one of your proffered gifts — wisdom which equips us both to recognise and also describe that 'gulf that divides aspiration from achievement, and the shadow that falls between the motion and the act'.

May you lead us today, through our perceptions and beyond our analyses — and point us again towards the way we must walk if we are to walk with you. Amen.

A Benediction
Grace, mercy and peace. . . be yours. Amen.

34

The mountain of humility

Reverence for the Lord is an education in itself. You must be humble before you can ever receive honours.

Obey the Lord, be humble, and you will get riches, honour and a long life.

Arrogance will bring your downfall, but if you are humble, you will be respected.

God resists the proud, but shows favour to the humble. Humble yourselves, then, under God's mighty hand, so that he will lift you up in his own good time.

I live in a high and holy place, but I also live with people who are humble and repentant, so that I can restore their confidence and hope.

I am pleased with those who are humble and repentant, who fear me and obey me.

My sacrifice is a humble spirit, O God; you will not reject a humble and repentant heart.

Humble yourselves before the Lord, and he will lift you up.

The greatest in the Kingdom of Heaven is the one who humbles himself and becomes like this child.

Live a life that measures up to the standard God set when he called you. Be always humble, gentle and patient. Show your love by being tolerant with one another.

You are the people of God; he loved you and chose you for his own. So then, you must clothe yourselves with compassion, kindness, humility, gentleness and patience.

The attitude you should have is the one that Christ Jesus had: He always had the nature of God, but he did not think that by force he should try to become equal with God. Instead of this, of his own free will he gave up all he had, and took the nature of a servant. He became like man and appeared in human likeness. He was humble and walked the path of obedience all the way to death — his death on the cross. For this reason God raised him to the highest place above and gave him the name that is greater than any other name.

If my people who are called by my name will humble themselves and pray. . . then I will hear. . . forgive. . . and heal.

Proverbs 15: 33, GNB; Proverbs 22: 4, GNB; Proverbs 29: 23, GNB; 1 Peter 5: 5-6 GNB; Isaiah 57: 15, GNB; Isaiah 66: 2, GNB; Psalm 51: 17, GNB; James 4: 10, GNB; Matthew 18: 4, GNB; Ephesians 4: 1-2, GNB; Colossians 3: 12, GNB; Philippians 2: 5-9, GNB; 2 Chronicles 7: 14, RSV)

We live in a world of successful, bright, rich, good looking people. These are the ones who make headlines, who are the famous, the stars, the examples. To be humble in a self-exalting world is seen as the way to failure.

Even in the church the successful, the growers, the high flyers are paraded before us in Christian media — do this, do that, follow their example, succeed. This is the age of the positive thinker, possibility thinking, church growth, meeting challenges and achieving. This is God's new age — let us be great for God!

Church members seek roles of status, authority and control. Pastors look to succeed by moving to bigger churches or better ministries. Sometimes we downgrade notions of servanthood, ignore the sin of pride, devalue humility. We are tempted to listen to the message of the popular song — 'O Lord it's hard to be humble, when you're perfect in every way'! — rather than the voice of our Servant-Lord. We forget that Christian humility is God-inspired, God-directed, God-enabled active service.

And then people like Mother Teresa call us from the slums of Calcutta, the jungles of Nicaragua, or the streets of Kings Cross — 'I tell you, whenever you refused to help one of these least important ones, you refused to help me' (Matthew 25: 45).

For those who would learn God's ways, humility is the first thing, humility is the second thing, humility is the third.

Augustine

Not a valley dark with shadow in which to hide,
not a cave in which to seek retreat,
not self-abasement lost in the dust of the bush, but a mountain to climb.
To struggle up winding paths, to rock, crag, scree and icy slope — against the wind of human nature, the hurricane of pride.

To go down the valley, retreat in the cave, be lost in the bush of self-denial, the worminess of human depravity and nothingness, is but a journey inward away from the world, and God, who loves, values and exalts his children.

Rather, climb the mountain of his glory, feel the pain of ascent, skinned knees and torn fingers, bruised and aching spirit, the fear of falling as the rope of ability frays.
Climb up with strength, skill and power and, when strength can climb no more, when his glory still before, unreached by human means, taunts the aching heart; he will come and carry.

Stand on the peaks, bathed in his light,
Hear him say, 'Well done. . .'
And, turning to the voice to claim the reward. . .
Find the mountain continues.

Clive Cook, 'The mountain of humility'

'I suppose you are quite a great lawyer?' I said.
'Me, Master Copperfield?' said Uriah Heep. 'Oh, no! I'm a very 'umble person. I am the 'umblest person going,' he went on modestly. 'Father and me was both brought up at a foundation school for boys. They taught

us all 'umbleness from morning to night, and to abase
ourselves before our betters. Father got the monitor medal
by being 'umble. So did I. "Be 'umble, Uriah, be 'umble,"
says Father to me, "and you'll get on. Be 'umble and
you'll do."'

Charles Dickens, *David Copperfield*

False humility is really a lie, and cannot be acceptable to
a God of truth.

William Plumer

Humility is often confused with the gentlemanly self-
deprecation of saying you're not much of a bridge player
when you know perfectly well you are. Conscious or
otherwise, this kind of humility is a form of gamesman-
ship. If you really aren't much of a bridge player, you're
apt to be rather proud of yourself for admitting it so
humbly. This kind of humility is a form of low comedy.
True humility doesn't consist of thinking ill of yourself
but of not thinking of yourself much differently from the
way you'd be apt to think of anybody else. It is the
capacity for being no more and no less pleased when you
play your own hand well than when your opponents do.

Frederick Buechner, *Wishful Thinking*

Humility is to have a just estimate of oneself, humility is
pure honesty.

Jack McAlister

True humility is to fully acknowledge your God-given gifts
and humbly use them for his glory in the service of others.

C.H. Spurgeon

Whoever would be great among you must be your servant,
and whoever would be first among you must be the slave
of all. Jesus. . . rose from supper. . . girded himself with
a towel. . . and began to wash the disciples' feet. He
said, 'Do you know what I have done to you?. . . I have
given you an example, that you should do as I have done
to you. If you know these things, blessed are you if you
do them.'

Mark 10: 43 and 44; John 13: 4, 5, 12, 15 and 17 — all RSV

No pretence of humility may make us decline our duty.
Matthew Henry

I had been brought up to believe that, for the Christian,
    service to humanity meant verbal proclamation.
I know I cannot ignore Christ's command to 'preach the
gospel'. What makes me think I can ignore his command
to 'wash feet'?

What my Lord seems to be saying is:
    'This is what it means to love your fellowman, your
    neighbour, as yourself. It means not simply your
    condescending
    willingness, but your eagerness to stoop to the
    humblest
    act of service on his behalf. This is what I have done
    in descending from heaven to stoop to your needs,
    in shedding the glory and power of divinity
    to become identified with your humanity.
    Now this is the manner in which you
    are to carry on my ministry. You are to meet your
    fellowman
    in loving concern and in utter humility at his point of
    need.'
It is difficult for me to consider foot-washing important
    in comparison to proclaiming the gospel.
Yet here it is, my Lord's command to wash feet,
    to serve the needs of people.

If I cannot comprehend the point of Christ's example
    I may never really discover the joy and meaning and
    purpose of redemption.
After all of Christ's exhortations and demonstrations
    and the examples of scores who followed him,
    I am still inclined to confine my religion
    to a set of spiritual exercises
    that I carry on in prayer closet or church sanctuary.
As long as I do this, I am still just about as self-centred

as those who have never heard about Jesus Christ,
and this in spite of my constant exposure to the gospel,
my professions of faith in Christ,
and my professional attempts to proclaim him to
others.

I am born to be a servant.
If I am truly to serve Christ, I may have to begin by
washing another's feet,
by engaging in a most humble and unspiritual act
of loving service to the person closest to me
or the neighbour next door.
If I refuse to be a servant, I shall live and die as a slave,
a slave to self-centredness,
from which I have never allowed Christ to set me free.
I have asked Christ to set me free.
I have claimed his redeeming power for that purpose.
If I am truly to discover that freedom,
I must act as a creature of freedom,
as one who has been set free in order to live for others.

Leslie Brandt, 'Go and Wash Feet'

O Lord,
My heart is not pure
My praise is not perfect.
I am trapped by the desires of the flesh,
The comforts of the world.

Money to spend, cars to drive,
The comfort of my bed,
The warmth of my morning coffee cup,
The luxury of soap and a hot shower,
My home, family — possessions in abundance.

Lord, to give these up for you:
To live in your world as Jesus did.
To identify with and support the poor,
The sick, the homeless, the lonely, widows and orphans.
Father, to do this seems to be

Beyond my physical and spiritual resources.

Father, my heart is not pure,
My praise is not perfect.
I am trapped by the desires of the flesh,
The ways of my world.

The old rabbits still jump, run
And burrow inside me.
Envy, jealousy, malice, pride.
And the others, Lord: anger, criticism, resentment,
Frustration, lust, greed, selfishness.

Lord, I want to serve you perfectly.
I want to love you wholly.
To know fully your love, joy, peace,
Faithfulness, kindness, goodness
Would be my greatest joy.
But Father, to do this seems to be
Beyond my physical and spiritual resources.

In the days I fail you, forgive me.
In the days I am weak, strengthen me.
In the days I am tempted, drive me to
seek your way of escape.
In the days of dryness, teach me to pray.
Father, my spirit is weak,
It is hungry, it struggles tired and worn.
Jesus, fill me with your spirit
That I may live in your world
An 'overcoming life',
That I may grow and be your person,
Your servant, in your world.

A Benediction

So climb the mountain of humility. It will be a lifetime struggle
that may end with a cross, the promise of eternal life, and
nothing more.

These rebellious powers
(Albert van den Heuvel)

The Lord asked Cain, 'Where is your brother Abel?' He answered, 'I don't know. Am I supposed to take care of my brother?' Then the Lord said, 'Why have you done this terrible thing? Your brother's blood is crying out to me.'

You know that among the gentiles those they call their rulers lord it over them, and their great men make their authority felt. Among you this is not to happen. No: anyone who wants to become great among you must be your servant, and anyone who wants to be first among you must be a slave to all. For the Son of man himself came not to be served but to serve, and to give his life as a ransom for many.

You call me Teacher and Lord, and it is right that you should do so, because that is what I am. I, your Lord and Teacher, have just washed your feet. You, then, should wash one another's feet. I have set an example for you, so that you will do just what I have done for you. I am telling you the truth: no slave is greater than his master, and no messenger is greater than the one who sent him. Now that you know this truth, how happy you will be if you put it into practice!

The Lord has told us what is good. What he requires of us is this: to do what is just, to show constant love, and to live in humble fellowship with our God.

Obey the really important teaching of the Law, such as justice and mercy and honesty.

We who are strong. . . ought to help the weak carry their burdens. We should not please ourselves.

(Genesis 4: 9-10, GNB; Mark 10: 42-45, JB; John 13: 13-17, GNB;

Micah 6: 8, GNB; Matthew 23: 23, GNB; Romans 15: 1, GNB)

'Power' once described ruling or conquering groups, such as nations and armies. Now it is also used in a more personal sense: the ability to affect, influence and change other persons.

Power and powerful people fascinate us. Sometimes we submit unquestioningly to charismatic leaders - 'mana-personalities' Jung called them - who radiate assurance and make wonderful promises.

Moses was one of these and, despite his excuse that he really had no power, that was precisely why he was chosen to set God's people free. 'Moses is like you and me', says Moltmann in a sermon in his book *The Power of the Powerless*. 'Liberation comes on limping, human feet. . . The Lord does not liberate people through miracles of power and eloquence or any other conjuring tricks which really paralyse the liberty of human beings. He frees people through people, with all their handicaps, with their signs of age and their disabilities.'

But liberation must be married to mysticism — what Schillebeeckx calls 'political holiness': 'Without prayer or mysticism politics soon becomes cruel and barbaric; without political love, prayer or mysticism soon becomes sentimental or uncommitted interiority. In an inseparable two-in-oneness, Christian faith thus has both a mystical and a political dimension'.

Power issues face all of us. For modern Western pastors, for example, there are at least three problems of power and powerlessness. First, as the influence of the church-as-institution is waning, clergy, too, are moving to the periphery of society. Within congregations, the pastor's role is less clear, so 'role ambiguity', 'role conflict', 'role confusion' are endemic in churches. Thirdly, there is an operational dimension to the question of power — the search for new patterns of congregational leadership that share power. Rather than the clergyperson exercising power *over* others he or she shares power *with* them.

We who are clergy are sometimes tempted like James

and John to covet power in Christ's kingdom, but we do it more subtly: by monopolising the leadership ministries of the church instead of giving them away — doing most of the preaching, baptising, blessing, and chairing. What the devil failed to do with Jesus he's succeeded in doing with us.

Justice is power used to enhance the well-being of others. *Injustice* is the misuse, abuse or non-use of power. Justice is the strong helping the weak. Injustice is causing another pain, or doing nothing to alleviate that pain. Each of us has the power to 'do justice'. Indeed, according to Micah and Jesus it is the first requirement if we are to do what God wants us to do in the world (and the church).

Evil is present, not only in human hearts, but also in human structures. And in those structures it can acquire an almost independent power of its own, so that good individuals with the best of intentions can be party to great corporate evil.

Robert McAfee Brown, *Creative Dislocation*

The greatest evils in the world are not committed by bad people, but by good people who do not know that they are not doing good.

Reinhold Niebuhr

Wherever persons hold unequal power in society they will strive to maintain it. They will use whatever means are most convenient to that end and will seek to justify them by the most plausible arguments they are able to devise . . . Those who benefit from social injustice are naturally less capable of understanding its real character than those who suffer from it.

Reinhold Niebuhr, *Moral Man and Immoral Society*

All social systems have their flaws. Capitalism has been a force for economic growth, but has failed to secure a just distribution of wealth. . . Communism has captured over one-fourth of the earth's population, but has not found a way to limit the power of the few or to answer divisive nationalism in its own ranks. Democratic socialism has produced cradle-to-grave security, but little solidarity with the less fortunate. . . So far no structures have proved a match for humanity's ingenuity in furthering our own advantage at the expense of others.

Jens-J. Wilhelmsen, *Man and Structures*

Middle-class white people in America generally see capitalism as a good thing because it has been good to them. My present inability to accept the basic structures of our society as truly just is a bequest from minority peoples who have forced me to see that although the system works to *my* benefit, it works against *theirs*. . . 'Healthy paranoia' [means] that whoever it is they are out to get, they will explain it in ways that sound as though they were doing their victims a favour. . . We [Americans] use our power not (as our rhetoric claims) to help others out of poverty, but to enhance our own wealth. . . Our task is clear: to engage in a quantum leap from being a 'voice for the voiceless' (a role I now realise as patronising) to moving over so that the voiceless can not only have space on the platform, but also get control of the mike. [We must] be more willing to trust the hurting.

It is important to get on record as opposing evil. It is also important to be effective in stopping evil. But if you can't stop it, at least oppose it. . . At the very least, things might have been worse if you had done nothing. . . And don't wait until all the facts are in before you act. The facts are never all in. . . Not to take sides is to take sides. The spectator, Elie Wiesel reminds us, ends up supporting executioners rather than victims.

Robert McAfee Brown, *Creative Dislocation*

People have an almost mysterious faculty for recognising demons in other houses, but regarding those at home as friends even when they are subject to them.

Albert van den Heuvel, *These Rebellious Powers*

Processes of growth have come into being which escape

our control: growth of industrial production, growth of environmental destruction, growth of populations, growth of the need for raw materials and energy, growth of man's dependence on a flood of outward stimuli, and his inward instability. These processes of growth goad one another on reciprocally. . . Unrestricted demands cannot be fulfilled with restricted potentialities. The limitless growth of claims for greater power and expanded rule has up to now been the inner fuel of 'progress'. We can now look ahead to the time when it will be the fuel of catastrophe as well.

Jurgen Moltmann, *The Church in the Power of the Spirit*

Love of neighbour, love of God, *caritas* without justice is a lie; even justice becomes an empty word if it does not lead to the establishment of a just social and political order. . . The churches must at all times be ready to challenge injustice (modestly but dauntlessly). . . This does not come about without a power struggle. . . [The church must] further truth and justice in the world in the way of spiritual power, a power which has as its mission keeping alive in the heart of humanity the will to form human society into a dwelling-place in which it is good for everyone to live, something which it is good to live for.

Edward Schillebeeckx, *Jesus in our Western Culture*

Why did the powers fight against Christ? Jesus had come as their Lord, in him they were created, and in him they met their master. Since they had become independent, however, and had set themselves up as gods, they could only attack Jesus. Their service structure had become a structure of domination. Neither politics nor religion were helping people to live according to God's will any longer. . . Paul points out that what Christ has done upon the cross is not only to take our sins upon himself, but also to liberate us from the tyranny of the powers.

Albert van den Heuvel, *These Rebellious Powers*

Conservatism and traditionalism are perverted powers:

they bind people to yesterday and do not let them be open to new demands. . . The alternatives, however, are not progressivism and change. The biblical alternatives are called covenant and eschatology. Without tradition, the church would have to live with today and tomorrow only. . . [but when] tradition becomes traditionalism, [it becomes] a perverted power.

Albert van den Heuvel, *These Rebellious Powers*

Lord of the church, where two or more are gathered in your name there are sometimes power struggles and conflicts. Some who have been 'sinned against' by other powers bring their frustrations to church and find there a place to exercise 'bad' power. Others who have been around for a long time wield power by becoming 'permission-witholders'. Still others use the power of special knowledge, or 'ordination', to exclude many from ministries of 'good' power.

Jesus, you came, not to make our lives more comfortable, but to redeem us from the evil powers, from alienation, and 'give us back to ourselves'. In the words of Dostoyevski's Grand Inquisitor: 'Instead of dominating conscience, you came to make it even more profound; instead of encircling human liberty, you came to make its horizon even wider. . . Your desire was to liberate people for love. Free, they ought to follow you, feel themselves attracted to you and as your prisoners. Instead of obeying the harsh laws of the past, people ought to begin as of now to decide in your presence what is good and what is bad, having your example before their eyes.'

Help us humans to know that any power we have is a derived power: the authority to exercise power ultimately belongs only to you, Lord God. May we use the power given to us in our creation for the good of the cosmos. May the authority we are given in our re-creation to become the children of God empower us to serve others, in the church and in the world. As Jesus lived among us in the power of the Spirit, may we, too, be receptive to the same kind of power, so that 'evil powers' will be banished and annulled in his strong name.

A Benediction

Now to him to whom power ultimately belongs, and whose love is constant;

> *who is the creator of all other powers;*
> *who in Jesus Christ has unmasked evil powers;*
> *who has power to help us stand firm in our faith;*
> *to him alone be glory, and power and dominion for ever and ever,* Amen.

36

The cosmic conflict

For our fight is not against human foes, but against cosmic powers, against the authorities and potentates of this dark world, against the superhuman forces of evil in the heavens.

Your father is the devil and you choose to carry out your father's desires. He was a murderer from the beginning, and is not rooted in the truth; there is no truth in him. When he tells a lie he is speaking his own language, for he is a liar and the father of lies.

Satan himself masquerades as an angel of light.

Awake! be on the alert! Your enemy the devil, like a roaring lion, prowls round looking for someone to devour.

The seventy-two came back jubilant. 'In your name, Lord,' they said, 'even the devils submit to us.' He replied, 'I watched how Satan fell, like lightning, out of the sky.'

Stand up to the devil and he will turn and run.

We know that the man we once were has been crucified with Christ, for the destruction of the sinful self, so that we may no longer be the slaves of sin, since a dead man is no longer answerable for his sin.

So far you have faced no trial beyond what man can bear. God keeps faith, and he will not allow you to be tested above your powers, but when the test comes he will at the same time provide a way out, by enabling you to sustain it.

The Son of God appeared for the very purpose of undoing the devil's work.

He has broken the power of death and brought life and immortality to light through the gospel.

For he is destined to reign until God has put all enemies under his feet; and the last enemy to be abolished is death.

(Ephesians 6: 12; John 8: 44; 2 Corinthians 11: 14; 1 Peter 5: 8; Luke 10: 17-18; James 4: 7; Romans 6: 6; 1 Corinthians 10: 13; 1 John 3: 8; 2 Timothy 1: 10; 1 Corinthians 15: 25-26 — all NEB)

I pulled my car into the side street to buy the flowers, not so much because I wanted them, but because the seller was young and attractive. As I paid for the flowers, I attempted to make conversation. 'How's business?' I asked. 'Business is good. I'm the second best seller of flowers in the city,' she easily replied. 'What's your secret?' I inquired, winking. Without hesitation, she responded with an answer that still haunts me. 'I'm a witch. I have the power to get people's attention as they drive by. I make them stop here and buy flowers just like you did. I have other powers, too.'

Did she really have that kind of power? I had been a Christian for years but never considered fighting Satan in anything but metaphorical terms. I wondered: just what kind of cosmic conflict is really going on?Since that time I have learned a little more about the cosmic conflict between God and Satan. I have learned that all of us are in it. The conflict is constant. There is never a lull. It is invisible. And it continues as long as we are alive.

But there is encouraging news. In Jesus' first coming to earth he defeated our three greatest enemies — sin, Satan and death. Sin is still in the world, but because of Jesus' forgiveness no-one needs to be enslaved to sin. Satan still has power, but because of the cross one no longer has to be controlled by him. Death still claims its victims, but we are no longer slaves to that fear because of Jesus' death and resurrection.

Therefore, sin, Satan and death have been *defeated* by Jesus' first coming. And when he comes again in glory, Jesus Christ will utterly *destroy* these foes. Yes, the battle will rage on while we still have breath. But we look to the return of the conquering Christ when the cosmic conflict will end in victory for the Lamb upon the throne.

There are two equal and opposite errors into which our race can fall about the devils. One is to disbelieve in their existence. The other is to believe, and to feel an excessive and unhealthy interest in them. They themselves are equally pleased by both errors.

C.S. Lewis, *The Screwtape Letters*

The devil's cleverest ruse is to make believe that he does not exist.

Donald Barnhouse, *The Invisible War*

We have seen that the devil is never quite so subtle, and never quite so successful, as when he succeeds in persuading people that he does not exist at all! That, as we have suggested, was his supreme masterpiece, and it is certainly a part of our problem at the present time. The tendency now is to say that we must not talk about 'the devil' but only about 'evil'. We must not tell people to 'renounce the works of the devil'; we must encourage them to 'resist the devil'. In other words, the whole tendency today is to say that our fight is only against a principle of evil that is in ourselves and in others, and perhaps in the very environment into which we are born. But it is not considered to be 'consistent with modern knowledge' to believe still in a personal devil. We must not even make that principle of evil positive. What has been called 'evil', we are told, is simply the absence of good qualities rather than something positive in and of itself!

D. Martyn Lloyd-Jones, *The Christian Warfare*

Often the kingdom (of God) is likened to a Caribbean cruise on a luxury liner. People change into their leisure clothes, grab their suntan lotion, and saunter down to the docks. What a shock it is when they find that entering the kingdom is really more like enlisting in the navy and doing battle with the enemy.

The enemy follows no rules of war. Satan considers

nothing unfair; he is not a gentleman. The sooner Christians understand this, the more serious they will become about being equipped and properly trained for the kingdom.

John Wimber, *Power Evangelism*

Satan knows that he has no legal right to any ground in the life of a believer, but if he can keep us from finding out this truth, he will have a field day in our lives.

We are told that Jesus 'disarmed' those hostile powers. That's just exactly what it means. Satan is like a toothless bulldog. He can growl and intimidate, but he has no authority to back up his threats in the life of a believer. If we don't know this or believe it, though, we will allow him to intimidate us, and he is a master at that. He loves to get Christians to cower or run from him in fear.

Hal Lindsey, *Satan is Alive and Well on Planet Earth*

We have been forewarned that an enemy relentlessly threatens us, an enemy who is the very embodiment of rash boldness, of military prowess, of crafty wiles, of unretiring zeal and haste, of every conceivable weapon and of skill in the science of warfare. We must, then, bend our every effort to this goal: that we should not let ourselves be overwhelmed by carelessness or faint-heartedness, but on the contrary, with courage rekindled, stand our ground in combat. Since this military service ends only at death, let us urge ourselves to perseverance.

Therefore, whatever men or Satan himself may instigate, God nevertheless holds the key, so that he turns their efforts to carry out his judgments. . . I confess, indeed, that it is often by means of Satan's intervention that God acts in the wicked, but in such a way that Satan performs his part by God's impulsion and advances as far as he is allowed.

But because that promise to crush Satan's head pertains to Christ and all his members in common, I deny that believers can ever be conquered or overwhelmed by him. Often, indeed, are they distressed, but not so deprived of life as not to recover; they fall under violent blows, but afterward they are raised up; they are wounded, but not fatally.   In short, they so toil throughout life that at the last they obtain the victory.

John Calvin, Institutes

The devil shapes himself to the fashions of all men.   If he meet with a proud man, or a prodigal man, then he makes himself a flatterer; if a covetous man, then he comes with a reward in his hand.   He had an apple for Eve, a grape for Noah, a change of raiment for Gehazi, a bag for Judas.   He can dish out his meat for all palates, he hath a last to fit every shoe; he hath something to please all conditions.

William Jenkyn

O God, your greatness towers above the mountains. Your love is deeper than the valleys of the oceans and as encompassing as the waters that cover the sea. Hear our pleas and listen to our appeals. We are pressed and hindered on all sides by the enemy. We feel almost overwhelmed, but we know you are faithful. Watch over our nights and fill our days with your presence. Cause our feet to stand on solid ground and give us vision for making proper choices. Our lives are in your keeping, O God. Hear us as we pray in the name of the one who rules at your right hand.

A Benediction
Now may the reigning king, Jesus Christ, protect you from the wiles of the evil one. May he keep you from being squeezed into the mould of this world. May he empower you with all the spiritual benefits of the citizens of heaven, in the name of the one who defeated sin, Satan and death. Amen.

37

Tempted to be Christian

(Harry Emerson Fosdick)

About noon, O king, as I was on the road, I saw a light from heaven, brighter than the sun, blazing around me and my companions. We all fell to the ground and I heard a voice saying to me in Aramaic, 'Saul, Saul, why do you persecute me? It is hard for you to kick against the goads!'

And I, when I am lifted up from the earth, will draw all to myself.

That I may know him, and the power of his resurrection, and the fellowship of his sufferings, being made conformable unto his death; if by any means I might attain unto the resurrection of the dead.

Not as though I had already attained, either were already perfect: but I follow after, if that I may apprehend that for which I am apprehended for Christ Jesus.

After this many of his disciples drew back and no longer went about with him. Jesus said to the twelve, 'Will you also go away?' Simon Peter answered him, 'Lord, to whom shall we go? You have the words of eternal life.'

Finally, brothers, whatever is true, whatever is noble, whatever is right, whatever is pure, whatever is lovely, whatever is admirable — if anything is excellent or praiseworthy — think about such things.'

(Acts 26: 13-14, NIV; John 12: 32, RSV; Philippians 3: 10-12, KJV; John 6: 66-68, RSV; Philippians 4: 8, NIV)

Stories of conversion to Jesus Christ, whether in the Bible, in history or today — and whether sudden, slow or in stages — are all stories of temptation. Temptation means a powerful attraction which draws a person away from previously determined goals. As Harry Emerson Fosdick has pointed out, however, the word 'temptation' is almost universally associated with evil. And there are good reasons why that is so.

Anyone who wants to live by the highest of goals becomes powerfully aware of forces — within and around — which divert, pressure, goad and suggest compromise, to settle, if not for evil, then at least for less than the best. You cannot read the story of Jesus' temptation, or the words of Paul about 'wrestling. . . with principalities and powers' without knowing that is so.

But in all accounts of temptation there must be an opposite temptation, to God and his will. Otherwise there is no struggle. Beauty, truth and goodness have a powerful winsomeness about them. Great books, music, art, inspiring human lives, friends, noble causes have a powerful magnetism for us. Paul said that, and told us to put ourselves in the way of *their* temptation.

It is all too easy to become overwhelmed and obsessed by the so obvious manifestations of evil, greed and violence. But the Bible's consistent message is that good is more powerful than evil, light than darkness, love than hatred. The resurrection confirms this by demonstrating forever that life has mastered death. Where sin abounds — grace much more abounds!

So, in evangelism, there are powerful factors on the side of the church and the witnessing Christian. God has not left himself without witness in the lives of those we seek to reach with the gospel of Christ; indeed, they were created in his image! That is the point of contact. That is the terminal which makes it possible again for the spark between God and any human soul to leap across again. John said of Christ, 'He was the true light which enlightens every person who comes into the world.'

Behind the final capitulation of Saul of Tarsus to Christ was a persistent and powerful temptation of God — through Stephen and many others — drawing Saul, in spite of his struggles, inexorably towards Christ. Otherwise what do the words 'It hurts you, doesn't it, to kick against the goad' mean?

Christ will not be ignored. When people oppose, blaspheme and misunderstand him, they are acknowledging that they cannot ignore him. He will not be evaded. Playwrights, musicians, philosophers, politicians and a host of others find that they cannot evade him.

As preachers of the gospel, and as followers trying to witness, we are in the business of temptation.

The most powerful temptation is not the attraction and magnetism of evil, strong and apparently irresistible though it is. It is God. It is God's will. It is Christ.

≈❀≈

I, too, became aware that there really had been a man, Jesus, who was also God I was conscious of his presence. He really had spoken those sublime words — I heard them. He really had died on a cross and risen from the dead. Otherwise how was it possible for me to meet him, as I did?

Malcolm Muggeridge, *Jesus Rediscovered*

Well, all I can say is, as one aging and singularly unimportant fellowman, that I have conscientiously looked far and wide, inside and outside my own head and heart, and I have found nothing other than [Jesus] and his words which offers any answer to the dilemmas of this tragic, troubled time. If his light has gone out, then as far as I am concerned, there is no light.

Malcolm Muggeridge, *Jesus Rediscovered*

You must picture me alone in that room at Magdalen, night after night, feeling, whenever my mind lifted even for a second from my work, the steady, unrelenting approach of him whom I so earnestly desired not to meet. That which I greatly feared had at last come upon me. In the Trinity Term of 1929 I gave in, and admitted that God was God, and knelt and prayed: perhaps, that night, the most dejected and reluctant convert in all England. I did not then see what is now the most shining and obvious thing; the divine humility which will accept a convert even on such terms. The Prodigal Son at least walked home on his own feet. But who can duly adore that love which will open the high gates to a prodigal who is brought in kicking, struggling, resentful, and darting his eyes in every direction for a chance of escape? The words *compelle intrare*, compel them to come in, have been so abused by wicked men that we shudder at them; but, properly understood, they plumb the depth of the divine mercy. The hardness of God is kinder than the softness of men, and his compulsion is our liberation.

C.S. Lewis, *Surprised by Joy*

I fled him, down the nights and down the days;
I fled him, down the arches of the years;
I fled him, down the labyrinthine ways
Of my own mind; and in the mist of tears
I hid from him, and under running laughter.

But with unhurrying chase, and unperturbed pace,
Deliberate speed, majestic instancy,
They beat — and a voice beat
More instant than the feet —
All things betray thee, who betrayest me.

Francis Thompson, *The Hound of Heaven*

The devil tempts that he may ruin.
God tempts that he may crown.

St Ambrose

Batter my heart, three person'd God; for, you
As ye but knock, breathe, shine and seek to mend.
Take me to you, imprison me, for I
Except you enthrall me, never shall be free,
Nor ever chaste, except you ravish me.

John Donne, *Holy Sonnets, xiv*

Lord Jesus, in the quietness of my own heart, and in your presence, I calmly assess how much you have become part of me. You are now part of my thinking processes, my emotions, my volitional faculties — in fact you have become part of the fibre of my very being.

It began to happen when I was first drawn to you, as you said I would be. 'If I am lifted up,' you said, 'I will draw everybody to myself.' I struggled. I still struggle. But finally I had to say 'yes' and I've been learning to say it ever since. In a way, I'm caught between wanting to escape from you into the freedom of making my own choices and pleasing myself and knowing that I am held captive by you. But I know deep down that the freedom to please myself is the ultimate bondage, and that I am only truly free in your captivity. Like Paul, and Peter, and a million others, you are now so much part of me that I could never go back to where I was before I met you. To wherever else could I go? In fact, how could I go away? I am 'apprehended' — you have placed me under arrest. But it is the arrest of love and truth.

I am deeply grateful, Lord, for the realisation that, however powerful the forces of evil are, they are a reminder that your drawing power is greater. Where sin abounds grace does the much more abound. Inwardly, this tells me when I am almost overwhelmed by the power of personal temptation, that your power to tempt for good is also drawing me — and you are the greater. You have laid a prior claim to me.

I strive with this realisation. But also in it, and in you, I rest. Because you will never take your hand from me. Thanks be to God. Amen.

A Benediction
Now to the one who can keep you from falling, and set you in the presence of his glory, jubilant and above reproach, to the only God our Saviour, be glory and majesty, might and authority, through Jesus Christ our Lord, before all time, now and for evermore. Amen.

Jude 24, NEB

38

Eternity in our hearts

But if they ask me what his name is, what am I to tell them? And God said 'I am who I am'.

I am the first and I am the last

From everlasting to everlasting you are God.

The eternal God is your dwelling place, and underneath are the everlasting arms.

He has made everything beautiful in its time. He has also set eternity in human hearts.

God is the strength of my heart and my portion forever.

For God so loved the world that he gave his only son, that whoever believes in him should not perish but have eternal life.

And eternal life is this: to know you, the only true God, and Jesus Christ whom you have sent.

And they that be wise shall shine as the brightness of the firmament; and they that turn many to righteousness as the stars for ever and ever.

The wages of sin is death, but the gift of God is eternal life in Christ Jesus our Lord.

The effect of righteousness is. . . confidence forever.

We know also that the Son of God has come and given us understanding, so that we may know him who is true. And we are in him who is true — even in his son Jesus Christ. He is the true God and eternal life.

I am Alpha and Omega, the beginning and the end, the first and the last.

And in the world to come, life everlasting.

(Exodus 3: 14, JB; Isaiah 44: 6, KJV; Psalm 90: 2, NIV; Deuteronomy 33: 27, RSV; Ecclesiastes 3: 11, NIV; Psalm 73: 26, NIV; John 3: 16, RSV; John 17: 3, JB; Daniel 12: 3, KJV; Romans

6: 23, NIV; Isaiah 32: 17, NIV; 1 John 5: 20, NIV; Revelation 22: 13, KJV; Luke 18: 30, KJV)

Without beginning or end: timeless: lasting forever — these are the phrases for which the compilers of one dictionary groped in trying to define the eternal. Eternity is a word beyond words, a concept beyond understanding, a reality beyond description, a truth beyond our experience. Yet to some people, eternity has been a force which has given meaning to the whole of life.

Arthur Stace, or 'Mr Eternity' as we kids used to call him, was one of Sydney's eccentrics. Eternity would be one of the last words anyone would ever have thought of in connection with Arthur Stace's very earthy life. He was born in 1884 in a Balmain slum of parents who died of drinking methylated spirits. His brothers died derelict alcoholics. His sisters were prostitutes. He had little schooling and by his mid-twenties he had only ever worked as a brothel pimp and a two-up school cockatoo, had a long police record and was already a chronic alcoholic.

One night he went to one of Archdeacon Hammond's meetings at St Barnabas' Broadway in Sydney because he had heard there was tea and hot pies after the service. That night, Arthur Stace was converted. For the next twenty-four years, he worked tirelessly, caring for derelicts and down-and-outers of all kinds, preaching in the open air and visiting mental institutions, men's hostels and the leprosarium.

In 1930, Arthur Stace heard John Ridley preach. 'I wish I could shout "Eternity" through the streets of Sydney,' Ridley called out. The words forcibly struck Arthur. Afterwards, outside on the footpath, he found a piece of chalk in his pocket. He felt a powerful urge and with the chalk wrote 'Eternity' on the pavement. 'The funny thing is,' he said later, 'that I could hardly write my own name. I couldn't have spelt "Eternity" for a hundred quid, but it came out smoothly and in a beautiful copperplate script. I couldn't understand it and I still can't.'

For the next thirty-seven years, Arthur chalked the word 'Eternity' onto the footpaths of Sydney and into the character of the city. He also chalked it into the minds and lives of countless people who testify to the power of his one-word sermon. My grandfather knew him and I was about six when he first showed me the word near the entrance to Central Railway Station, pausing as I hurried up the ramp clutching his hand and sample bags from the Sydney Show.

After that, 'Eternity' was always there. Later on I met Arthur Stace when he spoke at our church — a small, quiet man in an old suit. He said eternity was something for all of us, something to lift us out of our ordinariness, out of our sin and give us hope. He chose the following hymn:

> Out of my bondage, sorrow, and night,
> Jesus, I come! Jesus, I come!
> Into thy freedom, gladness, and light,
> Jesus, I come to thee!
> Out of my sickness into thy health,
> Out of my want and into thy wealth,
> Out of my sin and into thyself,
> Jesus, I come to thee!
>
> Out of my shameful failure and loss,
> Jesus, I come! Jesus, I come!
> Into the glorious gain of thy cross,
> Jesus, I come to thee!
> Out of earth's sorrows into thy balm,
> Out of life's storms and into thy calm,
> Out of distress to jubilant psalm,
> Jesus, I come to thee!
>
> Out of unrest and arrogant pride,
> Jesus, I come! Jesus, I come!
> Into thy blessed will to abide,
> Jesus, I come to thee!
> Out of myself to dwell in thy love,
> Out of despair into raptures above.

Upward for aye on wings like a dove
Jesus, I come to thee!

Out of the fear and the dread of the tomb,
Jesus, I come! Jesus, I come!
Into the joy and light of thy home,
Jesus, I come to thee!
Out of the depths of ruin untold,
Into the peace of thy sheltering fold,
Ever thy glorious face to behold,
Jesus, I come to thee!

W.T. Sleeper, 'Jesus, I come'

I was out of Australia in 1967 when Arthur Stace died. He was eighty-three. He had no relatives. He left his few possessions to the church and his body to the University of Sydney. He had written 'Eternity' somewhere between half a million and a million times on Sydney's pavements.

It was many years later that I first saw the Sydney Square redevelopment. It was beautiful, but not quite the Sydney I remembered. Between the cathedral and the town hall, I walked down the new steps towards the Sydney Square waterfall. There, set in the paving stones in letters about 21cm high in white wrought aluminium, was the old word 'Eternity' exactly as Arthur used to write it. Arthur Stace was still held in the city's memory.

Here we have no lasting city, but we seek the city which is to come. . . the city which has foundations, whose builder and maker is God.

Hebrews 13: 14; 11: 10; RSV

The God of Abraham praise
who reigns enthroned above,
ancient of everlasting days,
and God of love;
Jehovah, great I am
by earth and heaven confessed!

I bow and bless the sacred name
for ever blest.

He by himself hath sworn,
I on his oath depend:
I shall, on eagles' wings upborne,
to heaven ascend:
I shall behold his face,
I shall his power adore,
and sing the wonders of his grace
for evermore.

Thomas Olivers

Thine for ever! God of Love!
Hear us from thy throne above.
There for ever may we be
Here and in eternity.

Mary Fawler Maude

People have become accustomed to think of time as a fourth dimension of life, additional to the dimensions of space. The Bible tells us of a still further dimension, that of eternity. This is not just an extension of time in the sense of 'everlasting', but a new dimension, a new quality of life, which we can begin to have now, which is not terminated by physical death, and which will reach its perfection in the spiritual sphere. We Christians learn about this kind of life from Jesus Christ; more than that, he shares his own victorious, deathless life with all who will open their being to his Spirit.

George Appleton, *Journey for a Soul*

There, in that other world, what waits for me?
What shall I find after that other birth?
No stormy, tossing, foaming, smiling sea,
But a new earth.

No sun to mark the changing of days,
No slow, soft falling of the alternate night,
No moon, no star, no light upon my ways,
Only the Light.

No grey cathedral, wide and wondrous fair,
That I may tread where all my fathers trod.
Nay, nay, my soul, no house of God is there,
But only God.

Mary Coleridge

The preacher kept shouting 'Eternity! Eternity!' When I
left the church, 'Eternity' was ringing in my brain.

Arthur Stace

Thou takest the pen — and the lines dance. Thou takest
the flute — and the notes shimmer. Thou takest the brush
— and the colours sing. So all things have meaning and
beauty in that space beyond time where thou art. How,
then, can I hold back anything from thee?

Dag Hammarskjold, *Markings*

I have lived down here long enough to convince myself
that we were not made for the earth, that the earth is not
our paradise, and that it has been of service to us only as
a great preparation for something else. Above all, it carried within it the all-too-familiar seeds of decay, and as
the years pass I find it increasingly wearisome, while my
soul fixes its sights with assurance on the one who always
has the power to captivate the uniquely, truly and eternally
new: God.

Carlo Carretto, *In Search of the Beyond*

To those who really grasp Eternity, life gains a new
perspective. While we are strong and able, it inspires us
to live for others in continual consciousness of the eternal
dimension of life. To those of us privileged to live long
enough to know our work is done, it enables us to face
death, to long for it, to embrace it.

Lord, I am lonely
And the sun is shining,
Listless, while the wind
Shakes the ageing leaves.
The harvest has been gathered,

All is bagged and barned,
Silos burst with grain.
Why, Lord, must I still stand
Dropping blind seeds
Onto a barren soil?

Come, sweet Jesus, cut me down
With the sickle of your mercy,
For I am lonely
And a stranger in this land.

Cliff Ashby, 'A stranger in this land'

I want to join my Maker.

Arthur Stace

God take me to a better country.
If I die, I will go to heaven where Jesus is. I will be
happy there.
O heaven, that good place. I go there.

Christian Aboriginal children, dying of
European diseases in the 1850s

When I die I will just stop living on this earth and I
will live again in heaven.
It will be so nice in heaven!

If I should die very soon,
I will be glad — then I will live in this bright and
beautiful happiness that will never end and I will see
Jesus!

Joanne and Benjamin Marxhausen,
'If I should die, if I should live'

Never weather beaten sail
more willing bent to shore
Never tired pilgrim's limbs
affected slumber more
Than my weary spirit longs to fly
out of my troubled breast
Oh come quickly
Oh come quickly

Oh come quickly
O sweet Lord
and take my soul to rest

Ever blooming are the joys
of heaven's high paradise
Old age deafs not there our ears
nor vapour dims our eyes
Glory, there, the sun outshines
whose beams the blessed only see
Oh come quickly
Oh come quickly
Oh come quickly
O sweet Lord
and raise my soul to thee.

Thomas Campian

For it is in giving that we receive,
It is in loving that we are loved
and it is in dying that we are born to eternal life.

St Francis of Assisi

Eternal God, whose existence is everlasting and whose power is infinite, I bring you my mortality. I bring you my humanity. It is hard for me to feel beyond this flesh and blood, hard for me to reach out with human hands and grasp eternity. I come to you in the only way I can come. I come as a human trusting in your son, human and not-human, mortal and immortal, man and God. I come to you trusting in the death and resurrection of the Lord Jesus Christ, whom to know is life eternal. Amen.

A Benediction
Now to him who is able to keep you from falling and to present you without blemish before the presence of his glory with rejoicing, to the only God our Saviour through Jesus Christ our Lord, be glory, majesty, dominion, and authority, before all time and now and for ever. Amen.

Jude 24-25, RSV

39

Procure me possibility

(Sören Kierkegaard)

Do I make my plans like a worldly man, ready to say Yes and No at once? As surely as God is faithful our word. . . has not been Yes and No.

Test me, Lord, probe me, scrutinise my heart and mind: Your love is always my study, and your constancy my companion.

I mimic the deaf in hearing nothing, I mimic the dumb in not saying a word, I mimic the man who, since he hears nothing gives no sharp answer in return.

I mean to sing to the Lord all my life, I mean to play to my God as long as I live. May these thoughts of mine give the Lord as much delight as he gives me.

Dear friends, if our consciences do not condemn us, we approach God with confidence, and we obtain from him whatever we ask for, because we are obeying his commands and doing the things that please him.

My heart exults, my mind rejoices and my body can dwell secure, knowing that you will not hand me over to Sheol and not put your friend within danger of the grave. Instead you will show me the path of life, the unbounded joy of living in your presence.

The Son of God, Jesus Christ whom we preached to you. . . was not Yes and No; but in him it is always Yes. For all the promises of God find their Yes in him.

God is love and whoever continues to love keeps in union with God and God with him.

(2 Corinthians 1: 17-18, RSV; Psalm 26: 2-3, JB; Psalm 38: 13-14, JB; Psalm 104: 33-34, JB; 1 John 3: 21-22, Goodspeed; Psalm 16: 9-11, JB; 2 Corinthians 1: 19-20, RSV; 1 John 4: 16, Goodspeed)

It is prayer which alone makes *good* sense of the past, illumines the present and makes the future hopeful. In the first half of life we are immersed in doing. We test our strength and innocence against the flood of experience which comes upon us, even over us. We taste in order to become wise, we enter in so that we know, we seek in the hope of being found. There are so many possibilities presented to us that we hardly contain our impatience, an impatience which later surprises us, gives cause for regret. We don't call 'procure me possibility'; we hope only for sufficient time to buy up all the experience possible.

In the second half of life we emerge from this welter of sensation to find that our necessary immersion in the world has left scars upon us. There are some regrets, there is some emptiness and longing. We are not satisfied; whatever we were looking for, that was not it. Our successes have not filled us, though we own that they were worth the labour. Our failures have dimmed the bright image of ourselves we entertained. We look about us with a view both widened and restricted by our experience. The fine things we hear ourselves saying have no corresponding beauty within. We paint ourselves into a corner with the varnish of appearance, even as God troubles our hearts with truth.

Now is the time of emergence. God comforts us by leading us into prayer. Some old securities and certainties he renews with paradox. Pride and hardness of heart he commutes into vulnerability. The love which we dwelt upon but which was not within us he puts into hearts renewed in tenderness. The creation we largely ignored in pursuit of more glittering prizes he fills with grandeur. We were afraid of dying and he allowed it to touch us in failures and disappointments, and having fallen so far, he raises us to comfort and joy. He satisfies longing and makes it increase. The cry of wretchedness is the cry 'procure me possibility'. God knows the wretchedness, hears the cry, answers it in and by prayer. The life of prayer discovers true riches.

From the Christian point of view everything. . . should serve for edification. The sort of learning which is not . . . edifying is precisely for that reason unchristian. Everything that is Christian must bear some resemblance to the address which a physician makes beside the sick bed.

Sören Kierkegaard, *The Sickness Unto Death*

Salvation is humanly speaking the most impossible thing of all; but for God all things are possible. This is the fight of faith, which fights madly for possibility. For possibility is the only power to save. When one swoons, people shout for water, Eau-de-Cologne, Hoffman's Drops; but when one is about to despair the cry is, Procure me possibility, procure me possibility.

Sören Kierkegaard, *The Sickness Unto Death*

We are free when we are living in a homeland, not when we are straying and breaking away. We are free when we are obeying some deep, inward voice of religious belief. Obeying from within. We are free when we belong to a living, organic, believing community, active in fulfilling some unfulfilled, perhaps unrealised purpose.

D.H. Lawrence, *Studies in Classic American Literature*

For only to faith is God alone of value, and God is God in that he desires nothing but faith. . . and just as faith is a trust which reaches out into the darkness, so God is the presence, affirmed in spite of every experience of his absence, of the one being who is worthy of faith, never disappoints, never fails, and deserves total reliance.

Gerhard Ebeling, *Luther*

It is from within us, deep down within us, that the new life proceeds and that means that anything which is not an expression of us will not be an expression of God either. In some sense the converse is also true. What is not an expression of God will not be a true expression of us.

Simon Tugwell, *Reflections of the Beatitudes*

If the soul loves God, its heart will not be turned in upon itself or preoccupied with its own pleasure and glory.

Rather, it will be intent upon giving honour and glory to God and upon giving him pleasure.

Francis Kelly Nemeck and Marie Theresa Coombs,
The Spiritual Journey

We learn about sin only on the basis of the proclamation of grace and pardon.

Jacques Ellul, *The Subversion of Christianity*

He who is truly alive is free to die. . . the people who find death intolerable are those who have never been more than half alive. . . Death followed by resurrection, life through dying is the way things are. It is the principle of all existence. Hang on to what you have of life and you are lost. Let go, do the necessary dying and a fuller, richer quality of aliveness will be given to you.

John V. Taylor, *Weep Not For Me*

Being a child of yours, dear Father, is the best adulthood I've ever had! It's richer by far than any combination of status, promotion, glittering things, beauty prizes and being 'special'. It gives me liberty to laugh at myself with enjoyment. Indeed, now I can grin and bear, laugh and be happy because you appreciate the joke and the joy better than I do. I am freed from envying the talent which others possess. I can say 'I don't know' without feeling the world reddening with embarrassment. 'Truth in the inward part' is what you give and it's wonderful, it's freedom! I see that I'm more ordinary than I thought and that others are deeper, more interesting, more loveable than I used to think. And the poor, dear God, the poor! I see them, more and more. For these wonders and for all the possibilities that he will yet draw from them, may God be praised! Amen.

A Benediction

On your head let there be humour,
In your breast let there be peace,
Out of your eyes much seeing,
Out of your words much ease.

Theme: Perspective

. . .from the mountains

Those who trust in the Lord are like Mount Zion,
    which cannot be shaken but endures for ever.
As the mountains surround Jerusalem,
    so the Lord surrounds his people
    both now and for evermore. . .

Send forth your light and your truth,
    let them guide me;
let them bring me to your holy mountain,
    to the place where you dwell.
Then will I go to the altar of God,
    to God, my joy and my delight.
I will praise you with the harp,
    O God, my God.

Why are you downcast, O my soul?
    Why so disturbed within me?
Put your hope in God,
    for I will yet praise him
    my Saviour and my God.

Psalms 125: 1-2; 43: 2-5, NIV

40

To know God

All I want is to know Christ and to experience the power of his resurrection, to share in his sufferings and become like him in his death, in the hope that I myself will be raised from death to life.

So Jesus said to those who believed in him, 'If you obey my teaching you are really my disciples; you will know the truth, and the truth will set you free.'

You diligently study the scriptures because you think that by them you possess eternal life. These are the scriptures that testify about me, yet you refuse to come to me to have life.

If we obey God's commands, then we are sure that we know him. If someone says that he knows him, but does not obey his commands, such a person is a liar and there is no truth in him. But whoever obeys his word is the one whose love for God has really been made perfect. This is how we can be sure that we are in union with God: whoever says that he remains in union with God should live just as Jesus Christ did.

What he commands is that we believe in his Son Jesus Christ and love one another, just as Christ commanded us. Whoever obeys God's commands lives in union with God and God lives in union with him. And because of the Spirit that God has given us we know that God lives in union with us.

This is how we know what love is: Christ gave his life for us. We too, then, ought to give our lives for our brothers! If a rich person sees his brother in need, yet closes his heart against his brother, how can he claim that he loves God? My children, our love should not be just words and talk; it must be true love, which shows itself in action.

But the fruit of the Spirit is love, joy, peace, patience, kindness, goodness, faithfulness, gentleness, self-control; against such there is no law. And those who belong to Christ Jesus have crucified the flesh with its passions and desires. If we live by the Spirit let us also walk by the Spirit.

Not everyone who calls me 'Lord, Lord' will enter the Kingdom of Heaven, but only those who do the will of my heavenly Father. When that day comes, many will say to me, 'Lord, Lord, did we not prophecy in your name, cast out devils in your name, and in your name perform miracles?' Then I will tell them to their face, 'I never knew you: out of my sight, you and your wicked ways!'

(Philippians 3: 10-11, GNB; John 8: 31-32, GNB; John 5: 39-40, NIV; 1 John 2: 3-6, GNB; 1 John 3: 23-24, GNB; 1 John 3: 16-18, GNB; Galatians 5: 22-25, RSV; Matthew 7: 21-23, NEB)

The business of knowing God, and it is after all our chief business, is not so easily practised as it is talked about. For many of us 'knowing God' consists of having given intellectual assent to Christ's claims to duty and having accepted the fact that Christ died for *our* sins. We then blithely go through the routine of life, say a few mumbled prayers — perhaps even on a daily basis — study the Bible a little and regularly attend the services of the church. We might even be involved in volunteer ministry. We might just feel serious enough about the whole thing to tithe. For some, 'knowing God' may even have led them to attend Bible college or seminary — perhaps even to engage in 'full-time' Christian ministry. But is *this* what is really meant by 'knowing God'? 'Knowing God' goes far deeper.

We parrot the phrase 'having a personal relationship with Jesus Christ'. But do we really understand what we are talking about? Do we realise that those words refer to 'intimate, constant companionship'? It is a relationship very much like being in the presence of one's best friend *all day* long and constantly interrupting the work or the silence for conversation wherein you reveal the deepest longing, pains, fears, joys and sorrows that you've experienced. And it is two-way conversation. How often do we really listen to God? Do we study the Bible simply to have more and better Bible knowledge? Or, do we study the scriptures to hear and see and know the Person behind them? There is a world of difference.

And does our knowledge really change us in any way? Indeed, we may become more 'mystical', more 'spiritual', and 'free'. But how does our companionship with God change the way we act towards others? Do we love more deeply, with greater sensitivity, greater practicality? In God's name how have we loved? With greater mercy, compassion and generosity? Have we loved only with our tongues and not with food, clothing and shelter for the poor? Or, have we loved in action, only to let our razor tongues destroy another child of the Father?

How well do we know God? How well do we image Christ? It is to that extent, and no further, that true knowledge of God dwells in us.

❧

For you have made us for yourself, and our hearts are restless till they find their rest in you.

Augustine, *The Confessions*

Thy beloved is of that nature, that he will admit of no rival; but will have thy heart alone, and sit on his throne as king.

Thomas à Kempis, *The Imitation of Christ*

Instead of asking yourself whether you believe or not, ask yourself whether you have this day done one thing because he said, 'Do it', or once abstained because he said, 'Do not do it'. It is simply absurd to say you believe, or even want to believe in him, if you do not do anything he tells you.

George MacDonald, *Anthology*

Men. . . would rather receive salvation from God than God [who is] their salvation.

George MacDonald, *Anthology*

And here again we ought to observe that we are called to a knowledge of God: not that knowledge which. . . merely flits in the brain, but that which will be sound and fruitful if we duly perceive it, and if it takes root in the heart.

John Calvin, *Institutes*

Only [God] himself is completely and utterly sufficient to fulfil the will and longing of our souls. Nothing else can. The soul, when it is restored by grace, is made wholly sufficient to comprehend him fully by love. He cannot be comprehended by our intellect or any man's — or any angel's for that matter. For both we and they are created things. . . to the intellect, God. . . is forever unknowable . . . to love, he is completely knowable.

The Cloud of Unknowing

Lift up your heart to God with humble love: and mean God himself, and not what you get out of him.

The Cloud of Unknowing

A man may sink by such slow degrees that, long after he is a devil, he may go on being a good churchman or a good dissenter and thinking himself a good Christian.

George MacDonald, *Anthology*

Each man himself, as an individual, should render his account to God. No third person dares venture to intrude upon this accounting between God and the individual. . . the most ruinous evasion of all is to be hidden in the crowd in an attempt to escape God's supervision of him as an individual.

Sören Kierkegaard

Behind every saint stands another saint. . . I never learnt anything myself by my own old nose.

Baron von Hüegel

That is why the real problem of the Christian life comes where people do not usually look for it. It comes the very moment you wake up each morning. All your wishes and hopes for the day rush at you like wild animals. And the first job each morning consists simply in shoving them all back; in listening to that other voice, taking that other point of view, letting that other larger, stronger, quieter life come flowing in.

C.S. Lewis, *Mere Christianity*

This is the reason why we have no ease of heart or soul, for we are seeking our rest in trivial things that cannot satisfy, and not seeking to know God, almighty, all-wise, all good. He is true rest. It is his will that we should know him, and his pleasure that we should rest in him. Nothing less will satisfy us.

Julian of Norwich, *Revelations of Divine Love*

He alone is able to make himself known as he really is. We seek in reasoning and in the sciences, as in a bad copy, for what we neglect to see in an excellent original. . . We leave him for trifles, and disdain to hold converse with our king, who is always present in us. It is too little to love God and know him by what books tell us, or by what we feel within, through a few worshipful ideas, or some inspiration. We must. . . lift ourselves above all that which we feel, to worship God and Jesus Christ. . . as they are in themselves.

Brother Lawrence, *The Practice of the Presence of God*

Come, O Fount of every blessing,
tune my heart to sing your grace;
streams of mercy never ceasing
call for songs of loudest praise.

Jesus sought me when a stranger,
wandering from the fold of God;
he, to rescue me from danger,
interposed his precious blood.

To your grace how great a debtor
I become in all I do;
let that grace now, like a fetter,
bind my wandering heart to you.

Prone to wander — Lord, I feel it —
prone to leave the God I love,
take my heart, Lord, take and seal it,
seal it in your courts above.

Robert Robinson

A Benediction
O Lord our heavenly Father, almighty and everlasting God, who has safely brought us to the beginning of this day; defend us in the same with your mighty power; and grant that this day we fall into no sin; neither run into any kind of danger: but that all our doings may be ordered by your governance, to do always what is righteous in your sight, through Jesus Christ our Lord. Amen.

WEEK

Go under the mercy

(*Sheldon Vanauken*)

Have mercy on me, O God, according to thy steadfast love; according to thy abundant mercy blot out my transgressions. Wash me thoroughly from my iniquity, and cleanse me from my sin!

Behold my servant, whom I uphold, my chosen, in whom my soul delights. . . a bruised reed he will not break, and a dimly burning wick he will not quench.

'My soul magnifies the Lord, and my spirit rejoices in God my saviour, for he has regarded the low estate of his handmaiden. . . his mercy is on those who fear him from generation to generation.'

'Do not be anxious about your life, what you shall eat or what you shall drink, nor about your body, what you shall put on. Is not life more than food, and the body more than clothing? Look at the birds of the air. . . consider the lilies of the field. . . your heavenly Father knows (what you need). . . seek first his kingdom and his righteousness, and all these things shall be yours as well.'

We know that in everything God works for good with those who love him, who are called according to his purpose.

Have no anxiety about anything, but in everything by prayer and supplication with thanksgiving let your requests be made known to God. And the peace of God, which passes all understanding, will keep your hearts and your minds in Christ Jesus.

(Psalm 51: 1-2; Isaiah 42: 1-3; Luke 1: 46-48 and 50; Matthew 6: 25, 26, 28, 32 and 33; Romans 8: 28; Philippians 4: 6-7 — all RSV)

None of us could live but for the mercy of God. That is true for the believer and the unbeliever, although the believer is more likely to be aware of it than the unbeliever.

Abraham, in a foreign country, tried to save his own life from being taken by the king of that land who wanted his wife Sarah; Abraham tried to pass her off as his sister. Abimelech the king discovered the deception when God warned him in a dream. Abimelech let them both go. God helped the believer, Abraham, and the pagan king. Both were under his mercy.

Very often we know only later that God was our deliverer. If we take the time to reflect upon his obvious and (as we later learn) his hidden interventions, our faith will deepen. Should we fail to read his presence from experience and from the history of salvation preserved in scripture, we may come to trust too much our own judgments.

Noticing God in the affairs of our life and in the life of the world is a Christian exercise which keeps our spiritual muscles strong. He goes mercifully in the world. If he did not, there would be no hope for any of us.

❧

. . .Friends and acquaintances, Christian and otherwise, came by, sometimes bringing others — sometimes only for a few minutes, sometimes for hours. There were conversations upon almost every imaginable subject, yet sooner or later, it seemed, the talk would drift round to ultimate things and Christianity. . . No-one who was a part of that scene has ever quite forgotten it. And as a background, accepted, hardly noticed, yet a part of the texture of the hours, there were the bells of Oxford, ringing across the night. And [there were] the goodbyes, going down the narrow staircase and out into Pussey Lane to speed the departing friend with 'Goodbye, goodnight. Go under the Mercy.' The phrase comes from Charles Williams, and we all used it — indeed, still use it, some of us, after the years. There would be a halo round the gas lamp in the lane, and the slight English rain like a mist, and the

cobblestones of the lane would be glistening. 'Goodnight.
Go under the Mercy.' And the friend would say perhaps,
'Sleep under the Protection. Goodnight.' And then the
sound of the heels marching away into the Oxford night
and perhaps bells marking the midnight.

Sheldon Vanauken, *A Severe Mercy*

Here in the sand where someone laid him down,
The one known human signature is clear,
Whether woman or man, white-skinned or brown,
Whether the out-flung arms were so for fear,
Or agony, or weariness, or shame —
Here in one line athwart another line
Is briefly written the one, mutual name
A saviour's, or a thief's, or yours or mine.

Author unknown

If we were thinking of truth simply as an intellectual view,
then the vast majority of people would be left floundering
while a few razor-brained pioneers marched on. Let me
make the point by a quotation from MacIntyre's book,
assuming that his view would now be the same:

'But suppose that we could found belief in God on
arguments. It is not just that our freedom would be
taken away. It is also the fact that the road into the
kingdom of God would be one made easier for those
with a grasp of sound argument. But the qualifications for entry into the kingdom of God are after all
different from those required to pass an elementary
logic examination. God, if he is the God of Christian
theology, speaks to shepherds and fishermen, to tax-
collectors and scholars, to all sorts and conditions of
persons, equally and in the same way. The voice of
God has to be one that all can hear.'

Howard Williams, *My Word*

I suppose Archbishop William Temple was the most un-
forgettable person I knew. He had an astonishing
combination of gifts. He was not a technical scholar in
the sense of minutely detailed scholarship, but he did very

wide reading, had a capacious mind and the capacity to chew on a problem until he found the solution, as well as the gift of ready expression, as seen in his great book *Nature, Man and God*. He was an excellent preacher — surprisingly excellent for so academic a man. He was a great missioner: his mission at Oxford in 1931 has never been forgotten. He was a skilful chairman. He had a great gift of summing up the sense of a meeting. . . What many people did not know was his own interior life. He seemed to me to be a Christian of superbly childlike faith. Not that he hadn't had difficulty as a young man; he had. He'd fought through his intellectual problems, but in the end he really had the faith of a little child. That came out in his personal friendships, his prayer life and his preaching. So his death at the age of sixty-two was a tremendous loss to the worldwide church and a grave loss to me personally.

Bishop Stephen B. Neill

[After twenty-eighty years on his island, Robinson Crusoe one day saw a ship in close to land and a small boat with three badly-treated men cast off from it. Defoe tries to imagine what the three badly-treated men would be thinking; an uninhabited island, or else one of wild beasts, or of cannibals? But whatever their fears, they did not know Crusoe was behind the trees watching them and ready to help. Defoe writes,] So little do we see before us in the world, and so much reason have we to depend cheerfully upon the great Maker of the world, that he does not leave his creatures so absolutely destitute, but that in the worst circumstances they have always something to be thankful for, and sometimes are nearer their deliverance than they imagine; nay, are even brought to their deliverance by the means by which they seem to be brought to their destruction.

Daniel Defoe, *Robinson Crusoe*

I am pleading for what our fathers called an overruling Providence, as though wickedness, like a stream, could indeed go wild, break its banks, and let loose a torrential flood, but lo! there is a lie of the land that gets control in the end, a limit beyond which no stream's wildness can go, a contour to the landscape, a shape to the eternal hills, a declivity in the valleys, that at last bring even the wildest streams to terms and force them into channels that they did not choose. . . Thank God for that lie of the land that no overflowing flood can ultimately escape, but that will turn the wildest currents to channels that not they but God chooses!

Harry Emerson Fosdick, 'God Talks to a Dictator'

Gracious God, seat us, settle us, silence us, so that by memories and mysteries and mastery we may learn to live in faith and trust and to enjoy and celebrate the goodness we have received, for we pray in the name of Jesus Christ our Lord. Amen.

Richard C. Brand

O God, in whom there is no darkness at all, we thank you that though we walk in darkness, you have given us enough light in which to walk. As the sun dispels each morning the shadows of the night, so your mercies which surround us pierce the shadows of sin ever and again, and help us to see the meaning of our life. Give us grace to triumph over the confusion of impulse, in which we are so easily ensnared, and to walk in the way disclosed by your wisdom. Grant us clearness of vision especially when good is intertwined with evil, and when duty conflicts with desire, so that we may do your will this day and always. Amen.

Reinhold Niebuhr

A Benediction

The Lord be within you to strengthen you; over and around you to ward off your spiritual foes on every side; under you to hold you up in your goings; behind you to guard you from the assaults of the past; before you to lead you on. Amen.

42

Look at life as God sees it

(Michel Quoist)

'For my thoughts are not your thoughts, neither are your ways my ways,' declares the Lord.

The message of the cross is foolishness to those who are perishing, but to us who are being saved it is the power of God.

The foolishness of God is wiser than man's wisdom, and the weakness of God is stronger than man's strength.

Whoever wants to save his life will lose it, but whoever loses his life for me will find it. What good will it be for a man if he gains the whole world, yet forfeits his soul?

Do not worry about your life, what you will eat; or about your body, what you will wear. Life is more than food, and the body more than clothes.

If anyone wants to be first, he must be the very last, and the servant of all.

He who is least among you all — he is the greatest.

Love your enemies and pray for those who persecute you, that you may be sons of your Father in heaven.

Let God remould your minds from within, so that you may prove in practice that the plan of God for you is good.

Now we see but a poor reflection; then we shall see face to face. Now I know in part; then I shall know fully, even as I am fully known.

However, as it is written:

'No eye has seen, no ear has heard, no mind has conceived what God has prepared for those who love him' — but God has revealed it to us by his Spirit.

(Isaiah 55: 8, NIV; 1 Corinthians 1: 18, NIV; 1 Corinthians 1: 25, NIV; Matthew 16: 25-26, NIV; Luke 12: 22 and 23, NIV; Mark 9: 35, NIV; Luke 9: 48, NIV; Matthew 5: 44-45, NIV; Romans 12: 2, Phillips; 1 Corinthians 13: 12, NIV; 1 Corinthians 2: 9, NIV)

Have you read today's newspaper yet? How much of a mention did God get? Probably not a lot. A clergyman in trouble, a religious war, maybe even a scripture verse tucked away amongst the small ads. But no hint that world events and individual lives are acted out in the awesome presence of God. No suggestion that the one in whom we 'live and move and have our being' is directly involved in those situations which are so graphically reported. And maybe that isn't too surprising. As T.S. Eliot said, humankind 'cannot bear very much reality'.

That partial reality seems to come to us from every direction: the media, conversations at work, even our man-made environment. All, in a fallen world, give us a distorted picture of reality. So, like the navigation system of an aircraft, our map of reality needs constant and conscious correction. Wrong attitudes need to be challenged, existing priorities re-ordered, new values adopted. Only in that way will our map be accurate enough to enable us 'to negotiate the terrain of life' (M. Scott Peck).

God, in his grace, has provided those re-programming opportunities if only we will take them. Meditation on the scriptures, fellowship with the Holy Spirit in us, the re-orientation brought about in our worship together — none of them are new or original. All of them can be empty ritual. But when received gladly they are God's means of helping us to see things as they *really* are. And that involves no less than us having 'the mind of Christ' (1 Corinthians 2: 16).

❧❦❧

Patients tested for glaucoma are shown a circle which represents their visual field and then asked to point out the areas they can see. The disease typically darkens the centre of the field, while leaving some vision on the periphery. The fallen mind's view of the world is like that of a glaucoma patient. Its view of all things is darkened and distorted by sin, but it has a sort of twilight vision of the periphery of life. In the inner circle of ultimate concerns, however, it is in deeper darkness.

Richard Lovelace, *Renewal as a Way of Life*

[Bubu, a tadpole, argues with a frog about the reality of the world beyond the pond.] Something akin to pity filled the frog's eyes as he looked at him.

'But Bubu,' he said quietly, 'the world up above that I talk about is real. I can't explain it, but in a sense it's more real than the watery universe we live in.'

'More real *to you*.'

'More real to anybody, Bubu.'

'But not at all real to me.'

The frog had lost his bantering manner entirely.

'Bubu, the world would be there whether I could feel it or not. It's still there even though you don't believe in it.'

John White, 'Metamorphosis'

Fortunately, truth does not cease just because people give up believing it.

Edward Norman

In 1952 when I was twenty-one and still an atheist study-ing philosophy at Yale, I picked up a copy of Thomas Merton's *Seven Storey Mountain*. . . As I read, my mind became enlightened by the reality of the presence of God . . . it seemed as though a window in the depths of my consciousness, a window I had never seen before, had suddenly been opened, allowing a blazing glimpse of new orders of existence. My mind was suddenly filled with streams of thinking which reordered my understanding around the central fact of God, streams which I knew were not rising from any source within my natural awareness, which now seemed a desert by comparison.

Richard Lovelace, *Dynamics of Spiritual Life*

The real problem of the Christian life comes where people do not usually look for it. It comes the very moment you wake up each morning. All your wishes and hopes for the day rush at you like wild animals. And the first job each morning consists simply in shoving them all back, taking that other point of view, letting that other, larger, stronger, quieter life come flowing in. And so on, all day. Standing back from all your natural fussings and frettings; coming in out of the wind.

C.S. Lewis, *Mere Christianity*

To live in the Spirit is to be agonisingly aware of the contrast between what is and what should be.

John Taylor

For the religious man is forever bringing all affairs of the first level down into the Light, holding them there in the Presence, re-seeing them and the whole of the world of men and things in a new and overturning way, and responding to them in spontaneous, incisive and simple ways of love and faith.

Thomas Kelly, *A Testament of Devotion*

Do we, as Christians, mentally inhabit the world presented to us by the faith of the Church as the real world? Do we mentally inhabit a world with a Heaven above it and a Hell beneath it; a world in which we are called to live daily, hourly, in contact with the God whom neither space nor time can limit? Do we as Christians mentally inhabit an order of being which is superior to decay and death?

Harry Blamires, *The Christian Mind*

At present we are on the outside of the world, the wrong side of the door. We discern the freshness and purity of morning, but they do not make us fresh and pure. We cannot mingle with the splendours we see. But all the leaves of the New Testament are rustling with the rumour that it will not always be so. Some day, God willing, we shall get *in*.

C.S. Lewis, 'The Weight of Glory'

Where is the reality, Lord? Is it in the hourly radio headlines or the beckoning salesmen or the ambition of my friends? Where is it?

I guess it's the wrong question I've asked. I only know true reality when I think your thoughts, look at the world through your eyes. But how can I do that in the face of the onslaught that hits me every day? Who am I to resist those overpowering voices and listen to you?

Thank you for the fixed points, the times to take stock, to reorder my thinking, to see things as you see them. Forgive me for neglecting those times. And even more, forgive me for avoiding the reality I would rather not face. Help me today to see the world in the light of your truth. Amen.

A Benediction
Let the light of your face shine on us, O Lord.
For with you is the fountain of life;
in your light we see light.
Then give us power to grasp how long, and high, and deep is the love of Christ, and to know this love that surpasses knowledge. Amen.

Struggling on the scree slopes

These sufferings bring patience, as we know, and patience brings perseverance, and perseverance brings hope, and this hope is not deceptive, because the love of God has been poured into our hearts by the Holy Spirit which has been given us.

The Lord is faithful; he will strengthen you and guard you from evil. . . May the Lord direct your hearts to the love of God and to the steadfastness of Christ.

We prove we are servants of God by great fortitude in times of suffering, in times of hardship and distress.

You will need endurance to do God's will and gain what he has promised.

This calls for patient endurance on the part of the saints who obey God's commandments and remain faithful to Jesus.

Be watchful, stand firm in your faith, be courageous, be strong. Let all that you do be done in love.

All I can say is that I forget the past and I strain ahead for what is still to come; I am racing ahead for the finish, for the prize to which God calls us upwards to receive in Christ Jesus.

For as the heavens are high above the earth, so great is [God's] steadfast love toward those who fear him.

I call heaven and earth to witness against you this day, that I have set before you life and death, blessing and curse; therefore choose life, that you and your descendents may live, loving the Lord your God, obeying his voice, and cleaving to him.

'Fear not, Daniel, for from the first day that you set your mind to understand and humbled yourself before your God, your words have been heard and I have come because of your words.'

'Truly, truly, I say to you, if you ask anything of the Father, he will give it to you in my name. Hitherto you have asked nothing in my name; ask, and you will receive, that your joy may be full.'

Thus says the Lord: 'Stand by the roads, and look, and ask for the ancient paths, where the good way is; and walk in it, and find rest for your souls.'

(Romans 5: 4-5, JB; 2 Thessalonians 3: 3 and 5, RSV; 2 Corinthians 6: 4, JB; Hebrews 10: 36, JB; Revelation 14: 12, NIV; 1 Corinthians 16: 13-14, RSV; Philippians 3: 13, JB; Psalm 103:11, RSV; Deuteronomy 30: 19-20, RSV; Daniel 10: 12, RSV; John 16: 23-24, RSV; Jeremiah 6: 16, RSV)

Life is not all peaks or valleys; there is a lot of trudging and sweating on the tracks in between, and not infrequent slipping-back on the scree slopes of mundane life. Sometimes the rubble of outer pressures and criticisms, or inner frustrations and uncertainties, not only block our journey, but leave us feeling powerless, thwarted by the trivia as much as by the bigger 'humps' of life.

The problem is (to vary Kipling's words) 'to keep your *feet* when all about you are losing theirs', especially on the scree slopes of fragile human relationships and personal hopes and goals. Israel as a nation, and individuals in the Old Testament, knew the desolation of Yahweh's seeming absence; we can identify readily with their thoughts of discouragement, gloom and sadness, the deep-felt need to tap again into a reservoir of faith and hope and love. There are times when we wish Paul would visit us, to impart some spiritual gift to strengthen us. We would then know the mutual encouragement of each other's faith and a new-found confidence that life is indeed going somewhere. Yet God often breaks into our slippery, disconsolate uncertain territory with his gift of patience, endurance, perseverance and steadfastness. Christ's consoling presence renews again our peace and joy, despite external circumstances and inner doubts. Discouragement then withers and dies of malnutrition.

According to William Barclay, the term *hupomone* was

used in classical Greek for the ability of a plant to live in a harsh environment — literally in the deserts and rocky slopes. In later Greek and Jewish literature it was used to refer to the 'spiritual staying power' which enabled the faithful to die for their God. In the New Testament, the noun or its corresponding verb are used forty-five times, commonly in the context of patience and endurance in times of suffering, distress and hardship.

The steadfastness that God gives his people is the spirit 'which can bear things, not simply with resignation, but with blazing hope; it is not the spirit which sits statically enduring in the one place, but the spirit which bears things because it knows that these things are leading to a goal of glory. . . Chrysostom calls *hupomone* a. . . fruit that never withers, a fortress that is never taken.' It is the quality which keeps a man or woman on their feet, their face to the wind, when troubles and trials abound, because beyond the pain and impotence it sees the goal and purpose of the Christ-centred life. It is pure gift, simply of God's grace; it is waiting to be appropriated and, in God's great mystery, this is especially so when we feel most helpless.

❧

Still the question:
Shall I ever get there?
There where life resounds,
A clear pure note
In the silence. . .

Forward! Thy orders are given in secret. May
I always hear them — and obey.
Forward! Whatever distance I have covered,
it does not give me the right to halt.
Forward! It is the attention given to the last
steps before the summit which decides the value
of all that went before.

Dag Hammarskjold, *Markings*

No. . . climber among the precipices purposely exposes

himself to stormy wind. . . But spiritual mountaineers must; and at such an hour there must be 'some perseverance when we are tired, some resoluteness not to let ourselves off easily', something akin to the spirit of the world's mountaineers, 'a spirit firm and tenacious and ambitious enough to drive on the body to its seemingly last extremity'. There is no such thing as an easy or sheltered climb.

Amy Carmichael, *Gold by Moonlight*

My search is further.
There's still to name and know
beyond the flowers I gather
that one that does not wither —
the truth from which they grow.

Judith Wright, 'The Forest'

Say not the struggle naught availeth,
The labour and the wounds are vain,
The enemy faints not, nor faileth,
    And as many things have been, things remain.
If hopes were dupes, fears may be liars;
    It may be, in yon smoke concealed,
Your comrades chase e'en now the fliers,
    And, but for you, possess the field.
For while the tired waves, vainly breaking,
    Seem here no painful inch to gain,
Far back through creeks and inlets making,
    Comes silent, flooding in, the main.

Arthur Hugh Clough, 'Say Not the Struggle Naught Availeth'

Archimedes said, 'If I can find a fulcrum for my lever I can lift the universe', and in the same way we can lift the burden of this. . . deterministic world as long as we have the lever of self-determinism. As Romain Rolland said, 'Determinism in the world exists only when one has released one's hold upon one's self'.

Toyohiko Kagawa, *The Practising Christian*

Not a word of praise is given to the disciple for obeying the call [Mark 2: 14]. We are not expected to contemplate the disciple, but only him who calls, and his absolute authority. . . there is no other road to faith or discipleship — only obedience to the call of Jesus. . . The cross is laid on every Christian. It begins with the call to abandon the attachments of this world. . . We surrender ourselves to Christ in union with his death.

Dietrich Bonhoeffer, *The Cost of Discipleship*

Sometimes it is a matter of total perplexity as to just what God is doing with us. . . We reach. . . assurance in the same way that Paul and Jacob reached it – by hanging onto the God with whom we wrestle and refusing to let him go until he pours out on us his sustaining power and his comfort in every perplexity. . . One thing Jacob knew — that he fought with the one person who could give him all life and good. And he hung onto God and cried out in his struggle, 'I will not let you go until you bless me!'

Elizabeth Achtemeier, *Preaching as Theology and Art*

. . .there is really only the way forward, which does not seem a way and which no-one wants to tread. There is no way out; no escape which is more than a mirage, illusory. Go on. It has to be 'in faith'. . . and that faith in God, because human help whether medical, psychological or counselling fails. . . I can just with the tip of my finger touch the sense that God can and does so trust us that he leaves us to shoulder the load in a way which is appropriate to us and the world of our time.

J.B. Phillips

Oh my Lord! Your help is necessary here; without it one can do nothing. In your mercy do not consent to allow this soul to suffer deception and give up what was begun . . . Let the soul always heed the warning not to be conquered. . . if you should at times fall, don't become discouraged and stop striving to advance. For even from this fall God will draw out good.

Teresa of Avila, *The Interior Castle*

God, how we need your help!

Without you, life is like the Stony Desert;
with you, life is like the Channel Country
after abundant rains.
If we have become bare and unfruitful,
like a neglected paddock,
be to us as a plough in hard ground.
If we have wandered in waste places,
becoming lost and blinded in sandstorms,
lead us to some quiet, verdant gully,
where there is living water to refresh us. . .

Bruce Prewer, 'Without you, life is desert'

I don't know why my friend and neighbour is sick and dying and in constant pain. . . I can only tell him that the God I believe in did not send the disease and does not have a miraculous cure that he is witholding. But in a world in which we all possess immortal spirits in fragile and vulnerable bodies, the God I believe in gives strength and courage to those who, unfairly and through no fault of their own, suffer pain and the fear of death.

Harold S. Kushner, *When Bad Things Happen to Good People*

. . .have you ever considered that if you want absolute certainty you must give up freedom, love and hope?

Freedom means making choices and allowing other people to make choices.

Love arises spontaneously and is freely given. It cannot be coerced into being and produced on demand.

Hope can only exist where there is uncertainty. Absolute certainty means complete hopelessness. . . Life must be an uncertain business. That is what makes it worthwhile.

Dorothy Rowe, *Depression*

I go back to the one perfect summary of man's Godward life and call — the Lord's Prayer. Consider how dynamic and purposive is its character. Thy will be *done* — Thy kingdom *come*! There is energy, drive, purpose in these words; an intensity of desire for the coming of perfection into life. Not the limp resignation that lies devoutly in the road for the steamroller; but a total concentration on

the total interests of God, which must be expressed in
action.

Evelyn Underhill, *The Spiritual Life*

Where two or three come together and symphonise ('agree'
comes from the word 'symphonise'), asking anything in
his name, their prayers will be answered, even to the
extent of lifting a mountain and casting it into the sea.
And remember that mountains of hate and fear are as
gigantic and apparently immovable as rock and soil.

Glenn Clark, *Windows of Heaven*

Incarnate Word, in whom all nature lives,
Cast flame upon the earth: raise up contemplatives
Among us, men who walk within the fire
Of ceaseless prayer, impetuous desire.
Set pools of silence in this thirsty land:
Distracted men that sow their hopes in sand
Will sometimes feel an evanescent sense
Of questioning, they do not know from whence.
Prayer has an influence we cannot mark,
It works unseen like radium in the dark.
And next to prayer, the outward words of grace:
Humility that takes the lower place,
Serene content that does not ask for more,
And simple joy, the treasure of the poor,
And active charity that knocks on any door.
It's easy said — I wish my words might chime
With fitting deeds as easily as they rhyme
Yet somehow, between prayer and commonsense,
Hearts may be touched, and lives have influence.
And when the heart is once disposed to see,
Then reason can unlock faith's treasury.
To rapt astonishment is then displayed
A cosmic map Mercator never made.

James McAuley, 'A letter to John Dryden'

---

*Lord, there are times when my life, and my prayers, are like a
scree slope in the mountains — disconnected fragments, rubble*

without cohesion or foundation — and progress with you seems hard indeed. Forgive me for slipping back, complaining, feeling forsaken, directionless. My head says I can't blame you, but my soul is like sparse mountain grass, and my spirit a dried-up creek. 'Patience' and 'endurance' sound like alien words for foreign people, yet others ladle them upon me, laced with judgment, and etch my mind with guilt.

And yet. . . and yet you're still the Lord of life and hope, steadfast in your love beyond all my comprehension. You send soil and seed to bind the crumbling path, and sustenance for my struggling life. Thank you!

And almost before I realise it, you're calling me to pray for other wandering souls — those disinherited long ago, or recently lost in grief. Strange, to feel drawn to pray for others when I'm so weak. . . but perhaps that's your way. It leaves room for you to encourage my soul's sincere desire, for you to inject me with your staying power, so I can work along with you, not on my own. Once more I see that you surely are the way, the truth, and the life.

A Benediction
God keep you safe when the cliffs are sheer
God keep you safe when the night is drear
God keep you safe on the path you tread
God keep and be with you at your head.

David Adam, *The Edge of Glory*

44

Carey was a plodder, too!

I have fought the good fight, I have finished the race, I have kept the faith. Now there is in store for me the crown of righteousness, which the Lord, the righteous Judge, will award to me on that day — and not only to me, but also to all who have longed for his appearing.

Therefore, my dear brothers, stand firm. Let nothing move you. Always give yourselves fully to the work of the Lord, because you know that your labour in the Lord is not in vain.

Finally, be strong in the Lord and in his mighty power. Put on the full armour of God so that you can take your stand against the devil's schemes.

Sanballat and Geshem sent me this message: 'Come, let us meet together in one of the villages on the plain of Ono.' But they were scheming to harm me: so I sent messengers to them with this reply: 'I am carrying on a great project and cannot go down. Why should the work stop while I leave it and go down to you?'

Therefore, since we are surrounded by such a great cloud of witnesses, let us throw off everything that hinders and the sin that so easily entangles, and let us run with perseverance the race marked out for us. Let us fix our eyes on Jesus, the author and perfecter of our faith, who for the joy set before him endured the cross, scorning its shame, and sat down at the right hand of the throne of God.

Let us not become weary in doing good, for at the proper time we will reap a harvest if we do not give up.

Jesus Christ is the same yesterday and today and forever.

(2 Timothy 4: 7-8, 1 Corinthians 15: 58, Ephesians 6: 10-11, Nehemiah 6: 2-3, Hebrews 12: 1-2, Galatians 6: 9, Hebrews 13: 8 — all NIV)

We live in a world of thirty second commercials, fast foods, instant coffee, action replays, crash diets and instant gratification. Compare all this with the fact that we are called to live the Christian life which Paul likens to running a marathon race. It's not surprising that the qualities of endurance, faithfulness and persistence don't score highly in the values of our contemporary society. And yet these are the qualities that contribute to Christlikeness. Could it be that the enemy has subtly set about to reverse our values in order that discouragement may weaken our resolve rather than strengthen our character?

One of the ways I am seeking to combat this reversal of values is to include biographical studies from the scriptures and other books in my reading program. In doing so, I find that the heroes of the faith speak to me and stir me to faithfulness and endurance by the witness of their lives.

I'll never forget completing the gripping biography of William Carey who encountered major discouragements at many strategic points along the way. At the end of it all I was moved as I read, 'He claimed no other power than that of being a plodder. . . Nothing came easy to Carey. He only accomplished anything by toiling at it.' I thought to myself, 'Carey was a plodder, too.' Nothing moved him because he knew that any labour in the Lord was not in vain.

❧❧❧

Perhaps the best estimate of Carey's life is his own. He claimed no other power than that of being a plodder. Some people's lives seem easy. We say that they are born poets, painters or musicians, and they cannot help us much, because we were not born so. Nothing came easy to Carey. He only accomplished anything by toiling at it. His is a record of what can be done by hard work, by a life consecrated to God.

Percy H. Jones, in *William Carey*

General William Booth, of the Salvation Army, was once asked to reveal the secret of his success. The devout leader hesitated a moment, then, as tears came into his eyes and ran down his face, he replied: 'I will tell you the secret. God has had all there was of me to have. There may have been men with greater opportunities; but from the day I got the poor of London on my heart, and a vision of what Jesus Christ could do, I made up my mind that God would have all there was of William Booth. If there is anything of power in the Salvation Army today, it is because God has had all the adoration of my heart, all the power of my will, and all the influence of my life.'

Robert Coleman, *Songs of Heaven*

I have found there are three stages in every good work of God.
First it is impossible,
Then it is difficult,
Then it is done.

Hudson Taylor

What lies behind us
And what lies before us
Are tiny matters compared to
What lies within us.

Ralph Waldo Emerson

Love isn't an act, it's a whole life. It's staying with her now because she needs you. It's knowing you and she will still care about each other when sex and daydreams, fights and futures — when all that's on the shelf and done with. Love — well, I'll tell you what love is: It's you at seventy-five and her at seventy-one, each of you listening for the other's step in the next room, each afraid that a sudden silence, a sudden cry, could mean a lifetime's talk is over.

Brian Moore, *The Luck of Ginger Coffey*

If we are to achieve a worthwhile ambition it will require such a wholehearted abandonment as the orator Demosthenes displayed in pursuit of oratorical power. When Demosthenes first spoke in public he was hissed off the platform. His voice was harsh and weak and his appearance unprepossessing. He determined that his fellow citizens would yet hang on his words, and to this end he gave himself day and night to elocution. He shaved half his head so that he would not be drawn into the involvements of society. To overcome a stammer he recited with pebbles in his mouth. He matched his orations with the thunders of the Aegean Sea that his voice might gain volume. An ugly hitching of the shoulder he corrected by standing beneath a suspended sword. He corrected any facial distortions by practising in front of a mirror.

It is not surprising that when he next appeared in public, he moved the nation. He was speaking with another orator on a matter of vital moment to the nation. When his companion concluded his speech the crowd said, 'What marvellous oratory!' But when Demosthenes reached his peroration they cried with one voice, 'Let us go and fight Philip!'

J. Oswald Sanders, *A Spiritual Clinic*

What language shall I borrow
To thank thee, dearest friend,
For this, thy dying sorrow,
Thy pity without end?
O make me thine forever;
And should I fainting be,
Lord, let me never never
Outlive my love to thee.

J.M. Alexander

O thou who camest from above,
The pure, celestial fire to impart,
Kindle a flame of sacred love
On the mean altar of my heart.

There let it for thy glory burn,
With inextinguishable blaze;
And, trembling, to its source return
In humble love and fervent praise.

Jesus, confirm my heart's desire
To work and speak and think for thee;
Still let me guard the holy fire,
And still stir up thy gift in me;

Ready for all thy perfect will,
My acts of faith and love repeat,
Till death thine endless mercies seal,
And make the sacrifice complete.

Charles Wesley

A Benediction

Now to him who is able to do immeasurably more than all we
ask or imagine, according to his power that is at work within
us, to him be glory in the church and in Christ Jesus throughout
all generations, for ever and ever! Amen.

Ephesians 3: 20-21, NIV

Climb the highest mountain

Moses. . . came to Horeb, the mountain of God. . . God
. . . said, '. . .the place on which you are standing is
holy ground.'

Moses went up from the plains of Moab to Mount
Nebo. . . And the Lord showed him all the land.

The Lord called to him out of the mountain, saying,
'Thus you shall. . . tell the people of Israel: You have
seen. . . how I bore you on eagle's wings and brought
you to myself.'

The glory of the Lord went up from the midst of the
city, and stood upon the mountain.

Jesus took [them] and led them up a high mountain
apart. And he was transfigured before them, and his
face shone like the sun.

A cloud. . . overshadowed them. . . And a voice from
the cloud said, 'This is my son, my chosen. . . listen to
him.'

God has made him both Lord and Christ, this Jesus
whom you crucified.

Let us run with perseverance the race that is set before
us, looking to Jesus the pioneer and perfecter of our
faith.

He said to them, 'Follow me'.

It shall come to pass in the latter days that the mountain of the house of the Lord shall be established as the
highest of the mountains.

(Exodus 3: 1 and 5; Deuteronomy 34: 1; Exodus 19: 3; Ezekiel
11: 23; Matthew 17: 1-2; Luke 9: 35; Acts 2: 36; Hebrews 12: 1-2;
Matthew 4: 19; Isaiah 2: 2 — all RSV)

One of the recreations of urban dwellers is to go for a long drive into the country, or to the mountains. Do you find, as I do, that it is restful for the eyes to have an occasional long view, instead of the shorter, limited view of suburbia? We need these times to break away from the routine of family life, of business life, of church life, and to take a long view, an overview of our total lifestyle. Have my priorities of time been wisely allotted? Have I made enough time for communication with my spouse, my children, my parents — my Lord? Was that disturbance in my life so cataclysmic or, when viewed from the mountains, is it possible that God was shaking my earth just slightly so he could have more of my attention?

Think of some mountain-top experiences from scripture — Abraham, called to give his son, but the Lord's promise, 'I will provide'; Moses, terrified at being called to a new responsibility and the Lord's promise, 'I will be with you'; Jesus, on Mount Hermon, on the way to probable death, experiencing transfiguration and being affirmed by his Father that the way of the cross was the way that led to glory; the disciples on Mount Olivet who were assured by the ascending Christ of his power through the presence of the Holy Spirit.

We are called to follow the steps of the Master up whatever mountain he has chosen for us. A man climbed a mountain as far as he could, then he marked the place, and returned, exhausted. On bewailing his misfortune a wise listener reminded him that each climber who makes a path and leaves markers makes it easier for the next people to go further.

May we each faithfully climb our particular mountain, making paths for others to follow which will lead them to higher peaks. Then may we have compassion on those who are hemmed in by the valleys of spiritual short-sightedness, limited by boulders of self-centredness, trapped by the forest of an unforgiving spirit. May we be empowered by the spirit of unconditional love, taking to others the message of a new view of life, seen from the mountain of the Lord.

Christ of the upward way
My guide divine,
Where thou hast set thy feet
May I place mine;
And move and march wherever thou hast trod,
Keeping face forward up the hill of God.

Walter John Mathams

When you begin to pray aright you are on an ascending path. It will carry you to even greater heights, but as you climb you will become increasingly aware of your own littleness and of the immensity of the prospect. You will see your surroundings in relation to a higher heaven and a more distant horizon: mountains of difficulty will sink to molehills, ways will appear where no way declared itself and the sources of many streams be revealed.

Hugh Redwood, *Practical Prayer*

If one wants to climb mountains one must have a good base camp, a place where there are shelter and provisions, where one may receive nurture and rest before one ventures forth again to seek another summit. Successful mountain climbers know that they must spend at least as much time, if not more, in tending to their base camp as they actually do in climbing mountains, for their survival is dependent upon their seeing to it that their base camp is sturdily constructed and well stocked.

M. Scott Peck, *The Road Less Travelled*

I have often felt that my life was rather akin to mountaineering, with a clear goal to reach the highest peak. There may be a fairly long journey to reach the foothills before the real climb can be started. On the way up, the goal is often hidden from view by clouds, or by lesser peaks, but the original sight of the summit keeps us pressing on, despite weariness and even discouragement.

As I went down from the present peak into the valley between the mountains, I was often shadowed by the very peak I was enjoying. This I interpreted in a sense of failure and this often led to despair. . . I see now I was wrong. . .

The going down was merely an initial moving forward towards the next higher ground.

Helen Roseveare, *Give Me This Mountain*

There is a path of service in which I would lead you where the grass is green, the pastures verdant. No foot has preceded you there. It is virgin territory. You shall walk with me because there is none other gone before to mark the way.

O my child, you have crossed a bridge. Reach not back. Move on ahead and press into the fullness of all I have prepared for you. It is the blossoming of that which long ago was planted and for many years has been nurtured. It is waiting for you to step forward and receive.

As I have told you so often, keep your heart fixed on me. Only thus will you have the needed stamina to keep your own soul from falling into discouragement. Only by my power will you be able to stand. Focus on my footsteps.

Frances Roberts, *On the Highroads of Surrender*

How do you spot a miracle? Just look for a mountain. Look for a problem or a difficulty, because often the first way God reaches us is in a moment of pain.

Trouble never leaves you where it found you. It changes you, permanently. It either makes you bitter and tough and hard and cold and angry, or it'll turn you into a soft, gentle, compassionate, understanding, generous human being.

You know, if you've got a problem, I predict it's the beginning of a miracle, because what is the reason for mountains that God lets us run into? Some mountains are there to block us so that we won't run madly ahead and get ourselves in trouble. If a mountain is there to keep us from going into enemy territory, then the mountain indeed has been turned into a miracle.

Robert Schuller, *Living Positively*

She perceived that no-one who finds herself up on the slopes of the Kingdom of Love can possibly dogmatise about what is seen there, because it is only then that she comprehends how small a part of the glorious whole she sees. All she can do is to gasp with wonder, awe and thanksgiving, and to long with all her heart to go higher and to see and understand more. Paradoxical as it may seem, as she gazed out on dazzling vistas, so glorious that she could not look at them steadily or grasp their magnificent sweep, she often thought that the prayer which best expressed her heart's desire was that of the blind man, 'Lord, that I might receive my sight! Help me to open myself to more light. Help me to a fuller understanding'.

Hannah Hurnard, *Hind's Feet on High Places*,
an allegory of a girl, formerly crippled, now walking on the
High Mountains

Enlarge thou me in love, that with the inward palate of my heart I may taste how sweet it is to love, and to be dissolved and, as it were, to bathe myself in thy love.

Let me be possessed by love, mounting above myself, through excessive fervour and admiration.

Let me sing the song of love, let me follow thee, my beloved, on high; let my soul spend itself in thy praise, rejoicing through love.

Let me love thee more than myself, nor love myself but for thee; and in thee all that truly love thee, as the law of love commandeth, shining out from thyself.

Thomas à Kempis

Lord, forgive me for being blinded so often by the pressures of this world. Open my eyes so that I can see the mountain path up which you are calling me. Help me to keep my eyes on the risen Christ who knows the way I take and will never leave me comfortless. Thank you for your knowledge of me, of my gifts, of my dreams and for the way in which you incorporate them into your greater plans for your kingdom. Lord, I want to keep my eyes on the glistening peaks of your perfect will and your perfect love. I give myself to you again, for you to use on the mountains or in the valleys, as a guide or as a rescuer, as a sweeper of the paths or keeper of the rest-houses.

I praise you, Lord. I stretch out to reach you — and find that you are there, ready to hold my hand. I praise and worship you.

A Benediction
The grace of the Lord Jesus Christ, the love of God, and the fellowship of the Holy Spirit be with us all now and forever. Amen.

46

What Jesus did not say

They did not understand the saying which he spoke to them.

Jesus said to them, 'My food is doing the will of him who sent me, and finishing the work he has given me. Don't you say, "Four months more and then comes the harvest"? But I tell you to open your eyes and look at the fields — they are gleaming white, all ready for the harvest!'

This figure Jesus used with them, but they did not understand what he was saying to them.

Peter was hurt because Jesus asked him the third time, 'Do you love me?' He said, 'Lord, you know all things; you know that I love you.' Jesus said, 'Feed my sheep. I tell you the truth, when you were younger you dressed yourself and went where you wanted; but when you are old you will stretch out your hands and someone else will dress you and lead you where you do not want to go.' Jesus said this to indicate the kind of death by which Peter would glorify God. Then he said to him, 'Follow me!' Peter turned and saw that the disciple whom Jesus loved was following them. . . When Peter saw him he asked, 'Lord, what about him?' Jesus answered, 'If I want him to remain alive until I return, what is that to you? You must follow me.' Because of this, the rumour spread among the brothers that this disciple would not die. But Jesus did not say that he would not die; he only said, 'If I want him to remain alive until I return, what is that to you?'

He said to them, 'It is not for you to know times or seasons which the Father has fixed by his own authority. But you shall be my witnesses.'

(Luke 2: 50, RSV; John 4: 34-35, Phillips; John 10: 6, RSV; John 21: 17b-23, NIV; Acts 1: 7-8, RSV)

There were many times when Jesus' followers misunderstood him. Worse, there is evidence that they developed their own beliefs, theories and practices around their misunderstanding. Then they dignified their errors by claiming that they were acting by his word and with his authority and blessing.

Such phenomena have blighted the church in every period of history, including the present. We are probably all guilty of it to some extent.

After Peter had renewed his confession of love for Jesus, as they walked together by the Sea of Galilee, Peter became curious about what Jesus had in store for others. He enquired about John. Jesus replied, 'If John lives on until I come again, what business is that of yours?' That was the fact. But it didn't take long for the simple, direct word of Jesus to be woven into a theory about the second coming. The rumour spread that John would not die before Jesus came!

So when John was knocking ninety, speculation intensified and the air was filled with anticipation of an imminent Parousia! Some left their crops unsown and unreaped. Some deserted their families and neglected their houses. So the Gospel writer felt it was high time to set the record straight. 'Jesus did not say that John would not die,' he insisted. 'He said only that if John lives on until I come, what business is that of yours?'

Such beliefs are held sincerely. That makes them all the more damaging. Apartheid is held by many sincere people as a divinely ordained order of society. This kind of thing usually happens when law is exalted above love, doctrine above relationships, and orthodoxy is mistaken for faith.

Christianity is not about speculation and theory. It is about loving relationship, obedience and real life.

The main reason we 'go off on such a tangent' is that it avoids the real and costly demands of discipleship.

Sure, it is done unconsciously. It is a way of avoiding the 'follow me' demand. We take a word of Jesus, and rationalise it for our own comfort or prestige. Historically this has led to crusades, inquisitions and the proliferation of cults. Each claims the authority of the divine word.

But Jesus relentlessly brings us back to the issue, as he did with Peter. When the first disciples wanted to speculate about the time for the kingdom to come he said bluntly, 'It isn't for you to worry about times and seasons. These are set by the Father's authority. Here's the real issue — you are to be witnesses to me. Here, first, then beyond. And now!'

We must not build on what Jesus *didn't* say. We know what he *did* say, both to Peter and to us: that is — 'Follow me'!

Happy are the simple followers of Jesus Christ who have been overcome by his grace, and are able to sing the praises of the all-sufficient grace of Christ with humbleness of heart. Happy are they who, knowing that grace, can live in the world without being of it, who by following Jesus Christ, are so assured of their heavenly citizenship that they are truly free to live their lives in this world.

Happy are they who know that discipleship simply means the life which springs from grace, and that grace simply means discipleship. Happy are they who have become Christians in this sense of the word. For them, the word of grace has proved a fount of mercy.

Dietrich Bonhoeffer, *The Cost of Discipleship*

If we were willing to learn the meaning of real discipleship — and actually become disciples, the church in the West would be transformed, and the resultant impact on society would be staggering.

David Watson

History is a distillation of rumour.

Thomas Carlyle, *History of the French Revolution*

Rumour is a pipe
Blown by surmises, jealousies, conjectures
And of so easy and so plain a stop
That the blunt monster with uncounted heads
The still-discordant wavering multitude
Can play upon it.

William Shakespeare, *Henry IV, Part 2*

Cheap grace means grace as a doctrine, a principle, a system. . . Cheap grace is grace without discipleship, grace without the cross, grace without Jesus Christ, living and incarnate.

Dietrich Bonhoeffer, *The Cost of Discipleship*

Lord, when I confess you as the truth, I become painfully aware that there are mechanisms within my being which are there for my protection. They protect me from emotional overload. But I have learnt, ever since I was little, to use them for self-protection. I can shut off unpleasant and demanding thoughts, I can rationalise my own actions and words, I can even convince myself that what I think, believe and do is your will and command. If I were totally honest and open, I would have to admit that many of them are self-justification for my own will. I don't always read your word deeply and honestly enough, I put words into your mouth, I argue from your silences.

I don't do this to be evasive or dishonest. At least, not consciously or deliberately. It happens because, like Peter, I am too afraid to face up to what Jesus is really saying to me.

It's more comfortable to develop theories — even theologies — which enable me to spiritualise your demands. It eases my conscience when I commit myself to doing something which is good — but which is often a substitute for the best.

The words of yours I most need to hear are clear. They are not veiled in mystery. They are really too clear for my comfort.

But, like you did to Peter and to the rest of your followers, you relentlessly bring me back to the central issue. One by one you knock away the props of my excuses and rationalisations until it is again just you and me facing each other. No theories, no institutions, no programs, no techniques, no excuses and no bypaths open — nothing in between. And it is then that I am compelled to hear your two most disquieting words — 'Follow me'. I can no longer say, 'Lord, what about him? or her?' That's none of my business. I must follow. Please help me to be honest and faithful in my following.

And above all, remind me that following you also means being with you. And you in me. Following you means being in your presence, with your companionship, drawing on your strength.

May it be so today — in all my tasks and responsibilities, small or large. Amen.

A Benediction

May the God of peace, who brought up from the dead our Lord Jesus, the great shepherd of the sheep, by the blood of the eternal covenant, make you perfect in all goodness so that you may do his will. And may he make of us what he would have us be through Jesus Christ, to whom be glory for ever and ever. Amen.

Hebrews 13: 20-21 — NEB

47

Networking. . . working the net

. . .God who has been my shepherd from my birth to this day

. . .who has redeemed me. . .

The Lord is my shepherd; I lack nothing.

Give ear, O shepherd of Israel. . . appear. . . come to our help! Restore us. . .

Like a shepherd he pastures his flock: he gathers. . . carries. . . gently [he] drives. . .

As a shepherd seeks out his flock. . . so I will seek out my flock. . . I will look for the lost, I will bring back the strayed. . . I will sustain the weak. . .

(Genesis 48: 15; Psalm 23: 1; Psalm 80: 1-3; Isaiah 40: 11; Ezekiel 34: 12 and 16 — all Tanakh)

The good shepherd surrenders his life for his sheep (John 10: 11), but he does so in order to 'take it up again'. At this point, surely, he re-assumes his identity as our good shepherd (Hebrews 10: 13). He now shepherds us — giving his life for us and to us — in the Holy Spirit.

One of the exciting, even breathtaking, things I'm rediscovering is the immediacy of God: his participation in the day-to-day events of life. Thus I read something; and then someone refers to it, or says something which clarifies or amplifies it, very soon after. I meet someone — and then I'm linked up, often quite remarkably, with someone else who points me forward in my association with my new contact.

We love to talk about networking. It is the 'go-between God', to use John V. Taylor's evocative term for him, who initiates and fosters and is involved in our relationships.

God is always at work. Remember those who asked/demanded of Jesus a sign? The signs are all around us if we are 'open to God'; if we are tiptoe with expectancy as we wait to see where next, how next, he will participate in our lives.

Whether he links us with others; or with himself; or with our own self; or with events — it doesn't matter. In all these things he is working in us. Shepherding us, if you like!

❧

Why do people in churches seem like cheerful, brainless tourists on a packaged tour of the Absolute?

On the whole, I do not find Christians, outside of the catacombs, sufficiently sensible of conditions. Does anyone have the foggiest idea what sort of power we so blithely invoke? Or, as I suspect, does no-one believe a word of it? The churches are children playing on the floor with chemistry sets, mixing up a batch of TNT to kill a Sunday morning. It is madness to wear ladies' straw hats and velvet hats to church; we should all be wearing crash helmets. Ushers should issue life preservers and signal flares; they should lash us to our pews. For the sleeping god may wake some day and take offence, or the waking god may draw us out to where we can never return.

Annie Dillard, Teaching a Stone to Talk

It is true that the ten commandments had a central place in Judaism because they were believed to be an expression of the divine will. Obedience to the commandments is a test of human goodness. But the rich man (Mark 10) adopted a mechanical. . . view of salvation. Lochman has some perceptive words on this mechanical attitude to salvation. 'Salvation is found neither in a system nor as a system, but only wherever real life, freedom and happiness shatter the salvation systems, and the planned and the predictable can be expected to be disturbed.

Resurrection? Judgment? Grace?. . . These incisive questions, particularly the reference to resurrection, judgment and grace. . . bring us to the second aspect of the alienation of salvation in the life of society and the church, namely the one-dimensional view of salvation. All salvation systems and machines have this tendency. A one-dimensional view of salvation enables them to operate more smoothly, 'interference free' with 'painful' (or agreeable) 'precision'. Undimensional man is far easier to direct and control. Herbert Marcuse's analysis of human alienation along these lines is therefore to be taken very seriously. It fits all salvation machines, both Eastern style and Western!

The attitude of the rich man in the story of Jesus is representative of the many good and 'decent' Christians who de facto exclude the 'interference factor' by limiting the scope of such factors as faith, God, judgment and resurrection.

John Pobee, *Who are the poor?*

You need not choose evil; you have only to fail to choose good, and you drift toward evil. You do not need to say, 'I will be bad'; you only have to say, 'I will not choose God's choice', and the choice of evil is already settled.

W.J. Dawson

I told you once that I couldn't really regret the past. But now I do regret it, very much. It's as if absolution and communion and prayer let us through into a place where we get a horribly clear view — a new view — so that we see all the waste, and the cost of it, and how its roots struck deep down into the earth, poisoning the springs of our own lives and other people's. Such waste, such cost in human and spiritual values. The priest says, 'Go in peace, the Lord has put away thy sin.' But of course one doesn't go in peace, and in one sense he can't put it away; it has done its work. You can't undo what's done. Not all the long years of happiness together, of love and friendship and almost perfect companionship (in spite of its background) was worth while. It cost too much, to us and to other people. I didn't know that before, but I do now.

If only I had refused, and gone on refusing. It's not a

question of forgiveness, but of irrevocable damage done. Perhaps I shall mind more and more, all my life. Is this what absolution and communion do to one? I see now why belief in God fades away and has to go, while one is leading a life one knows to be wrong. The two can't live together. It doesn't give even intellectual acceptance its chance.

Rose Macauley, *Letters to a Friend*

Once, many years ago, there was a child of nine who loved Walter Milligan. One Saturday morning she was walking in the neighbourhood of her school. She walked and thought, 'The plain fact is — as I have heard so many times — that in several years' time I will not love Walter Milligan. I will very probably marry someone else. I will be untrue; I will forget Walter Milligan.'

Deeply, unforgettably, she thought that if what they said about Walter Milligan was true, then the rest went with it: that she would one day like her sister, and that she would be glad she had taken piano lessons. She was standing at the curb, waiting for the light to change. It was all she could do to remember not to get run over, so she would live to betray herself. For a series of connected notions presented themselves: if all these passions of mine be overturned, then what will become of me? Then what am I now?

She seemed real enough to herself, willful and conscious, but she had to consider the possibility, the likelihood, even, that she was a short-lived phenomenon, a fierce, vanishing thing like a hard shower, or transitional form like a tadpole or winter bud — not the thing in itself but a running start on the thing — and that she was being borne helplessly and against all her wishes to suicide, to the certain loss of self and all she held dear. Herself and all that she held dear — this particular combination of love for Walter Milligan, hatred of sister and piano lessons, etc. — would vanish, destroyed against her wishes by her own hand.

When she changed, where will that other person have gone? Could anyone keep her alive, this person here on the street, and her passions? Will the unthinkable adult that she would become remember her? Will she think she is stupid? Will she laugh at her?

She was a willful one, and she made a vow. . . I will until I die love Walter Milligan and hate my sister and read and walk in the woods. . .

Foremost in her vow was this, that she would remember the vow itself.

Anne Dillard, *Teaching a Stone to Talk*

The whole business of communion with God [is] so age-old, so irrepressible, so partially achieved, so always sought after.

Source unknown

One of the main purposes of meditation is to expose us to the reality of the Father in such a way that we can become the kind of people who are able to love. His life radiating through us cleanses, heals and transforms us. Then we can truly love in the way that Jesus asked of us. He did not tell us that we are his followers when we are great at meditating and religious activities, but only when we love one another as he loved us. This is the ultimate criterion of our lives, which can be fully realised only as we turn inward and open ourselves to God.

The most basic premise for giving love is knowing the person one loves. Before there can be any real love, one must find out what the other person is like. One has to become aware, conscious of the person's true being, in order to love that very person and not some image of one's own that one projects upon the other. It is altogether too easy to believe that I really love someone when all I am doing is enjoying my own ideal of what I would like that person to be. And probably the surest way of finding out the difference is by listening to the other person, allowing oneself to be open and sensitive to the person's real reactions.

Morton Kelsey, *The Other Side of Silence*

The Industrial Revolution has given way to a revolution in information technology. . . transforming yesterday's blue-collar worker into a fully-fledged information worker and blurring the distinction between worker and foreman, foreman and manager. As the workforce becomes more educated and sophisticated, hierarchical management from the top down will have to be replaced by a participative system of relatively autonomous computer operators organised from the bottom up.

We have recognised the inefficiency of authority to motivate and lead people in the new information environment. We can no longer control people by authority, by bureaucracy, and by rules.

Naisbitt and Aburdene, *Re-inventing the Corporation*

This need for security is basic to all of us. There is no escape from it. The question is where and in what fashion we place the trust that will bring it. There seem to be very strong movements to place it in key elements of our external and internal world.

Internally, as reason begins to develop, the locus of that trust tends to be in the understanding and categories by which each individual orders and masters the world. Knowledge and understanding born of learning are of prime importance, but so are the categories, prejudices and particular world views which we inherit from parents, family and local community. These tend to give us a basis for judgment, especially regarding our everyday life that we must live in the midst of persons and things that need to be dealt with and ultimately controlled. This internal organisation tends to delude us into thinking that we have that absolute control or mastery of our world. But in so doing it narrows and constrains, and in the long run can make us incapable of moving beyond, of risking the novel, the uncertain.

In the external order we look to certain persons and things to provide the same security. It can be money, position and all the comfortable security that they provide. Perhaps more restraining, yet seemingly securing, is the adoption of certain roles which each of us plays and expects those who relate to us to play. There is a certainty and security if I can name who someone is, who I am, and then live a related life in terms of those roles. There is no risk of uncertainty in terms of the future, and a comfortable sense of security is achieved.

James Grace in *Spirituality Today*

The hero is one who kindles a great light in the world, who sets up blazing torches in the dark streets of life for others to see by. The saint is the one who walks through the dark paths of the world, himself a light.

Felix Adler

I search the Psalms —
Those Psalms of David that delighted him,
Learned in his childhood speech,
Repeated to me at night
While the others slept.
None reached, he said, the depths of spirit
David touched, nor built a surer rock
Of song to climb upon. I remember. . .
Why art thou cast down, O my soul?
And why art thou disquieted within me?
Hope thou in God; for I shall still praise him
Who is the help of my countenance, and my God.
He hears my thoughts. Lifting his head
He wills his love towards me.
His parched lips move with mine:
All thy waves and thy billows are gone over me,
I will say unto God, my rock, Why hast thou forgotten me?
Why go I mourning because of the oppression of my enemy?
Seeing him revive and hearing 'God',
The crowd renews its mocking: 'He saved others:
Himself he cannot save!' *For thy sake*
I have borne reproach, his lips continue.
I am become a stranger unto my brethren
And an alien unto my mother's children.
For the zeal of thy house hath eaten me up,
And the reproaches of them that reproach thee
Are fallen on me. For the first time
He turns to his mother,
Mary of Nazareth, on her shelf of rock.

'Woman' — linking us with his eyes —
'Behold your son.' The voice is effort.
'Son, behold your mother.'
His lips part for a new psalm:
My God, my God, why hast thou forsaken me?
Still in the northern form: 'Eloi! Eloi!'
None understands but I. To his enemies
He calls Elijah. To his few friends
He is drowning in despair. Only I know —
Know he controls despair
By giving shape to it, a mould of words,
Finds in undying beauty
Assurance that the spirit which gave it birth
Is also deathless. *O my God,*
I cry in the day-time and thou hearest not,
And in the night season and am not silent. . .
A Pharisee, standing near the cross,
Has caught his words, and caps them, jeering:
He trusted in the Lord that he would deliver him,
Let him deliver him. Ignoring him,
My friend continues:
The assembly of the wicked has enclosed me:
They pierced my hands and feet,
They parted my garments among them
And cast lots upon my vesture.
Be not thou far from me, O Lord!
O my strength; haste thou to help me!
I follow him through the long Psalm
To its triumphant climax:
All the ends of the world shall remember
And turn unto the Lord.
He gazes at me for the last time,
Defeat defeated.
Then aloud, with great expense
Of power: 'It is finished.'

Clive Sanson, 'John'

See me through this day, Lord — me and those I'm linked with.
Tie things together for us. We for our part will tie together

what things we can, wherever it lies in our power to do so.

You have already offered meaning and purpose to this day. Help us to see — and then to choose — authentic meanings, ennobling purposes. Provide us in our pilgrimage today with glimpses of new horizons; and grant us the vision and strength to pursue them. You know that we long to live in accord with this prayer; first, so as to glorify your name and honour your presence among us; and then, so that our lives in being graced by you may have the potential to bless the lives of others. Hear us, Lord, we ask in Jesus' name. Amen.

A Benediction

May the God of ongoing involvement invite you, this day, to be again involved with him in the working of his net. May you see him as the networker par excellence — and delight in the opportunity to drag in the net with him. Amen.

48

The freedom of those who love
(Helmut Thielicke)

When you buy a Hebrew slave, he shall serve six years, and in the seventh he shall go free, for nothing. . . But if the slave plainly says, 'I love my master, my wife and my children; I will not go free,' then his master shall bring him to God, and he shall bring him to the door or the doorpost; and his master shall bore his ear through with an awl; and he shall serve him for life.'

And he came to Nazareth, where he had been brought up; and he went to the synagogue, as his custom was, on the sabbath day. And he stood up to read; and there was given to him the book of the prophet Isaiah. He opened the book and found the place where it was written, 'The Spirit of the Lord is upon me, because he has anointed me to preach good news to the poor. He has sent me to proclaim release to the captives and recovering of sight to the blind, to set at liberty those who are oppressed, to proclaim the acceptable year of the Lord.'

Jesus then said to the Jews who had believed in him, 'If you continue in my word, you are truly my disciples, and you will know the truth, and the truth will make you free.' They answered him, 'We are descendants of Abraham, and have never been in bondage to any one. How is it that you say, "You will be made free"?' Jesus answered them, 'Truly, truly I say to you, every one who commits sin is a slave to sin. The slave does not continue in the house for ever; the son continues for ever. So if the Son makes you free, you will be free indeed.'

Now the Lord is the Spirit, and where the Spirit of the Lord is, there is freedom.

(Exodus 21: 2, 5-6; Luke 4: 16-19; John 8: 31-36; 2 Corinthians 3: 17 — all RSV)

Most Sunday afternoons before I was married, our living room was the scene of a theological battle. My father was an amateur theologian and my fiancé was a theological student, but they were seldom in agreement. The conflict ranged far and wide throughout the scriptures and beyond, but in the end it usually focussed on one major point of contention: Is liberty the basic component of the Christian gospel or is love?

My father contended that liberty must have priority for it is impossible for love to flourish unless it is free. Love cannot be forced or manipulated. It cannot truly be love unless it is love freely given. Even God does not force his love upon a resisting person.

On the other hand, my fiancé argued that love must take first place for it is only out of an attitude of love that liberty can be granted. As long as there is self-interest or suspicion or rivalry, we will try to force people to our own ends. When we truly love people we are willing to grant them freedom. After all, is it not the proof of God's prior love for us that he allows the freedom to accept him or reject him?

It was a circular argument, a bit like the chicken and the egg. Each quality is dependent on the other. In fact, they must be coexistent if they are to exist in any absolute sense. Love is the atmosphere in which true liberty exists, while liberty creates and increases the opportunity for love. Paul tells us that where the Spirit of the Lord is, there is liberty. His presence liberates us from the human bonds which enslave us. He is reflecting the manifesto of Jesus in Luke 4: 18. Does this mean that where there is no liberty, the Spirit of the Lord is not present? That could be a sobering thought. But Paul also tells us that the Spirit of the Lord produces certain qualities in our lives and the foremost of these is love. Love, liberty and the presence of the Holy Spirit seem to go together.

This kind of thinking worries some people. Surely

without a code of law, human weakness will run riot and the Christian's life will collapse into chaos.

Yet love is not wishywashy. It is tough. Our love restricts our liberty and prevents it from bursting out into selfish licence. If we love our Christian brothers and sisters we will not try to force them into our mould as though we alone had access to the Spirit of God. We will care enough for them to set them free to work out God's plan for them, whatever that may be.

Love will not allow us to exercise our liberty in such a way as to harm another, even it if means we have to make sacrifices ourselves. Love will not allow us to be judgmental or divisive. We are not free *from* our brothers and sisters, but free *for* them. In the same way we are not free *from* the world, but we are free *for* the world.

Our love for our Lord releases us into his service. When we bow the knee to him he does not take our freedom from us, but he wills us to be free. We show our love by surrendering to his will and in that surrender we gain a freedom we had never dreamed of.

As always, the truth lies in paradox. The old illustration in the book of Exodus expresses it all. No-one is more free than a voluntary slave. Yet even there Jesus has the last word. We may see ourselves as slaves, but God sees us as his children — free children in his household.

✿

Everything depends not on our merely reacting, but rather upon our learning to undergo that transformation of vision that took place in the eyes of Jesus when he looked at his enemies, upon seeing in the functionaries and fanatical ideologists the hidden brothers and sisters of our Lord, for whom he died and whom he bought with a great price.

If we allow him to give us that vision we shall experience a miracle: will become inwardly free from the other's oppression and our witness will gain in authority. Nothing like this ever happens anywhere else in the world with its law of retaliation. It happens only where Jesus Christ rules and calls us to the freedom of those who love.

Helmut Thielicke, *The Freedom of the Christian Man*

If freedom is truth in action and if Jesus Christ and God are one, then freedom in the life of any Christian must be simply God in action. God in action, freeing the human mind from the need to follow the herd, from the need to despise, from the need to prejudge, from the need to love inadequately. . . God in action on behalf of our release from all that binds us, from all that makes us stupid, insensitive; from all that makes us mimics, erratic half-doers, living only on the surface and in the margins of life.

Eugenia Price, *Where God Offers Freedom*

The commandment 'love your enemies' has always constituted a certain offence to the ordinary human mind. In the first place, how can anybody command me to love? Is not love a spontaneous act which occurs *of itself* quite independent of any external pressure? So how can I be enjoined to love, of all people, my enemies?. . .

When Jesus prayed for them and thus broke through to love for his enemies, this was not based upon an act of will that led to victory over himself. It was rather the result of a new way of seeing, a real act of seeing. . . He saw through and beyond the functions they were then performing against him and recognised in them the real human design that God intended, namely children of his Father in heaven and thus his brothers.

Helmut Thielicke, *The Freedom of the Christian Man*

Why then, doesn't Jesus Christ free Christians to disagree in love, to shun prejudice, to be sensitive, to share the sheer joy of knowing God? Why is it then that the one common indictment against us by the rest of the world is, that we tend to huddle in our parlours in self-righteous intensity over the God who said he came to set men free to live their lives in his strength and his love and his balance?

Eugenia Price, *Where God Offers Freedom*

Four tests of freedom:
1. Are you overly concerned about what others think

of you?
2. Are you willing to become involved in the world's problems?
3. Are you primarily interested in others for what they can do for you?
4. Are you concerned about who is going to get the credit?

Howard Keeley

Freedom is a gift which God gives his people when they accept his love for them in Jesus Christ. The authentic mark of the Christian style of life is that we live in God's freedom and transmit it to others. Yet we find ourselves living all too often not as free persons but as slaves. We fear to live freely because it means risking rejection, ridicule, the loss of others' love. We pretend, posture, cover up and live dishonestly. It is tragic that so many of us who have talked about God's unconditional love in Christ still continue to live closed lives before friends and fellow Christians.

Bruce Larson, *Setting Men Free*

A Christian is the most free lord of all and subject to none. A Christian is the most dutiful servant of all and subject to everyone.

Martin Luther

Pledge taken by the members of the non-violence movement led by Dr Martin Luther King:
1. Meditate daily on the teachings and life of Jesus.
2. Remember always that the non-violent movement in Birmingham seeks justice and reconciliation, not victory.
3. Walk and talk in the manner of love, for God is love.
4. Pray daily to be used by God in order that all might be free.
5. Sacrifice personal wishes in order that all might be free.
6. Observe with both friend and foe the ordinary

rules of courtesy.
7. Seek to perform regular service for others and for the world.
8. Refrain from violence of fist, tongue or heart.
9. Strive to be in good spiritual and bodily health.
10. Follow the directions of the movement and of the captain of the demonstration.

Martin Luther King

When you most belong to him, you most belong to yourself. Lowest at his feet you stand straightest before everything else. Bound to him you walk the earth free. Fearing him you are afraid of nothing else. You bow to him, but you do not bow to anything else. You are God's freeman, for you are God's slave. The strongest persons are those most surrendered to God; the weakest persons are those most surrendered to themselves.

E. Stanley Jones

I love, I love my Master, I will not go out free,
For he is my redeemer; he paid the price for me.
I would not leave his service, it is so sweet and blest;
And in the weariest moments he gives the truest rest.

My Master shed his life-blood my vassal life to win,
And save me from the bondage of tyrant self and sin.
He chose me for his service and gave me power to choose
That blessed perfect freedom which I shall never lose.

Frances Ridley Havergal

Lord God, whom we freely choose to love and serve, we are astonished that you should choose not only to accept our service, but also to grant us total freedom as your sons and daughters. Help us to live in that freedom with love as our aim.

Teach us that freedom is not something to be grasped for ourselves, but something to be given freely to others. Since you do not bind burdens upon us, teach us not to bind burdens on others. Instead let us share the ministry of Jesus — proclaiming good news to the poor, release to the captives, sight to the blind and liberty for the oppressed. Let the year of Jubilee begin!

A Benediction
May God, whose freedom is absolute and whose nature is love, teach us to show the world the freedom of the children of God. May the love of Jesus motivate our actions, and his mind control our thoughts. May the Holy Spirit find liberty in us so that his will may be done in our lives as it is in heaven. Amen.

49

Climb ev'ry mountain

Bless the Lord, all his angels, creatures of might who do his bidding. Bless the Lord, all his hosts, his ministers who serve his will. Bless the Lord, all created things, in every place where he has dominion. Bless the Lord, my soul.

And God gave Solomon depth of wisdom and insight, and understanding as wide as the sand on the sea-shore, so that Solomon's wisdom surpassed that of all the men of the east and of all Egypt.

The Lord was with Joseph and he prospered. He lived in the house of his Egyptian master, who saw that the Lord was with him and was giving him success in all that he undertook.

But the Almighty we cannot find; his power is beyond our ken, and his righteousness not slow to do justice. Therefore mortal men pay him reverence, and all who are wise look to him.

O Lord our sovereign, how glorious is thy name in all the earth!

O Lord, who savest man and beast, how precious is thy unfailing love!

You are, I know, eager for gifts of the Spirit; then aspire above all to excel in those which build up the church.

And now I will show you the best way of all. I may speak in tongues of men or of angels, but if I am without love, I am a sounding gong or a clanging cymbal.

(Psalm 103: 20-23; 1 Kings 4: 29-30; Genesis 39: 2-3; Job 37: 23-24; Psalm 8: 1; Psalm 36: 7; 1 Corinthians 14: 12; 1 Corinthians 12: 31b - 13: 1 — all NEB)

Excellence, in the biblical sense, is possible. It is not to be confused with the worldly notion of 'success', which can so easily and uncritically be adopted by Christians, both individually and corporately.

It is a perversion of the gospel to interpret this excellence in terms of the status symbols of worldly success, which include in our culture such things as wealth, positions of responsibility and status (including in the church) size (of buildings, cars etc.), popularity numbers within the groups we lead, and so on. Rather, the gospel stands against the so-called wisdom which decrees that 'life' is to be found in achieving a perceived elevation in power. The gospel offers fulfilment and joy in the conscious reversal of the values of the world by calling us to engage in the gracious handing over of power and the symbols of power.

The call of God is for us to climb the mountain of true excellence with him. This is the path of self-denial which is saturated in his love, and ours. How different is this call! We are not called to a competition based on frantic ego-activity whereby 'success' is measured in terms of self-fulfilment, no matter who else is hurt in the endeavour. We are called to embrace the 'higher way' of love.

This call of God is also to be embraced by his people corporately. It is hardly the intention of God that we should adopt the destructive strategies of the world in determining how we relate to other groups of Christian people. Our group — congregation, assembly, denomination — has no mandate to engage in self-promotion, or to gloat over the difficulties experienced by other groups of Christians, or to have glib feelings of Pharisaic self-righteousness about doctrine or practice. How can a Christian group ever think it has reached the top of the pile, when 'the pile' is steeped in humility? If the Kingdom of God is the sphere of loving service, of delighting in preferring others above one's own self or group, what place is there for feelings of superiority, or for the practice of undermining others who are God's people?

We are the people of the rainbow, the children of promise. We live in the tension of the 'not yet'. We have not arrived. Our dream takes our acting, our loving, our praying and our witnessing beyond the tinsel of this present time into the reality of God's future. We dream of a new heaven and of a new earth, and we devote ourselves without reserve to that dream.

❧❧

If I had my life to live over again,
I'd try to make more mistakes next time. . .
I would be crazier, I would be less hygienic.
I would take more chances.
I would take more trips.
I would climb more mountains, swim more rivers and watch more sunsets. . .   Source unknown

Success is a shining city, a pot of gold at the end of the rainbow. We dream of it as children, we strive for it through our adult lives, and we suffer melancholy in old age if we have not reached it.

Success is the place of happiness. And the anxieties we suffer at the thought of not arriving there give us ulcers, heart attacks and nervous disorders. If our reach exceeds our grasp, and we fail to achieve what we want, life seems meaningless and we feel emotionally dead.

Anthony Campolo, *The Success Fantasy*

Success focusses its attention on the external — becoming the taskmaster for the insatiable appetites of the conspicuous consumer.

Excellence beams its spotlight on the internal spirit, becoming the quiet, but persuasive, conscience of the conscientious who yearn for integrity.

Success engenders fantasy and a compulsive groping for the pot of gold at the end of the rainbow.

Excellence brings us to reality, and a deep gratitude for the affirming promise of the rainbow.

Success encourages expedience and compromise, which prompt us to treat people as means to our ends.

Excellence cultivates principles and consistency, which ensure that we will treat all persons as intrinsically valu-

able ends — the apex of our heavenly Father's creation. . .
Success pales in the brilliance of excellence.

Jon Johnston, *Christian Excellence — An Alternative to Success*

Success exposes us to the pressure of people and thus
tempts us to hold onto his gains by means of fleshly
methods and practices, and to let ourselves be ruled wholly by the dictatorial demands of incessant expansion.

Success can go to our heads. . . unless we remember
that it is God who accomplished the work, that he can
continue to do so without our help whenever he wants
to cut us out.

Charles Spurgeon

The highest offices of State and Church resemble a
pyramid whose top is accessible to only two sorts of
animals — eagles and reptiles.

John Wesley

The famous conductor Leonard Bernstein was once asked,
'What is the most difficult instrument to play?' Without
hesitation he replied, 'Second fiddle.' Then he explained,
'I can get plenty of first violinists, but to find one who
plays *second* violin with as much enthusiasm or *second*
French horn or *second* flute, now that's a problem. And
yet if no-one plays second, we have no harmony.'

Charles Swindoll, *Improving Your Serve*

I will seek elegance rather than luxury,
    refinement rather than fashion.
I will seek to be worthy more than respectable,
    wealthy and not rich.
I will study hard, think quietly,
    talk gently, act frankly.
I will listen to stars and birds,
    babes and sages, with an open heart.
I will bear all things cheerfully, do all things
    bravely await occasions and hurry never.
In a word I will let the spiritual, unbidden
    and unconscious grow up through the common.

William Ellery Channing, 'My Symphony'

Lord, I find it difficult to accept that you accept me without reserve in Christ, and that you delight to embrace me as a father welcomes his prodigal child. Help me to experience that acceptance deep within, and to relish your presence. Deliver me from thinking that I have to prove myself, whether to you, or to others, or to myself.

Grant me an openness of spirit so that I can be freed of the shackles of self-expectation and take whatever risks you desire for me today.

I confess that self-promotion is a sin which clings so closely, and I claim your forgiveness and the gift of your self-giving Spirit.

Be pleased to renew us with a fresh compassion for others in need, and a new desire and ability to share our wealth, power and status symbols.

Hear my cry for a deeper love for you and for my neighbour.

A Benediction
Lord, enable us to show a deeply generous attitude to all we meet, serve, love and listen to, in the name of the Father, the Son and the Holy Spirit. Amen.

50

Holy bravado

In the small hours Jesus went out to them, walking on the water of the lake. When the disciples caught sight of him walking on the water they were terrified. 'It's a ghost!' they said, and screamed with fear. But at once Jesus spoke to them. 'It's all right! It's myself, don't be afraid!' 'Lord, if it's really you,' said Peter, 'tell me to come to you on the water.' 'Come on, then,' replied Jesus. Peter stepped down from the boat and did walk on the water, making for Jesus. But when he saw the fury of the wind he panicked and began to sink, calling out, 'Lord save me!' At once Jesus reached out his hand and caught him, saying, 'You little-faith! What made you lose your nerve like that?'

'If you can do anything, please take pity on us and help us.' 'If you can do anything!' retorted Jesus. 'Everything is possible to the one who believes.' 'I do believe,' the boy's father burst out. 'Help me to believe more!'

Shadrach, Meshach, and Abednego answered, 'Your Majesty, we will not try to defend ourselves. If the God whom we serve is able to save us from the blazing furnace and from your power, then he will. But even if he doesn't, Your Majesty may be sure that we will not worship your god, and we will not bow down to the gold statue that you have set up.'

(Matthew 14: 25-31, Phillips; Mark 9: 23-24, Phillips; Daniel 3: 16-18, GNB)

It must have been painful for Peter to be reminded of the times when he goofed!

In fact it is one of the subtle miracles of the New Testament, that the stories of Peter's failure became incorporated in the Gospel accounts. Surely they should have been edited out! At the time of the compilation of Matthew's Gospel, Peter had been a respected figure in the church. He had a reputation for strong leadership. The flocks looked to him for pastoral wisdom. He was a rock on which Christian communities depended for stability.

In Matthew 14 we have the embarrassing story of Peter climbing out of the boat with holy bravado, then sinking in the waters of his panic. It's all so unbecoming!

Certainly the story would have been encouraging to the young churches experiencing the first fierce winds of persecution. The account reminded them that in the midst of such storms the Lord Christ would come to them through the storm. He was never far away even though his people may have felt alone and unprotected.

It was so typically impulsive of Peter: 'Lord, let me come to you on the water.' It was bold, rash and enthusiastic. If he'd thought a moment more he may have stayed in the boat. But Jesus' coming to them made him feel confident. A kind of brash faith.

It was not the kind of thing we would do. . . surely! We'd need to weigh it up carefully, taking soundings, put it to the vote, call for a feasibility study, test the idea in controlled conditions!

But Peter failed. Spectacularly. His confidence could not keep him afloat. And with wise theological hindsight we nod our heads and damn him for lack of trust. It was foolhardy anyhow, we tell him.

The feeling is familiar. We've dreamed of making a mark for God. Our ardour for his kingdom encouraged us to take bold steps for him. But then we lost our nerve and the initiative failed.

So, once bitten, next time we are more careful. And we become tentative, a little less enthusiastic about the kingdom. Our love becomes tepid. We begin to feel that we are not quite as keen to do *anything* our Lord may want us to do. Perhaps *almost* anything. . . given the right situation and if the project seems viable. We cool off. We become formal. Our Christianity loses its sense of adventure.

It's not safe outside the boat, you see.

Good for you, Peter. You had a go. You failed, that's true. So what?

At least you got out of the boat!

❦

I find that your will knows no end in me. And when old words die out on the tongue new melodies break forth from the heart.

Rabindranath Tagore

Keep your feet on the ground, but let your heart soar as high as it will. Refuse to be average or to surrender to the chill of your spiritual environment.

A.W. Tozer, The Root of the Righteous

He was a gambler, too. . .
And, sitting down, they watched him there,
The soldiers did;
There, while they played with dice,
He made his sacrifice,
And died upon the cross to rid
God's world of sin.
He was a gambler, too, my Christ,
He took his life and threw
It for the world redeemed.
And ere his agony was done,
Before the westering sun went down,
Crowning that day with its crimson crown,
He knew that he had won.

G.A. Studdart Kennedy, The Unutterable Beauty

Nothing before, nothing behind;
  The steps of faith
Fall on the seeming void, and find
  The rock beneath.

John Greenleaf Whittier

Not daring to care,
Not caring to share;
Not seeing a want,
Not wanting to know;
Not trying to think,
Not thinking to try;
Not hearing a cry,
Not crying for change;
Not living a hope,
Never hoping to live.
. . . Dare to Live!

Chris Ledger

On the earlier occasion of storm on the lake, Jesus had been with them in the ship. Now he withdraws, as though to teach them to battle alone and to rely upon an aid they could not see; he sends them into the tumult and darkness without his visible presence. God often does this. It is his will that we should grow to spiritual maturity and trust where we cannot see. Too often in such situations of testing, past lessons are forgotten, and fear banishes faith. But God is always in the shadows, keeping watch over his own. We have only to cry out and he is by our side.

E.M. Blaiklock, *Bible Characters and Doctrines*

Risk means the refusal to be shaped by the world as it is. It is a refusal to be cowed by tradition, realism, 'the facts' or social pressure. It is an act of freedom and a breaking of bondage. It is an insistence on reopening situations that appear closed, on following a third alternative when only two seem to be available. . . Maybe the situation is closed. But maybe not! If God himself can enter human history in Jesus Christ, if God can carry out the Great Miracle, the resurrection from the dead, then anything is possible.

David W. Gill, *Peter the Rock*

If someone had come up to Jesus when he was on the cross and asked him if he hurt, he might have answered, like the man in the old joke, 'Only when I laugh.' But he wouldn't have been joking. Faith dies, as it lives, laughing.

Faith is better understood as a verb than as a noun, as a process than as a possession. It is on-again-off-again rather than once-and-for-all. Faith is not being sure where you're going but going anyway. A journey without maps.

Frederick Buechner, Wishful Thinking

Life opens up. Instead of the stuffy, ponderous life of Ur in the Chaldees — rich, oppressive, monotonous — there is a wind-blown life in the austere desert, a place that is empty of human achievement, but full of opportunity to respond to the great invisibles of grace and love and hope. Life becomes adventure, growth, exploration, faith.

Abraham was the person for whom the invisible was more real than the visible. What God said to him was more important than what others said about him. He chose to live extravagantly and recklessly by promise rather than cautiously on a guaranteed income from the Chaldean banks. He chose to live the free life.

Eugene Peterson, Travelling Light

Half of the failures in life arise from pulling in one's horse as he is leaping.

Julius and Augustus Hare, Guesses at Truth

It is faith that lifts us up to heaven. It is faith that saves us from the flood tide of fear. It is faith that sets us free from our prisons, extinguishes the burning fire that threatens us, feeds us when we are hungry, raises us from death and makes nobodies into somebodies.

Aphraates of Persis

Those who are free to fail are the most free. Fear of failure inhibits freedom; the freedom to fail encourages it. The life of faith encourages the risk-taking that frequently results in failure, for it encourages human ventures into crisis and the unknown. When we are in situations where we are untested (like Peter at the arrest of Jesus) or un-accustomed (like Peter on the Mount of Transfiguration), we are sometimes going to fail, sometimes ignominiously. These failures, though, are never disasters because they become the means by which we realise new depths of our humanity and new vistas of divine grace.

Eugene Peterson, *Travelling Light*

Nothing ventured,
Nothing gained.

Old proverb

Have faith. The faith that uproots trees, moves mountains, calms the sea, extinguishes fire, heals the sick, raises the dead. Have faith. Live selflessly while others are trying to profit from everything. Be poor, while others are thinking only about increasing their wealth. Work, while others are neglecting their duties. Serve the people, while others are just wanting to be served. Be charitable, while others are thinking only about themselves. Stay in the shadow, while others are striving to glitter in the limelight. Have faith.

Father Malinski

May we live our lives conscious of our past and true to our heritage, keeping ablaze the fires our prophets lit.

May we, like our fathers, still stand out against the multitude, protesting with all our might against its follies and its fears.

May a divine discontent give colour to our dreams, and a passion for holy heresy set the tone of our thoughts.

May the soul of the rebel still throb in us as it throbbed in our forefathers that, refusing to be silenced, we may take the part of those without a voice.

And may our ultimate loyalty be only to you, that we may never surrender to the threat of falsehood, or capitulate to the idols, caesars and powers of this world.

Terry Falla, *Be our Freedom Lord*

Save me Lord, I'm sinking!
I'm sinking. . .
in trivia and detail

> *in soft and safe options*
> *in church politics*
> *in shuffling papers*
> *in the avoidance of bold decisions*
> *in familiar well-worn things*
> *by meeting people's expectations*
> *by keeping machinery oiled*
> *by doing what is normal and predictable*
> *by propping things up that have outlived their usefulness.*
> *I don't think I can tread water much longer.*

Let me know you will catch me and pull me out. Help me to really believe you are there, your arm still strong to save.

Lord Jesus, I feel safe in the boat. Especially when the wind is blowing so hard. I enjoy the fellowship; it's so supportive.

But I feel compelled to ask whether there's something new you want me to do. I'm rather hoping you'll be willing to leave me where I am and as I am. But maybe there is something more.

You know I love you. I've told you so. Do you really want me to show you?

If you need to shake me from complacency and half-hearted devotion, I'm willing for that.

Help me to climb out and walk to you.

A Benediction

Take a step today. Not too many. Enough to know you're heading in the right direction. Keep your eyes on Jesus.

May the Lord reassure you that he is there with you. And even if you fail, be encouraged that he is strong enough to hold you.

Place your confidence in him.

51

Living with ambiguity

My thoughts are not your thoughts
and your ways are not my ways,
declares Yahweh.
For the heavens are as high above earth
as my ways are above your ways,
my thoughts above your thoughts.

We know only imperfectly. . . When I was a child, I used to talk like a child, and see things as a child does, and think like a child; but now that I have become an adult, I have finished with childish ways. Now we see only reflections in a mirror, mere riddles. . . Now I can know only imperfectly.

The marriage relationship is doubtless a great mystery, but I am speaking of something deeper still — the marriage of Christ and his church.

So, then, where does that leave the wise? or the scholars? or the skilful debaters of this world? God has shown that this world's wisdom is foolishness!

How great are God's riches! How deep are his wisdom and knowledge! Who can explain his decisions? Who can understand his ways? As the scripture says,

'Who knows the mind of the Lord?
Who is able to give him advice?
Who has ever given him anything,
so that he had to pay it back?'

For all things were created by him, and all things exist through him and for him. To God be the glory for ever! Amen.

(Isaiah 55: 8-9, JB; 1 Corinthians 13: 11-12, JB; Ephesians 5: 32, JB; 1 Corinthians 1: 20, GNB; Romans 11: 33-36, GNB)

God is mystery. We can never encompass him in thoughts or words. When we talk about God we are trying to describe the divine from the point of view of the human, the eternal from the standpoint of the temporal, the infinite in finite terms, the absolute from the severely limited perspective of the relative.

Rudolf Otto describes the sacred as 'mysterium tremendum et fascinans', the awe-inspiring mystery which fascinates us. We are tempted to hide from the fearful majesty of God, but also to gaze in wonder at his loveliness.

We encounter mystery in the descriptions of the ways of God in the Bible, in the sacraments, liturgies and rites of the church, in nature, and in the events of history. Mystery pervades the whole of reality. Indeed, true knowledge and freedom are not possible without an experience of mystery.

In the languages of literature, art, music, we touch the hem of God's garment and feel a little tingle of power, but God will always remain incomprehensible.

Mystery also surrounds the human creatures who are both made in the image of a mysterious God and who have, by their sinning, marred that image. Pascal says this doctrine of the Fall offends us, but yet, without this mystery, the most incomprehensible of all, we are incomprehensible to ourselves.

So Christianity, says Kierkegaard, is 'precisely the paradoxical'. (Paradox — from the Greek *para* and *doxa*, 'against opinion'.) The idea of mystery invites us to think more deeply, not to abandon thinking; to reject the superficial, and the simplistic.

Prejudice is, in essence, idolatry: the worship of my — or my group's — ideas, even ideas of God. If I know all the answers I would be God, and 'playing God' is the essence of idolatry. One of my greatest dangers is to relax my vigilance against the possibility of prejudice in my own life, or to suffer from the delusion that I can ever be really free from it. We human beings are more rationalising than rational. Thomas Merton said somewhere, 'No-one is so wrong as the one who knows all the answers.' Alfred North Whitehead says, 'Religions commit suicide when they find their inspiration in their dogmas.' 'If you understand everything, you must be misinformed,' runs a Japanese proverb. People who are always right are always wrong. The dilemma is summed up by W.B. Yeats — 'While the best lack conviction, the worst are full of certainty and passionate intensity.'

The key lies in distinguishing between faithless doubt and creative doubt. Faithless doubt, as Kahlil Gibran put it, 'is a pain too lonely to realise that faith is his twin brother'. Or it is a cop-out to save us being committed to anything. Its accomplice, neutrality, is also evil: the apathy of 'good' persons results in the triumph of evil. The worst evils in the world are not committed by evil people, but by good people who do not know they are not doing good. The authentic Christian is willing to listen, as well as to save.

Creative doubt, on the other hand, is 'believing with all your heart that your belief is true, so that it will work for you; but then facing the possibility that it is really false, so that you can accept the consequences of the belief.' (John Reseck).

So faith is not about certainty (certainty makes faith invalid and unnecessary). Its core is the mystery — and the reality — of the Eternal coming into time: 'Our God contracted to a span, incomprehensibly made man' (Wesley). The essence of Christianity is not dogmatic systems of belief, but being apprehended by Christ. True faith holds onto Christ, and for all else is uncommitted. It is about a *relationship* with Christ (and all meaningful relationships involve risk). The true God does not give us an immutable belief-system, but *himself*. He became one of us to 'make his light shine in our hearts, to bring us the knowledge of God's glory shining in the face of Christ' (2 Corinthians 4: 6). Alleluia!

�✿�

The essential difference between orthodox Christianity and the various heretical systems is that orthodoxy is rooted in paradox. Heretics, as Irenaeus saw, reject paradox in favour of a false clarity and precision. But true faith can only grow and mature if it includes the elements of orthodoxy that God cannot be known by the mind, but is known in the obscurity of faith, in the way of ignorance, in the darkness. Such doubt is not the enemy of faith, but an essential element within it. For faith in God does not bring the false peace of answered questions and resolved paradoxes. Rather, it can be seen as a process of 'unceasing interrogation'.

Kenneth Leech, *True God*

'Stage 5' faith involves going beyond explicit ideological systems and clear boundaries of identity; accepting that truth is more multidimensional and organically independent than most theories or accounts of truth can grasp; symbols, stories, doctrines and liturgies are inevitably partial, limited to a particular experience of God and incomplete. This position (i.e. that an appreciation of mystery and ambiguity is the essence of maturity) implies no lack of commitment to one's own truth tradition. Nor does it mean a wishy-washy neutrality or mere fascination with the exotic features of alien cultures. . . Rather, each genuine perspective will augment and correct aspects of the other in a mutual movement toward the real and the true.

James Fowler, *Stages of Faith*

I believe, because it is absurd. . . it is certain, because it is impossible.

Tertullian

Nicolas of Cusa expressed what the human heart had always surmised: all opposites coincide in God. This insight has weighty implications for any attempt to speak about divine realities. The closer we come to saying something worthwhile, the more likely that paradox will be the only way to express it. 'When I am weak, then I am strong' (2 Corinthians 12: 10). 'In losing one's life one will find it' (Matthew 10: 39). 'In spite of that, we call this Friday good' (T.S. Eliot, *Four Quartets*).

David Steindl-Rast, *Gratefulness, the Heart of Prayer*

Most of us find it very easy to hurl an epithet or fashion a label. We like to smooth out wrinkles, sand down rough edges, simplify the mysteries that are threatening precisely because they defy categorisation. There is certainly enough confusion in our lives, we reason. Shouldn't it facilitate our day to day living if we are clear on what is good or bad, who is left or right, what is profound or drivel? The fact is that those who have attempted to nail down or write off mystery end up 'undone' by the very pride which leads them to play God in the first place. . . the Pharisees did not rest until they had nailed an upstart dissenter to a tree.

Donald J. Foran, *Living with Ambiguity*

If you want to attempt to travel through life without trouble, believe everything (be gullible) or believe nothing (be cynical), and don't be committed to anything (be 'neutral').

Source Unknown

Whilst we might deplore [any] lack of openness to any new thing God is doing, nevertheless this is the psychology of the human creatures God has made. Those whose thinking is rooted in 'simplicity this side of complexity' must not be too harsh with others who enjoy 'complexity the other side of simplicity'. Ideally, we are all moving towards 'simplicity the other side of complexity', but we must be patient with one another on the way there.

Rowland Croucher, *Recent Trends Among Evangelicals*

There's a wideness in God's mercy,
    Like the wideness of the sea:
There's a kindness in his justice,
    Which is more than liberty.
For the love of God is broader
    Than the measures of man's mind:
And the heart of the Eternal
    Is most wonderfully kind.
But we make his love too narrow
    By false limits of our own;

And we magnify his strictness
With a zeal he will not own.

F.W. Faber

The ultimate gift of conscious life is a sense of the mystery
that encompasses it.

Lewis Mumford

The most beautiful experience we can have is the
mysterious. It is the fundamental emotion which stands
at the cradle of true art and true science.

Albert Einstein

If they [the ministers of the church] had no doubts, they
would hardly be very good Christians, because the intellectual life is as ambiguous as the moral life. . . The
element of doubt is an element of faith itself. . . What
the church should do is to accept someone who says that
the faith for which the church stands is a matter of one's
ultimate concern. . . Dogma should not be abolished, but
interpreted in such a way that it is no longer a suppressive
power which produces dishonesty or flight.

Paul Tillich, *A History of Christian Thought*

At ebb tide I wrote
A line upon the sand
And gave it all my heart
And all my soul.
At flood tide I returned
To read what I had inscribed
And found my ignorance upon the shore.

Kahlil Gibran

---

*Lord God, the God of security and the enemy of security too; I
come to you, confused, needing the reassurance of your gracious
acceptance; broken, needing your healing — or else the promise
of your presence; thirsting for reality, to the fountain of life;
desolate, yearning for a loving touch as from a parent.*

Help me to love you above everything else; to trust your

goodness when I do not understand your ways, to affirm your constancy in spite of my fickleness; my times are in your hands.

Eternal God, the light of the minds that know you, the joy of the hearts that love you, and the strength of the wills that serve you; grant that I may know you, that I may truly love you, and so to love you that I may fully serve you, whom to serve is perfect freedom, in Jesus Christ our Lord. Amen.

St Augustine of Hippo

In this day, may my thoughts, words and deeds betray a little more of your image in me, less of the influence of the world, the flesh and the devil, so that all I meet I shall treat as Christ and be as Christ to them. Amen.

A Benediction
Knowing the love of Christ, which is beyond knowledge, [may] you be filled with the utter fullness of God (Ephesians 3: 19, JB).

Dreams and visions

Where there is no vision, the people perish.

And the Lord answered me: 'Write the vision; make it plain upon tablets, so he may run who reads it. For still the vision awaits its time; it hastens to the end — it will not lie. If it seems slow, wait for it; it will surely come, it will not delay.'

Now Joseph had a dream, and when he told it to his brothers they only hated him the more. He said to them, 'Hear this dream which I have dreamed: behold, we were binding sheaves in the field, and lo, my sheaf arose and stood upright; and behold, your sheaves gathered round it, and bowed down to my sheaf.'. . . They said to one another, 'Here comes this dreamer. Come now, let us kill him and throw him into one of the pits; then we shall say that a wild beast has devoured him, and we shall see what will become of his dreams.'

But as he considered this, behold, an angel of the Lord appeared to him in a dream, saying, 'Joseph, son of David, do not fear to take Mary your wife, for that which is conceived in her is of the Holy Spirit; she will bear a son, and you shall call his name Jesus, for he will save his people from their sins.'

(Proverbs 29: 18, KJV; Habakkuk 2: 2-3, RSV; Genesis 37: 5-7, 19-20, RSV; Matthew 1: 20-21, RSV)

'Here comes this dreamer.' Joseph is remembered in the biblical story as a dreamer and interpreter of dreams. He sees what others cannot yet see and pictures what others cannot yet imagine. In his dreaming he is the bearer of a divine vision; the vision of God's new future which is of God's new future which is about to break into the history of Israel and transform it.

In something like this sense, Christians are called to be dreamers, people captured and captivated by the vision of the new creation which God is working in history. We are bearers of the dream of the kingdom which was incarnate in Jesus and which has been reflected and refracted, forgotten and recovered, in all the generations since. Until now, in our time, we become visionaries of God's justice and mercy, seers of God's love and peace.

But the dream is threatening. The dreamer dangerous. Joseph's brothers react angrily to his dream of the sheaves (and the stars, the sun and the moon!). They want to be rid of him and his troublesome visions. 'Come let us kill him,' they say.

The revelation of God always meets with resistance. For the dream of God's coming future inevitably challenges the finitude and fallibility of our present realities and complacencies. It happened to Jesus, whose coming into the world was announced by the angel to that other Joseph in another dream. Jesus, God's self-revelation, his dream incarnate, precipitated the same violent reaction.

'Come, let us kill him before his dream undoes the world as we know it and control it.' Every disciple thereafter who has sought to become a secondary bearer of the vision of Christ has found the same: to be a dreamer after God's heart means to take up a cross.

'And we shall see what shall become of his dreams.' There is irony in these last words of the brothers. They were determined that Joseph's dream would come to nothing and so leave their world unchallenged and untouched. But their very actions against him became the impetus that set in motion that long journey which took Joseph to Egypt and to power; power which, years later, put him in a position to supply food and shelter to his family now in desperate need. The sheaves *did* come and bow down. The vision was fulfilled. God's revelation reaches its goal even — indeed especially — through the cross.

But how strangely. Never for a moment did the young (and arrogant!) dreamer suspect the tortuous dance his dream would lead him. The rejection of his family, the faked death, the horrible pit, the slave auction, refugee status in Egypt, poverty, false accusation, sexual harassment, prison, the threat of execution, years of hard labour. All this lay between the dream and its fulfilment. And only in the treading out of that journey did the vision prove its power.

So it was with Jesus. Announced in the initial dream as 'saviour of his people', he had to make that long journey from Nazareth to Calvary before the vision declared itself finally, bursting forth on resurrection morning in unquenchable light and irrepressible life.

Vision, conflict, sacrifice, fulfilment. These are the dynamics of revelation in the world. And they are the dynamics we will discover when we venture to take up the dream, the dream of God's grace and truth in the person of Jesus Christ.

❧❧

Be thou my vision, O Lord of my heart,
Be all else but naught to me, save that thou art;
Be thou my best thought in the day and the night,
Both waking and sleeping, thy presence my light.

Ancient Irish

The world is charged with the grandeur of God.
　It will flame out, like shining from shook foil;
　It gathers to a greatness, like the ooze of oil
Crushed. Why do men then now not reck his rod?
Generations have trod, have trod, have trod;
　And all is seared with trade; bleared, smeared with toil;
　And wears man's smudge and shares man's smell: the soil
Is bare now, nor can foot feel, being shod.

And for all this, nature is never spent;
　There lives the dearest freshness deep down things;
And though the last lights off the black West went
　Oh, morning, at the brown brink eastward, springs —
Because the Holy Ghost over the bent

World broods with warm breast and with ah! bright
wings.

Gerard Manley Hopkins, 'God's Grandeur'

When we are open we find that the depths of ourselves
are revealed to us. God presents us with ourselves, and
then, as we work with him to understand and grow, he
draws us closer to himself. Dreams and the understanding
of them seem to be one way in which God pours out his
love upon us and helps us become what we are capable
of becoming.

Morton Kelsey, *Dreams: A Way to Listen to God*

Of course, the great change that has overtaken the theology
of sleep is that the ancients believed dreams to be
premonitory of the unborn future, whereas we moderns
regard them rather as uprisings from the half-buried past.
But this difference of interpretation does not at all affect
Christianity's main contention that God can be with us
even in our dreams. We are too apt to think that our
dreams come to us by mere chance, that there is no rhyme
or reason about them; yet such a notion is quite as much
opposed by the modern Freudians as by the ancient sooth-
sayers. Again, we think that we have no control over our
dreams, and it is indeed true that we have no direct control
over them — we cannot, as we lie awake, decide what
we are going to dream about after we go to sleep. Nevertheless, we can be certain that the power which controls
our dreams is the same power that controls our life as a
whole. If we have surrendered our hearts to God in the
sunlight, he will be with us no less during the hours of
darkness.

John Baillie, *Christian Devotion*

The characteristic way of a prophet in Israel is that of
poetry and lyric. The prophet engages in futuring fantasy.
The prophet does not ask if the vision can be implemented,
for questions of implementation are of no consequence
until the vision can be imagined. The *imagination* must
come before the *implementation*. Our culture is competent

to implement almost anything and to imagine almost nothing. The same royal consciousness that makes it possible to implement anything and everything is the one that shrinks imagination because imagination is a danger. . . It is the vocation of the prophet to keep alive the ministry of imagination, to keep on conjuring and proposing alternative futures to the single one the king [i.e. the powers of the *status quo*] wants to urge as the only thinkable one.

Walter Brueggemann, *The Prophetic Imagination*

The notion of revelation describes the condition. . . by which I mean that something profoundly convulsive and disturbing suddenly becomes visible and audible with indescribable definiteness and exactness. One hears — one does not seek; one takes — one does not ask who gives: a thought flashes out like lightning, inevitably without hesitation — I have never had any choice about it.

Friedrich Nietzsche, *Ecce Homo*

Revelation means the moment in our history through which we know ourselves to be known from beginning to end, in which we are apprehended by the knower: it means the self-disclosing of that eternal knower. Revelation means the moment in which we are surprised by the knowledge of someone there in the darkness and void of human life; it means the self-disclosure of light in our darkness. Revelation is the moment in which we find our judging selves to be judged not by ourselves or our neighbours, but by one who knows the final secrets of the heart; revelation means the self-disclosure of the judge. Revelation means that we find ourselves to be valued rather than valuing and that all our values are transvaluated by the activity of a universal valuer.

When a price is put upon our heads, which is not our price, when the unfairness of all the fair prices we have placed on things is shown up; when the great riches of God reduce our wealth to poverty, that is revelation. When we find out that we are no longer thinking him, but that he first thought us, that is revelation.

H. Richard Niebuhr, *The Meaning of Revelation*

A Christianity which does not resist the cross of reality, but rather takes it up, communicates to society the power of the spirit — the spirit which, in the midst of temptations, ruptured relationships, pain and absurdity, gives the miracle of endurance and continuance; the spirit of hope where there was nothing to hope for, the spirit of him who gives life to the dead and calls into existence the things that do not exist (Romans 4: 17f). Faith which stands the test of love, verifies the presence of this spirit. There is no other spirit in which the present social reality can be brought into relationship with the absolute, with God. Without this spirit, the 'fury of disappearing' confronts humanity.

Jurgen Moltmann, *Hope and Planning*

O Lord, for the power and persistence and glory of your vision, given through the ages to prophets, seers, dreamers and visionaries, we give you thanks. For those moments when something of that same great vision has dawned, bold and vivid, upon our own hearts, we are grateful. We pray now that the power of your revelation, present in our history in Jesus Christ, may revitalise our stale customs, challenge and transform our unjust politics and create anew our tired and self-centred religion.

Forgive us the dullness of mind that blurs the sharp freshness of your dream, and the timidity of heart that would rather play safe with the familiar than risk the adventure of a new path. Forgive the inertia of self-interest that beats against the movement of your spirit because it asks for the taking up of a cross in the journey of faith. Forgive us for the times when we confuse the petty dreams of our own imagination with the great vision of the new creation in Jesus Christ.

Reveal yourself to us again, O God. Show us your glory. Revive that vision without which we perish. Let the reality of your kingdom, manifest in the words and deeds and destiny of Jesus, break in upon us and upon our world, judging, healing, reconciling and restoring. Grant us courage not merely to see that vision, nor merely to celebrate it in word and song, but to

live it out in the great and small moments of our daily lives.
And to your name be all honour and glory and power, now and
forever. Amen.

A Benediction
Let us go out
from our customs and our habits
and learn to hope from the Bible.
Let us go out
and cross the frontiers
so that we may infect life with hope.
Let us ignore the barriers,
and look only to the one who breaks them down.
He is risen.
Jesus is risen indeed.
Blessed be the Lord for ever and ever.

Jurgen Moltmann, The Power of the Powerless

Postlude

THERE IS A CHINESE STORY of an old farmer who had an old horse for tilling his fields. One day the horse escaped into the hills and, when all the farmer's neighbours sympathised with the old man over his misfortune, the farmer replied, 'Misfortune? Good fortune? Who knows?'

A week later, the horse returned with a herd of wild horses from the hills and this time the neighbours congratulated the farmer on his good fortune. His reply was, 'Good fortune? Misfortune? Who knows?'

Then, when the farmer's son was attempting to tame one of the wild horses, he fell off its back and broke his leg. Everyone thought this very bad misfortune. Not the farmer, whose only reaction was, 'Misfortune? Good fortune? Who knows?'

Some weeks later, the army marched into the village and conscripted every able-bodied youth they found there. When they saw the farmer's son with his broken leg, they let him off. Now was that good fortune? Misfortune? Who knows?

Everything that seems on the surface to be an evil may be a good in disguise. And everything that seems good on the surface may really be an evil. So we are wise when we leave it to God to decide what is good fortune and what misfortune, and thank him that all things turn out for good with those who love him. Then we shall share something of that marvellous mystical vision of Julian of Norwich who uttered what for me is the loveliest and most consoling sentence I have ever read: *'And all things shall be well; and all things shall be well; and all manner of things shall be well!'*

Anthony de Mello, Sadhana

Anthony de Mello, *Sadhana; A Way to God*,
Gujarat Sahitya Prakash, Anand, 1979, p.134

Abbreviations

Abbreviations of versions of the Bible used in this book

GNB: *Good News Bible*, The Bible in Today's English Version, The American Bible Society, 1976

Goodspeed: Edgar J. Goodspeed, *The New Testament*, University of Chicago Press, 1923

JB: *Jerusalem Bible*, Darton, Longman and Todd, 1968

KJV: *The Holy Bible*, King James Version, 1611

LB: *The Living Bible*, Tyndale House, 1971

NEB: *The New English Bible*, OUP and CUP, 1970

NIV: *Holy Bible, New International Version*, International Bible Society, 1973

NJB: *The New Jerusalem Bible*, Doubleday, 1985

Phillips: J.B. Phillips, *The New Testament in Modern English*, The MacMillan Company, 1958

RSV: *Revised Standard Version*, Thomas Nelson and Sons, 1952

Tanakh: *Tanakh, the Jewish Bible*, Jewish Publication Society, 1985

Bibliography

Other sources used in weekly readings

Week 1
St Augustine of Hippo, in *The Hodder Book of Christian Prayers*, Tony Castle (comp.), Hodder & Stoughton, 1986, Nos. 20 and 557
Karl Barth, *Evangelical Theology*, Wiedenfeld and Nicolson, 1963, pp.6-7, 10-11 and 79
John Claypool, *Opening Blind Eyes*, Meyer Stone, 1983, p.96 and *The Light Within You*, Word, 1983, pp.197-198
Meister Eckhart, from a sermon, 'Letting God be God in you', in Matthew Fox, *Breakthrough: Meister Eckhart's Creation Spirituality in New Translation*, Doubleday, 1980, pp.207-208
John Fowles, *The French Lieutenant's Woman*, Pan, 1987, p.86
C.S.Lewis, in Clyde S. Kilby (ed.), *A Mind Awake*, Geoffrey Bles, 1968, p.81
George Maloney, *Alone with the Alone*, Ave Maria Press, 1982, pp.197-198
H. Richard Niebuhr, *The Meaning of Revelation*, Macmillan, 1974, pp.138-139
Michael Ramsay, *Be Still and Know*, Collins, 1982, p.59
Wes Seeliger, 'I Love You', *Faith at Work*, October 1977, p.23
Charles Haddon Spurgeon, in G.N.M Collins, *The Goodness and Severity of God*, IVF, 1947, p.14

Week 2
Gary Browning, 'Restore', December 1982. Record of interview entitled 'Forum', p.9ff
M.R. Carothers, *Power in Praise*, Logos, 1972, p.98
W.L. Duewel, *Touch the World through Prayer*, Zondervan, 1986, pp.138ff, 142
Editorial, 'Restore', December 1982, p.3
Graham Kendrick, 'Real Worship' in *New Day*, October 1987, p.17
Fred Mitchell, *At Break of Day*, Kingsway, 1981, p.8
Nestorian Liturgy, in J.O. Sanders, *Prayer Power Unlimited*, World Wide Publications, 1977, p.10
David Watson, *Fear No Evil*, Hodder & Stoughton, 1984, p.59
W. Wiersbe, *Real Worship*, Kingsway, 1987, p.166

Week 3
Dietrich Bonhoeffer, *Life Together*, Harper and Row, 1954, pp.76 and 77
John L. Casteel, *Renewal in Retreats*, Association Press, 1959, pp.15 and 17
Charles de Foucauld, in R. Job and N. Shawchuck, *A Guide to Prayer*, The Upper Room, 1983, p.34
Thomas à Kempis, *Of the Imitation of Christ*, Thomas Nelson, pp.42, 44 and 45
Elizabeth O'Connor, *Call to Commitment*, Harper and Row, 1963, pp.66 and 67
J.R.R. Tolkien, 'The Fellowship of the Ring', in the *The Lord of the Rings*, Houghton Mifflin Company, 1974, pp.237 and 243

Evelyn Underhill, 'The Need of Retreat', in *Light of Christ*, Longmans, Green and Co., 1956, pp.102, 104 and 105

Week 4

Mark Bubek, *The Adversary*, Moody, 1975, p.102

John R. Claypool, 'Worship as Involvement', sermon preached 23 September 1973, p.5

Stuart A. Frayne, *What is Worship*, p.23 — privately published, undated

Mary Artemisia Lathbury and Alexander Groves, 'Break thou the Bread of Life', in *Christian Hymns*, Evangelical Movement of Wales, 1977, No. 320

C.S. Lewis, *The Screwtape Letters*, Fontana, 1966, pp.45-46

Ian Malins, *Come let us Worship*, Christian Books Melanesia, 1983, pp.31-32

A.W. Tozer, *Great Quotes and Illustrations*, George Sweeting (comp.), Word, 1985, p.269

A.W.Tozer in *The Best of A.W. Tozer*, Warren Wiersbe (comp.), Baker, 1978, p.17

Warren Wiersbe, *The Integrity Crisis*, Oliver Nelson, 1988, p.130

Week 5

Samuel Crossman, 'My song is love unknown', *Hymns of Faith*, Scripture Union and C.S.S.M., 1964, No. 169

George Goodman, 'God commends His love. . .', *Hymns of Faith*, No. 347

W.W. How, 'It is a thing most wonderful. . .', *Hymns of Faith*, No. 302

Guy H. King, *A Day at a Time*, Marshall, Morgan and Scott, 1956, p.181

Kathryn Kuhlman, *I Believe in Miracles*, Lakeland, 1962, p.16

Alexander Maclaren, quoted in *Streams in the Desert*, Mrs Charles Cowman, Oriental Missionary Society, 1942, p.58

Michael Ramsey in Margaret Duggan (ed.), *Through the Year with Michael Ramsey*, Hodder and Stoughton, 1975, pp.38, 46 and 47

Isaac Watts, 'When I survey the wondrous cross', *Hymns of Faith*, No. 281

G.R. Harding Wood, 'Why did He love me?. . .', *C.S.S.M. Choruses*, Scripture Union and C.S.S.M., 1936, No. 411

Week 6

George Herbert, 'The Collar', *The Temple*, Seeby and Co. Ltd., 1906, p.194

Gerard Manley Hopkins, Poem 51, *Poems and Prose of Gerard Manley Hopkins*, Penguin, 1953, p.67

C.S. Lewis, *Till We Have Faces*, Geoffrey Bles, 1956, p.319

Michel Quoist, *Prayers of Life*, Gill and Macmillan, 1963, p.94

Evelyn Underhill, *Collected Papers*, Longmans Green and Co., 1946, p.48

David Watson, *Fear No Evil*, Hodder and Stoughton, 1984, p.49

Week 7

Leslie F. Brandt, 'Psalm 23', *Psalms/Now*, Lutheran Publishing House, 1976, p.32

Carlo Carretto, *Letters from the Desert*, Darton, Longman & Todd, 1972, xviii-xx

John Dryden, 'Horace', Book III, Ode xxix (translated), in *Dictionary of Quotations*, OUP, 1985, p.194

Richard Foster, *Freedom of Simplicity*, Triangle/SPCK, 1981, pp.3, 123

Archibald D. Hart, *The Success Factor*, Revell, 1984, p.10

Henri Nouwen, *Making All Things New: an Invitation to the Spiritual Life*, Harper and Row, 1981, pp.24-26, 41-43

Lewis B. Smedes, *How can it be all*

right when everything is all wrong?,
Harper and Row, 1980, pp.120-121
Isaac Watts, 'O God, our help in
ages past', *The Australian Hymn
Book*, Collins, 1977, No. 46

Week 8
John Baillie, *Our Knowledge of God*,
Charles Scribner's Sons, 1959,
p.244
Andrew Bonar, *A Commentary on
Leviticus*, The Banner of Truth
Trust, 1966, pp.218-219
Jerry Bridges, *The Pursuit of
Holiness*, NavPress, 1978, pp.21
and 143
Emil Brunner, *The Christian
Doctrine of God*, Westminster, 1950,
p.161
John Calvin, in R.C. Sproul, *The
Holiness of God*, Tyndale House,
1985, p.68
Stephen Charnock, *The Existence
and Attributes of God*, Sovereign
Grace Publishers, 1971, p.526
Cardinal Suenens, in John Stott,
Understanding Christ, Zondervan,
1979, p.144

Week 9
Findley B. Edge, *The Greening of
the Church*, Word Books, 1971
Neville Farmer, Pathology
Laboratory Manager, Melbourne
Brad Lovegrove, 'The Cult of the
Individual', *On Being*, June 1983,
p.6
Quentin Questnell, *The Authority
for Authority*, in 'Pulpit Resource',
Media Com.
Owen Salter, 'Can Church
Members be More Than
Strangers?', in *On Being*, June
1983, p.4f

Week 10
N. Douglas, 'An Alumanac', in
E.F. Murphy (ed.), *The Macmillan
Treasury of Relevant Quotations*,
Macmillan, 1980, p.165
Anne Frank, *The Diary of Anne
Frank*, Pan, 1955, p.111

Os Guinness, *The Dust of Death*,
IVP, 1973, pp.381-387
M. Luther, *Christian Freedom*,
Fortress, 1970, p.30
H.J.M. Nouwen, D.P. McNeill,
D.A. Morrison, *Compassion*, D.L.T.,
1982, pp.6 and 133
D. Sheppard, *Built as a City*,
Hodder and Stoughton, 1975,
p.318

Week 11
William Barclay, *Flesh and Spirit*,
SCM, 1962, p.66
William Faber, *The Australian
Hymn Book*, Collins, 1977, No. 72
C.S. Lewis, *Mere Christianity*,
Collins, 1952, p.116
George Macdonald, 'Love Thy
Neighbour', in C.S. Lewis, *George
Macdonald, An Anthology*, Geoffrey
Bles, 1946, p.39
Stephen Neill, *The Christians' God*,
Lutterworth, 1954, pp.50 and 51
Anders Nygren, *Agape and Eros*,
SPCK, 1957, p.118
David Prior, *The Message of 1
Corinthians*, IVP, 1985, p.228
Ulrich Schaffer, in John Powell,
Unconditional Love, Argus
Communications, 1978, p.83
Lewis Smedes, *Love Within Limits*,
Lion, 1979, pp.17 and 114

Week 12
Christopher Bryant, *The Search for
God in Depth*, Darton, Longman
and Todd, 1978, p.142
Irene Claremont de Castillejo,
Knowing Woman, Harper and
Row, 1973, p.21
Graeme L. Chapman, *Being
Together in the World*, College of
the Bible of Churches of Christ in
Australia, 1985, pp.11-14
William Clemmons, *Discovering
the Depth*, Broadman, 1976, p.105
Kahlil Gibran, *The Prophet*,
William Heinemann, 1964, pp.69
and 70
Andrew M. Greeley, *The
Friendship Game*, Image Books,

1971, pp.44 and 149
Ann Morrow Lindbergh, *Gift from the Sea*, Hogarth, 1985, p.114
Henri Nouwen, *Out of Solitude*, Ave Maria, 1974, p.34
John V. Taylor, *The Go-Between God*, SCM, 1972, p.18
Katie F. Wiebe, 'Alone — A Search for Joy', in Marion Stroud, *The Gift of Friends*, Lion, 1983

Week 13
William Barclay, *The Letters to the Galations and Ephesians*(Daily Study Bible), St Andrews, 1959, pp.136-137
Yves Congar, *Diversity and Communion*, John Bowden (tr.), SCM, 1984
Rowland Croucher, *Recent Trends Among Evangelicals*, Albatross, 1986, p.23
James Dunn, *Unity and Diversity in the New Testament*, SCM, 1977, p.372
David Ehrenfeld, 'Thirty million cheers for diversity', *New Scientist*, 12 June 1986, p.38
Ralph Waldo Emerson, *Journals, 1841*, quoted in *The International Thesaurus of Quotations*, R.T. Tripp (comp.), Harper and Row, p.450
Harry Emerson Fosdick, 'God of Grace and God of Glory', *The Hymnal*, Aylesbury, 1978, No. 359
Arthur Gunn, 'Ulrick Zwingli, the unknown reformer', in *Australian Presbyterian Life*, February 1984, p.31
Richard F. Lovelace, *Dynamics of Spiritual Life*, IVP, 1979, pp.16-17
John Macquarrie, *The Humility of God*, SCM, 1978, p.52
G.D. Matheson in George Appleton (ed.), *The Oxford Book of Prayer*, OUP, 1985, pp.371-372
Stephen Neill, *On the Ministry*, SCM, 1952, pp.112-113
Archbishop Keith Raynor, from an address edited by 'See', Anglican church in Melbourne and Bendigo, March 1988, p.1

Shylock, in William Shakespeare, *The Merchant of Venice*
Cardinal Sin of Manila, in a quote in 'The Age', Melbourne, Australia, 24 October 1981

Week 14
Matthew Arnold, 'A Summer Night', in Kenneth Allott, *Matthew Arnold: A Selection*, Penguin, 1954, p.171
John Bodycomb, 'The Prototype', in Nigel Watson (ed.), *The Heart of the Matter*, Joint Board of Christian Education, 1980, p.61
Bonaventure, 'The Soul's Journey into God', and 'The Tree of Life', in *Bonaventure*, The Classics of Western Spirituality, Paulist, 1978, pp.112 and 144
Corrie ten Boom, 'March 24th', in *Each New Day with Corrie ten Boom*, Kingsway, 1977
Amy Carmichael, *Gold by Moonlight*, SPCK, 1937, p.163
Neville Clark, *Interpreting the Resurrection*, SCM, 1967, p.60
John Donne, 'Resurrection', in John Hayward (ed.), *John Donne*, Penguin, 1958, p.166
Louis Evely, in Charles Ohlrich, *The Suffering God*, Triangle/SPCK, 1983, p.12
Graeme Griffin, 'Faith and Fear', in Nigel Watson (ed.), *The Heart of the Matter*, Joint Board of Christian Education, 1980, p.32f
Gerard Manley Hopkins, 'God's Grandeur', in W.H. Gardner (ed.), *Gerard Manley Hopkins: A Selection of his Poems and Prose*, Penguin, 1960, p.27
Thomas à Kempis, *The Imitation of Christ*, Penguin, 1956, p.38f
Sue Monk Kidd, 'Easter Sunday', in *Daily Guideposts*, Guideposts, 1983, p.122
Wilfred Noyce, *South Col*, Heinemann, 1954, pp.103 and 209
Charles Ohlrich, *The Suffering God*, Triangle/SPCK, 1983, p.118
Albert Schweitzer, *Quest of the*

Historical Jesus, quoted by Davis McCaughey, 'The Mystery of the Resurrection', in Nigel Watson (ed.), *The Heart of the Matter*, Joint Board of Christian Education, 1980, p.28
Vincent Taylor, *Jesus and His Sacrifice*, Macmillan, 1951, pp.255, 257 and 258

Week 15
Dom Helder Camara, a quotation personally written inside the cover flap of his book *Hoping Against All Hope*, Orbis/Dove, 1984
Dom Helder Camara, *Hoping Against All Hope*, Orbis/Dove, 1984, pp.9 and 10
William Cowper, 'Sometimes a Light Surprises', *Australian Hymn Book*, Collins, 1977, No. 55
Hassan Dehquani-Tafti, a poem published in *Bible Lands*, No. 12, Vol. 20, Autumn 1980, The Jerusalem and the Middle East Association, p.325
St Francis of Assisi, in Joyce Huggett, *Approaching Easter*, Lion, 1987, p.51
E. Stanley Jones, *Christ and Human Suffering*, Hodder and Stoughton, 1933, pp.243-244
Archbishop Robert Runcie, *Windows on to God*, SPCK, 1983, p.215
Archbishop Desmond Tutu, *Crying in the Wilderness*, Mowbray, 1982, pp.32-33

Week 16
Eberhard Arnold, *God's Revolution*, Paulist, 1984, p.195
Jonathan Edwards, *Religious Affections*, Multnomah, 1984, pp.3-4
Charles Elliott, *Praying the Kingdom*, Darton, Longman and Todd, 1985, p.78
John Gunstone, *The Lord is Our Healer*, Hodder and Stoughton, 1986, p.48
Joyce Huggett, *Listening to God*,

Hodder and Stoughton, 1986, pp.208-209
Mikail Khorev, in Keston College (eds.), *Religious Prisoners in the USSR*, Greenfire, 1987, p.64
Peter Kreeft, *Making Sense Out of Suffering*, Hodder and Stoughton, 1986, p.154
L.S. Thornton, *The Common Life in the Body of Christ*, Dacre, 1941, p.37
Jean Vanier, *Community and Growth*, St Paul, 1979, p.119

Week 17
Robert Girard, *My Weakness: His Strength*, Zondervan, 1981, pp.89 and 168
Archibald Hart, *Coping With Depression in the Ministry and Other Helping Professions*, Word, 1984, pp.11 and 15
Gordon MacDonald, *Restoring Your Spiritual Passion*, Highland Books, 1987, p.175
Vera Phillips and Edwin Robertson, *The Wounded Healer — J.B. Phillips*, SPCK, 1984, p.106
Michel Quoist, *Prayers of Life*, Gill Macmillan, 1963, p.51
John White, *The Masks of Melancholy*, IVP, 1982, p.226
H. Norman Wright, *Now I Know Why I'm Depressed*, Harvest, 1984, pp.14 and 16

Week 18
C.S. Lewis, *The Four Loves*, Harcourt, Brace, Janovich, 1960, pp.167-168 and 169
C.S. Lewis, *The Problem of Pain*, Macmillan, 1962, pp.7, 47-48 and 96-97
George MacDonald, in C.S. Lewis (ed.), *George MacDonald: An Anthology*, Macmillan, 1947, pp.46-47, 76 and 126
George MacDonald, in Rolland Hein (ed.), *Life Essential: The Hope of the Gospel*, Harold Shaw, 1974, p.54
George MacDonald, *Unspoken Sermons* in C.S. Lewis, *The Brother*

of Pain, Macmillan, 1962, p.7
Katharina von Schlegel, 'Be Still
my Soul', in *The Methodist Hymnal*,
The Methodist Publishing House,
1964, No. 209

Week 19
Matthew Arnold, 'A Tomb
Among the Mountains', in
Kenneth Allott, *Matthew Arnold:
A Selection*, Penguin, 1954, p.131
Dietrich Bonhoeffer, *Letters and
Papers from Prison*, Fontana, 1953,
p.173
Amy Carmichael, *Rose from Brier*,
SPCK, 1933, p.67
Glenn Clark, *Windows of Heaven*,
Arthur James, 1959, p.50
Archibald Hart, *Coping With
Depression in the Ministry and
Other Helping Professions*, Word,
1984, pp.4, 10 and 144
Gerard Manley Hopkins, 'Carrion
Comfort', in W.H. Gardner (ed.),
*Gerard Manley Hopkins: A Selection
of His Poems and Prose*, Penguin,
1960, p.60
Toyohiko Kagawa, *The Practising
Christian*, Hodder and Stoughton,
1937, p.21
Morton T. Kelsey, *Companions on
the Inner Way*, Crossroad, 1983,
p.66
D.H. Lawrence, 'The hands of
God', in *The Ship of Death and
Other Poems*, Faber, 1952, p.60
Bruce Prewer, 'When we are
feeling down', in *Australian
Psalms*, Lutheran, 1979, p.59
Bruce Prewer, 'Searching and
Finding', in *Australian Prayers*,
Lutheran, 1983, p.43
Dorothy Rowe, *Depression: The
Way Out of Your Prison*, Routledge
and Kegan Paul, 1983, p.129
Angelus Silesius, in David Adam,
The Cry of the Deer, Triangle, 1987,
p.126
Evelyn Underhill, *The Spiritual
Life*, Mowbray, 1984, p.42f
Chris Wallace-Crabbe, 'Stanzas
written in Connecticut', in

*Anthology of Australian Religious
Poetry*, selected by Les A. Murray,
Collins Dove, 1986, p.85
Leslie D. Weatherhead, *Why Do
Men Suffer?*, SCM, 1935, p.143f

Week 20
Scott Wesley Brown, *My Treasure*,
Spotlight Music, 1981
John Eddison, *The Troubled Mind*,
Scripture Union, 1972, p.67
Brother Jeremiah, in Ted W.
Engstrom, *The Pursuit of
Excellence*, Zondervan, 1982, p.90
Thomas à Kempis, *The Imitation of
Christ*, Moody, 1980, p.104
Brother Lawrence, *The Practice of
the Presence of God*, H.R. Allenson,
1906, p.37
Calvin Miller, *The Table of
Inwardness*, IVP, 1984, p.22
Gail Morgan, *Promise of Rain*,
Virago, 1985, p.125
Henri Nouwen, *Reaching Out*,
Collins-Faust Paperbacks, 1980,
p.35
John Piper, *Desiring God:
Meditations of a Christian Hedonist*,
Multnomah, 1986, p.36
Sheldon Vanauken, *Under the
Mercy*, Hodder and Stoughton,
1985, p.260

Week 21
Carlo Carretto, *I Francis*, Collins,
1983, p.121
Joan Clarke, *Motherhood Principles
and Labour Pains: Women and
Families*, International Project on
Family & Community,
Melbourne, 1987, p.18
Collect for Ordinary Sunday 34,
An Australian Prayer Book,
Anglican Information Office,
Sydney, 1978, p.266
Maryanne Confoy, 'Challenges to
Faith in Life's Journey', *Compass
Theology Review*, Autumn 1987,
p.12ff
Bill Cosby, 'Time Flies', in *Time*, 16
November 1987, p.52
Anthony de Mello, 'The Desert',

Wellsprings: A Book of Spiritual Exercises, Gujarat Sahitya Prakash, 1984, p.74
Karl Rahner, 'Reflections on the Experience of Grace', *Theological Investigations III*, in Confoy, *op.cit.*
George F. Will, 'On Turning 40', *Newsweek*, 27 April 1981, p.33

Week 22
Eugene C. Bianchi, *Aging as a Spiritual Journey*, Crossroad, 1984, p.220
Clarice Bowman, quoted by Bianchi, *op.cit.*, p.241
Desiderata, in *Encounter* 76, Vol.7, No.8, p.1
Peter de Rosa, *Not I, not I, but the wind that blows through me*, Argus Communications, 1975, Dedication.
John Tracey Ellis, in Eugene Bianchi, *op.cit.*, p.226
Charles J. Fahey, 'Spiritual Well-Being of the Elderly in Relation to God', in Eugene Bianchi, *op.cit.*, p.167
Dag Hammarskjold, *Markings*, W.J. Auden and Lief Sjoberg (tr.), Faber and Faber, 1964, p.89
George Herbert, 'The Flower', *Poems and Prose*, Penguin, 1973, p.111
Abraham J. Heschel, *The Old Person and the Family in the Perspective of Jewish Tradition*, in Bianchi, *op.cit.*, p.164
Lawrence Jones, in Eugene Bianchi, *op.cit.*, pp.228 and 242
Dorothy McMahon, 'Called to be Human', in Patricia Baker (ed.), *Listen to the Wind*, The Joint Board of Christian Education, 1986, p.21
Anna Letitia Waring, *Living Praise*, Marshall Morgan & Scott, 1983, No. 106
W.B. Yeats, 'Sailing to Byzantium', in J.A. and J.K. McKenzie (eds), *The World's Contracted Thus*, Heinemann, 1975, p.216

Week 23
Lucien Deiss, *Biblical Prayers*, World Library Publications, 1976, p.9
John Donne, 'Holy Sonnets VI', from *The Breviary*, p.573
Thomas H. Green S.J., *Opening to God*, Ave Maria, 1977, p.81
George W. Hughes, *God of Surprises*, Darton, Longman & Todd, 1985, pp.100-101
Jolande Jacobi (ed.), *C.G. Jung-Psychological Reflections*, Ark, 1986, pp.243, 344 and 365
C.G. Jung, *Modern Man in Search of a Soul*, Routledge & Kegan Paul, 1978, pp.271-273 (selections)
Morton Kelsey, *The Other Side of Silence*, Paulist, 1976, pp.51, 272 and 276
George Scott Moncreiff, 'Prayer of the Badger', in Mary O'Hara (ed.), *Celebration of Love*, Hodder & Stoughton, 1985, p.18
M. Scott Peck, *The Road Less Travelled*, Century, 1978, p.131

Week 24
Mark Buntain, *Miracle in the Mirror*, Bethany, 1981, pp.82 and 122-126
C.S. Lewis, *Mere Christianity*, Fontana, 1952, pp.161-162, 171 and 128-129
Kathryn Kuhlman, *I Believe in Miracles*, Lakeland, 1962, p.203
Bill Volkman, *The Wink of Faith*, Union Life, 1983, pp.114-115
John Wimber, *Power Healing*, Hodder and Stoughton, 1986, pp. 275 and 111-112

Week 25
Pierre Teilhard de Chardin, in Alice and Waldon Howard, *Exploring the Road Less Travelled*, Simon and Schuster, 1985, p.119
Victor Frankl, *Man's Search For Meaning*, Simon and Schuster, 1962, p.65
Chaim Potok, *The Chosen*, Penguin, 1980, pp.214-215

Ira Progoff, *At a Journal Workshop*, Dialogue House Library, 1980, pp.213-214

David Steindl-Rast, *Gratefulness, the Heart of Prayer*, Paulist, 1984, pp.80 and 83

John V. Taylor, *A Matter of Life and Death*, SCM, 1986, p.63

Helmut Thielicke, *The Prayer that Spans the World*, James Clarke and Co., 1978, pp.155-156

Paul Tournier, *The Seasons of Life*, SCM, 1964, p.58

Week 26

Bohemian Brethren Hymn, in Dietrich Bonhoeffer, *Life Together*, SCM, 1954, p.28

Dietrich Bonhoeffer, *op.cit.*, pp.28-29

Merle Davis, 'Morning Prayer', in Francis Byrne (ed.), *An Anthology of Christian Verse*, Rigby, 1983, p.12

Eleanor Farjeon, 'Morning Has Broken', *The Australian Hymn Book*, Collins, 1977, No. 91, v.1 and 3

Emily Henrietta Hickey, 'Beloved, it is Morn', *The Oxford Book of Quotations*, OUP, 1953, p.248

Eugene H. Peterson, 'The Pastor's Sabbath', in *Leadership 85*, Spring Quarter

Bruce Prewer, *Australian Prayers*, Lutheran, 1983, p.70

Reformation hymn, in Dietrich Bonhoeffer, *op.cit.*, p.27

J.M. Talbot, 'Come to the Quiet', Cherry Lane Music Co. and Sparrow Records.

Week 27

Leslie F. Brandt, *Psalms Now*, Lutheran, 1976, pp.47-48

Carlo Carretto, *The Desert in The City*, Crossroad, 1982, p.39

Andre Louf, *Teach Us To Pray*, Paulist, 1974, p.18

Don Postema, *Space for God*, Bible Way, 1983, pp.71 and 90

David Steindl-Rast, *Gratefulness, The Heart of Prayer*, Paulist, 1984,

pp.29-31 and 26-27

Week 28

Amy Carmichael, *Gold by Moonlight*, SPCK, 65-66 and 74 (words quoted are by Prebendary Webb-Peploe)

Amy Carmichael, *Rose from Brier*, SPCK, 1933, pp.76-77 and 116

Charles Colson, *Born Again*, Hodder and Stoughton, 1976, pp.370-371

C.S. Lewis, *Mere Christianity*, Fontana, 1952, p.170

Barbara Miller and Charles Paul Conn, *Kathy*, Spire, 1980, p.130

Harold Morris, *Twice Pardoned*, Word, 1986, p.94

John Smith, 'Praise or Pain?', *On Being*, December 1987 — January 1988, p.69

Bill Volkman, *The Wink of Faith*, Union Life, 1983, pp.134, 187-188, 195 and 202

Marion Bond West, 'Marion's Marriage', *Guideposts*, January 1988, p.17

John Wimber, *Power Healing*, Hodder and Stoughton, 1986, p.187

Week 29

Blessing at the Consecration of Coventry Cathedral, quoted in George Appleton (ed.), *The Oxford Book of Prayer*, OUP, 1986, p.172

Clovis Chappell, 'The Great Thirst', in *Sermons from the Psalms*, Abingdon, 1931, pp.164ff

David L. Frost, John Emerton and Andrew Macintosh, *The Psalms, a New Translation for Worship*, Collins, 1976, 1977

George Herbert, 'Love', *The Poems of George Herbert*, OUP, 1952

Light through the Curtains, Philip Walters & Jane Balengarth (comp.), Keston College, 1985

Edwin McNeill Poteat, Exposition Psalm 63, *Interpreter's Bible*, Vol.4, Abingdon, 1955, p.329

Week 30
An Australian Prayer Book,
Anglican Information Office, 1978,
pp.33 and 108
John Baillie, 'Night Thoughts', in
Christian Devotion, OUP, 1962, p.66
John Baillie, 'The Theology of
Sleep', in *Christian Devotion,* OUP,
1962, pp.71 and 77
Dietrich Bonhoeffer, *Life Together,*
SCM, 1954, p.56
Elizabeth Barret Browning in
Baillie, *op.cit.,* pp.73-74
Kenneth T. Crotty, 'Nature Has
Ended Another Day', in Francis
Byrne (ed.), *Anthology of Christian
Verse,* Rigby, 1983, p.106
Paul Gerhardt in Bonhoeffer,
op.cit., p.54
Brother Laurence, *The Practice of
the Presence of God,* in Baillie, *op.cit.*
Eugene H. Peterson, 'The pastor's
sabbath', in *Leadership 85,* Spring
Quarter, pp.53-54
Bruce Prewer, 'Vespers by the
Murray River' and 'God of the
Evening', in *Australian Prayers,*
Lutheran, 1983, pp.20 and 76

Week 31
Anselm, *Parish Prayers,* Hodder &
Stoughton, 1967, p.367
Geoffrey Bull, *When Iron Gates
Yield,* Hodder & Stoughton, 1960,
p.188
John Donne, *Poems,* OUP, 1945,
p.299
John Donne, *Sermons,* OUP, 1968,
p.224
Matthew Henry, *Commentary,*
Vol.1, Kensit, p.114
'Iona Community', *The Hodder
Book of Christian Prayers,* Tony
Castle (comp.), Hodder &
Stoughton, 1986, p.51
Thomas R. Kelly, *A Testament of
Devotion,* Hodder & Stoughton,
1943, p.50
Francis Thompson, *The Hound of
Heaven,* OUP, 1948, pp.92 and 94
Charles Wesley, 'Come, O thou
traveller unknown', in *The Oxford
Book of Christian Verse,* OUP, 1941,
p.329
Samuel Zwemer, *The Glory of the
Cross,* Oliphants, 1954, p.39

Week 32
Richard Gillard, *The Servant Song,*
Scripture in Song, 1977
Robert K. Hudnut, *This People,
This Parish,* Zondervan, 1986,
pp.112-113
Leander E. Keck, *The Bible in the
Pulpit: The Renewal of Biblical
Preaching,* Abingdon, 1978,
pp.118-120
Ray and Anne Ortlund, *The Best
Half of Life,* G/L Regal, 1976, p.74
David S. Schuller in *Youth Sings,*
Praise Book Publications, No. 76
David S. Schuller et al, *Ministry in
America,* Harper and Row, 1980,
p.30
J. Dawson Smith, poem on a 1950s
threepenny card
John R.W. Stott, *I Believe in
Preaching,* Hodder & Stoughton,
1982, pp.312-313
Isaac Watts, 'Jesus Shall Reign
Where'er the Sun', in *Australian
Hymn Book,* Collins, 1977, No. 136

Week 33
Annie Dillard, *Teaching a Stone to
Talk,* Pan, 1984, pp.69-70
Freeman Dyson, *Disturbing the
Universe,* Pan, 1988, pp.155 and 157
James P. Grace, 'A Philosophical
Basis for Abandonment', in
Richard Woods (ed.), *Spirituality
Today,* Autumn 1986, Vol. 38,
No. 3, pp.236-237
Morton Kelsey, *The Other Side of
Silence,* SPCK, 1977, p.67
Barry Lopez, *Arctic Dreams,*
Macmillan, 1986, pp.414-415
Rose Macauley, in Constance
Babington Smith (ed.), *Letters to a
Friend 1950-1952,* Collins, 1961,
p.97
Clive Sansom, 'John', in *The
Witnesses and Other Poems,*
Methuen, p.54

Week 34
Augustine, in John Blanchard,
Gathered Gold, Evangelical Press,
1934, p.155
Leslie Brandt, 'Go and Wash Feet',
in *Great God Here I am,* Concordia,
1969, p.62
Frederick Buechner, *Wishful
Thinking: A Theological A.B.C.,*
Harper and Row, 1973, p.40
Charles Dickens, *David Copperfield,*
in *The Readers' Digest,* 1966, pp.275
and 358
Matthew Henry, in John
Blanchard, *op.cit.,* p.156
Jack McAlister, in John Blanchard,
op.cit., p.156
William Plumer, in John
Blanchard, *op.cit.,* p.156
C.H. Spurgeon, in John Blanchard,
op.cit., p.156

Week 35
Robert McAfee Brown, *Creative
Dislocation — the Movement of
Grace,* Abingdon, 1980, pp.48-49,
57, 58, 72, 74, 98 and 99
Dostoyevski's Grand Inquisitor,
quoted in Leonardo Boff, *Jesus
Christ Liberator,* SPCK, 1980, p.98
John C. Harris, *Stress, Power and
Ministry,* Alban Institute, 1977,
Chapter 4, pp.44 ff
Albert van den Heuvel, *These
Rebellious Powers,* SCM, 1966,
pp.42-43, 73 and 84
Rollow May, *Power and Innocence,*
Norton, 1972, p.100
Jurgen Moltmann, *The Church in
the Power of the Spirit,* SCM, 1977,
p.172
Reinhold Niebuhr, *Moral Man and
Immoral Society,* Scribner's, 1932,
1960, pp. 34 and 80
Edward Schillebeeckx, *Jesus in our
Western Culture,* SCM, 1987,
pp. 74, 75, 77 and 78
Jens — J. Wilhelmsen, *Man and
Structures,* Grosvenor, 1977, p.viii

Week 36
Donald Barnhouse, *The Invisible*

War, Zondervan, 1965
John Calvin, *Institutes of the
Christian Religion,* Westminster,
1960, Vol. I, Book 1, 18:1-2, 19:18
William Jenkyn, in I.D.E. Thomas
(ed.), *The Golden Treasury of
Puritan Quotations,* Moody, 1975,
p.76
C.S. Lewis, *The Screwtape Letters,*
Macmillan, 1961, p.3
Hal Lindsey, *Satan is Alive and
Well on Planet Earth,* Zondervan,
1972, p.239
D. Martyn Lloyd-Jones, *The
Christian Warfare,* Baker, 1977,
p.108
John Wimber, *Power Evangelism,*
Harper and Row, 1986, p.8

Week 37
John Donne, 'Batter my heart', in
Sir Herbert Grierson (ed.), *The
Poems of John Donne,* OUP, 1933,
p.299
C.S. Lewis, *Surprised by Joy,*
Fontana, 1966, pp.182-183
Malcolm Muggeridge, *Jesus
Rediscovered,* Fontana, 1969, pp.8,
110
Francis Thompson, 'The Hound of
Heaven', from *Dictionary of
Quotations,* OUP, 1985, p.544
St Ambrose, in *The Hodder Book of
Christian Quotations,* Tony Castle
(comp.), Hodder and Stoughton,
1985, p.237

Week 38
George Appleton, *Journey for a
Soul,* Fontana, 1974, p.224
Cliff Ashby, 'A Stranger in this
land', in D. Davie (ed.), *The New
Oxford Book of Christian Verse,*
OUP, 1981, p.297
Carlo Carretto, *In Search of the
Beyond,* Darton, Longman and
Todd, 1975, p.49
Mary Coleridge, 'There' in H.
Gardner (ed.), *The Faber Book of
Religious Verse,* Faber and Faber,
1972, p.295
Dag Hammarskjold, *Markings,*

Faber and Faber, 1964, p.105
Joanne and Benjamin
Marxhausen, *If I Should Die, If I
Should Live*, Concordia, 1975
Mary Maude, 'Thine for ever, God
of love', *Golden Bells*, Scripture
Union, 1925, No. 331
Thomas Olivers, 'The God of
Abraham Praise', *Australian Hymn
Book*, Australian Hymn Book Pty
Ltd, 1977, No. 53
W.T. Sleeper, 'Jesus I come', in Ira
D. Sankey (ed.), *Sacred Songs and
Solos*, No. 487

Week 39
Gerhard Ebeling, *Luther*, Fontana,
1975, p.256
Jacques Ellul, *The Subversion of
Christianity*, Eerdmans, 1986, p.151
Soren Kierkegaard, *The Sickness
Unto Death*, Princeton University
Press, 1974, pp.142 and 172
D.H. Lawrence, *Studies in Classic
American Literature*, Penguin, 1977,
p.12
Francis Kelly Nemeck, Maree
Theresa Coombs, *The Spiritual
Journey*, Michael Glazier, 1987,
p.196
John V. Taylor, *Weep Not For Me*,
WCC, 1987, p.42
Simon Tugwell, *Reflections on the
Beatitudes*, Darton, Longman and
Todd, 1980, p.96

Week 40
Augustine, *The Confessions*,
Zondervan, 1971, p.1
The Book of Worship, The United
Methodist Publishing House,
1964, p.381
*The Cloud of Unknowning and Other
Works*, Clifton Wolters (tr.),
Penguin, 1961, pp.61 and 63
John Calvin, in John T. McNeill
(ed.), *Institutes of the Christian
Religion*, Westminster, 1960, Vol. 1,
61-62
Baron van Huegel, in Jerome M.
Neufelder and Mary C. Coelho
(ed.), *Writings of Spiritual

Direction*, Seabury, 1982, p.8
Julian of Norwich, in Clifton
Wolters (ed.), *Revelations of Divine
Love*, Penguin, 1966, p.68
Thomas S. Kepler (ed.), *Selections
from the Writings of Soren
Kierkegaard*, The Upper Room,
1952, p.28
Thomas à Kempis, *The Imitation of
Christ*, Grosset and Dunlap, Book
2, p.95; Book 3, p.128
Brother Lawrence, *The Practice of
the Presence of God*, Thomas
Nelson, p.83
C.S. Lewis (ed.), *George
MacDonald: An Anthology*,
Macmillan, 1947, pp.64, 73 and 105
C.S. Lewis, *Mere Christianity*,
Macmillan, 1960, p.169
Robert Robinson in *Australian
Hymn Book*, Collins, 1977, No. 152

Week 41
Richard C. Brand Jr., in *Expository
Times*, July 1984, p.311
Daniel Defoe, *Robinson Crusoe*,
Collins, 1953, p.206
Harry Emerson Fosdick, in
Riverside Sermons, Harper and
Brothers, 1958, pp.339-340
Alisdair MacIntyre, in Howard
Williams, *My Word*, SCM, 1973,
p.35
Stephen B. Neill, from an
interview reported in *The Christian
Century*, 4 June 1975
Reinhold Niebuhr, *Justice and
Mercy*, Harper and Row, 1974, p.74
Sheldon Vanauken, *A Severe
Mercy*, Hodder and Stoughton,
1979, pp.119-120

Week 42
Harry Blamires, *The Christian
Mind*, SPCK, 1963, p.76
T.S. Eliot, 'Burnt Norton', in *Four
Quartets*, Faber
Thomas Kelly, *A Testament of
Devotion*, Hodder and Stoughton,
1957, pp.33-34
C.S. Lewis in 'The Weight of
Glory', in J.T. Como (ed.), *C.S.*

Lewis at the Breakfast Table, Collins, 1980, p.34
C.S. Lewis, *Mere Christianity*, Fontana, 1955, p.165
Richard Lovelace, *Dynamics of Spiritual Life*, IVP, 1979, p.229
Richard Lovelace, *Renewal as a Way of Life*, Paternoster, 1985, p.134
Edward Norman, 1978 Reith Lectures
M. Scott Peck, *The Road Less Travelled*, Century, 1987, p.44
Michel Quoist, *Prayers of Life*, Gill, 1963, p.10
John Taylor, in *Lion Handbook of Christian Belief*, Lion, 1982, p.356
John White, 'Metamorphosis', in *The Race*, IVP, 1984, p.98

Week 43
Elizabeth Achtemeier, *Preaching as Theology and Art*, Abingdon, 1984, p.140f
David Adam, *The Edge of Glory: Prayers in the Celtic tradition*, Triangle/SPCK, 1985, p.52
William Barclay, *A New Testament Wordbook*, SCM, 1955, pp.59-61
Dietrich Bonhoeffer, *The Cost of Discipleship*, SCM, 1948, pp.50 and 73
Amy Carmichael, *Gold by Moonlight*, SPCK, p.67
Glenn Clark, *Windows of Heaven*, Arthur James, 1959, p.136
Arthur Hugh Clough, 'Say Not the Struggle Naught Availeth', *The Concise Oxford Dictionary of Quotations*, O.U.P., 1964, p.64
Dag Hammarskjold, *Markings*, Ballantyne, 1983, pp.1 and 124
Toyohiko Kagawa, *The Practising Christian*, Hodder and Stoughton, 1937, p.30
Harold S. Kushner, *When bad things happen to good people*, Pan, 1982, p.76
James McAuley, 'A letter to John Dryden', in Les A. Murray, *Anthology of Australian Religious Poetry*, Collins Dove, 1986, p.173
J.B. Phillips, in a letter in Vera

Phillips and Edwin Robertson, *The Wounded Healer — J.B. Phillips*, Triangle, 1984, p.80f
Bruce Prewer, 'Without you, life is desert', *Australian Prayers*, Lutheran Publishing House, 1983, p.29
Dorothy Rowe, *Depression: The way out of your prison*, Routledge and Kegan Paul, 1983, p.128
Teresa of Avila, *The Interior Castle*, Paulist, 1979, p.51f
Evelyn Underhill, *The Spiritual Life*, Mowbray, 1984, p.77
Judith Wright, 'The Forest', in Les A. Murray, *Anthology of Australian Religious Poetry*, Collins Dove, 1986, p.221

Week 44
J.W. Alexander, *Baptist Hymn Book*, Psalms and Hymns Trust, 1962, No. 145, verse 3
Robert Coleman, *Songs of Heaven*, Revell, 1980, p.43
Calvin Coolidge, in George Sweeting, *Great Quotes and Illustrations*, Word, 1985, p.201
Percy H. Jones, in S. Pearce Carey, *William Carey*, Hodder and Stoughton, 1923, p.41
Brian Moore, *The Luck of Ginger Coffey*, McClelland and Stewart, New Canadian Library, 1972, p.243
J. Oswald Sanders, *A Spiritual Clinic*, Moody, 1958, pp.116-117
Charles Wesley, *Baptist Hymn Book*, Psalms and Hymns Trust, 1962, No. 519

Week 45
Hannah Hurnard, *Hind's Feet on High Places*, Olive Press, 1977, p.237
Thomas à Kempis, *The Imitation of Christ*, Collins, p.128
Walter John Mathams, *The Baptist Hymn Book*, Psalms and Hymns Trust, 1962, No. 538
M. Scott Peck, *The Road Less Travelled*, Simon & Schuster, 1978, p.167

Hugh Redwood, *Practical Prayer*,
Hodder & Stoughton, 1938, p.36
Frances Roberts, *On the Highroads
of Surrender*, The King's Press,
1973, pp.55, 85 and 104
Helen Roseveare, *Give Me This
Mountain*, IVP, 1966, p.6
Robert Schuller, *Living Positively:
one day at a time*, Crystal Cathedral
Ministries, 1982, September 22

Week 46

Dietrich Bonhoeffer, *The Cost of
Discipleship*, SCM, 1966, pp.35, 36
and 47
Thomas Carlyle, in *Dictionary of
Quotations*, OUP, 1985, p. 126
William Shakespeare in *Dictionary
of Quotations*, OUP, 1985, p.441
David Watson, in *The Hodder Book
of Christian Quotations*, Hodder
and Stoughton, 1984, p.63

Week 47

W.J. Dawson, in E.S. Grover (ed.),
The Book of Courage
Annie Dillard, *Teaching a Stone to
Talk*, Pan, 1984, pp.40, 41, 163 and
164
James P. Grace, 'A Philosophical
Basis for Abandonment', in
Richard Woods (ed.), *Spirituality
Today*, Autumn 1986, Vol. 38, No.
3, p.236
Morton Kelsey, *The Other Side of
Silence*, SPCK, 1977, p.165
Rose Macauley, in Constance
Babington Smith (ed.), *Letters to a
Friend — 1950-1952*, Collins, 1961,
pp.61-62
Naisbitt and Aburdene,
Re-inventing the Corporation,
Macdonald, 1986, pp.100-101
John S. Pobee, *Who are the poor?*,
WCC Publications, 1987, pp.34-35
Clive Sansom, *The Witnesses and
other poems*, Methuen, pp.52-53

Week 48

Frances Ridley Havergal, 'I love, I
love my Master', Keswick Hymn
Book, Marshall Morgan and Scott,

No. 52
E. Stanley Jones, *The Way to Power
and Poise*, Hodder and Stoughton,
1950, p.73
Howard Keeley, in Bruce Larson,
Setting Men Free, Zondervan, 1967
Martin Luther King, in Kenneth
Slack, *Martin Luther King*, SCM,
1970, pp.76-77
Bruce Larson, *op cit.*, pp.81-82
Martin Luther, in Frank S. Mead
(ed.), *Encyclopedia of Religious
Quotations*, Peter Davies, 1965,
p.404
Eugenia Price, *Where God Offers
Freedom*, Oliphants, 1966, pp.30-31
and 186
Helmut Thielicke, *The Freedom of
the Christian Man*, 1963, pp.218
and 131-132

Week 49

Anthony Campolo, *The Success
Fantasy*, Victor, 1980, p.9
William Ellery Channing, in Jon
Johnston, *Christian Excellence —
An Alternative to Success*, Baker,
1985, p.104
Charles Spurgeon, in J. Oswald
Sanders, *Spiritual Leadership*,
Moody, 1967, p.23
Charles Swindoll, *Improving Your
Serve*, Word Books, 1981, p.34
John Wesley, in Johnston, *op.cit.*,
p.29

Week 50

Aphraates of Persis, as
paraphrased by David Winter, in
Faith under Fire, Harold Shaw,
1977, p.18
E.M. Blaiklock, *Bible Characters and
Doctrines*, Vol II, Scripture Union,
1974, p.32
Frederick Buechner, *Wishful
Thinking*, Harper and Row, 1973,
p.25
Terry Falla, *Be our freedom Lord*,
Lutheran, 1981, p.172
David W. Gill, *Peter the Rock*, IVP,
1986, p.60
John Greenleaf Whittier in

Treasury of Religious Verse, Fleming
Revell, 1966, p.174
Julius and Augustus Hare,
'Guesses at Truth', in Dictionary of
Quotations, Penguin, 1960, p.183
Chris Ledger, in Your will be done,
op.cit., p.66
Father Malinski, in Light through
the curtain, Lion, 1985, p.64
Eugene Peterson, Travelling Light,
IVP, 1982, pp.96 and 102
G.A. Studdart Kennedy, The
Unutterable Beauty, Hodder and
Stoughton, 1964, p.104
Rabindranath Tagore, in Your will
be done, Christian Conference of
Asia, Singapore, September 1984,
p.91
A.W. Tozer, in Gems from Tozer,
Send the Light Trust, 1969, p.48

Wondering, Holt Rinehart, 1981,
p.203
Kenneth Leech, True God: An
exploration of spiritual theology,
Sheldon Publishers, 1987, p.25
Lewis Mumford, in R.T. Tripp
(comp.) The International Thesaurus
of Quotations, Harper & Row, 1970,
p.105
Blaise Pascal, Pensees, No. 434
John Reseck, in James L. Christian,
op.cit., p.195
David Steindl-Rast, Gratefulness,
the Heart of Prayer, Paulist, 1984,
p.210
Tertullian, in Arthur Cohen and
Marvin Halverson (eds), A
Handbook of Christian Theology,
Abingdon, 1958, p.261
Paul Tillich, A History of Christian
Thought, SCM, 1968, p.xvi

Week 51

Augustine of Hippo, adapted
from a prayer in Tony Castle
(comp.), The Hodder Book of
Christian Prayers, Hodder and
Stoughton, 1986, p.18
Rowland Croucher, Recent Trends
Among Evangelicals, Albatross,
1986, p.40
Albert Einstein, in Melvin Konner,
The Tangled Wing: Biological
Constraints on the Human Spirit,
Heinemann, 1982, p.431
F.W. Faber, 'There's a wideness in
God's mercy', The Baptist Hymn
Book, Psalms and Hymns Trust,
1964, No. 419
Donald J. Foran, Living with
Ambiguity: Discerning God in a
Complex Society, Alba House, 1971,
p.xvi
James Fowler, Stages of Faith,
Dove, 1981, pp.186-187
Kahlil Gibran, in James L.
Christian, Philosophy: An
Introduction to the Art of

Week 52

'Be Thou my vision', Baptist Hymn
Book, Psalms and Hymns Trust,
1962, No. 462
John Baillie, Christian Devotion,
OUP, 1962, pp.76-77
Walter Brueggemann, The
Prophetic Imagination, Fortress,
1978, p.45
Gerard Manley Hopkins, 'God's
Grandeur', in Alan Swallow (ed.),
The Rinehart Book of Verse, Holt,
Rinehart and Winston, 1965, p.312
Morton Kelsey, Dreams: A Way to
Listen to God, Paulist, 1978, p.99
Jurgen Moltmann, Hope and
Planning, SCM, 1971, p.150
Jurgen Moltmann, The Power of the
Powerless, SCM, 1983, p.126
H. Richard Niebuhr, The Meaning
of Revelation, Macmillan, 1960,
pp.152-153
Friedrich Nietzsche, 'Ecce Homo',
in The Philosophy of Nietzsche, The
Modern Library, 1954, p.896

Contributors

Personal profiles of contributors

Neil Adcock is pastor of the Canberra Baptist Church, before which he ministered in Adelaide, Sydney, Melbourne and Perth. He is a past President of the Baptist Union of New South Wales and of South Australia. For many years, he has been involved in all sections of the media, especially radio. He and his wife, Joan, have three married children.

Lewis Born, senior minister of a Church of Christ congregation in Victoria, has spent most of his life and pastoral ministry in Queensland. During his years as State Director of the Uniting Church Department of Christian Education, he was also Moderator of the Queensland Uniting Church Synod, and involved in broadcasting. He and Betty have five children and eight grandchildren.

Vaughan Bowie is a lecturer at Macarthur Institute of Higher Education, Bankstown, New South Wales, and a member of Greenacre Church of Christ. He is married to Deidre, a fellow lecturer at Macarthur Institute.

Chris Bullard has been senior minister for the Church of Christ in Overland Park, Kansas (USA) since 1980. He is a frequent lecturer in biblical archaeology and historical geography. He and his wife, Maxine, have three children.

Ross Clifford is a Baptist pastor at Gymea in Sydney's southern suburbs. Prior to entering the ministry, he practised as a solicitor and barrister in Sydney and the Northern Territory. He has completed graduate study in apologetics, and Church and State. Ross and Beverley have two children.

Clive Cook is a pastor in a rural church in northern Victoria.

Educated and ordained at Burleigh College in South Australia, he is now studying towards a Master's degree. His hobby: a volunteer Country Fire Authority firefighter. He and Valerie have four children.

Rowland Croucher, following a career in school teaching and pastoral ministries in New South Wales, Victoria and Canada, is now a 'ministry consultant' with World Vision, encouraging clergy and church leaders throughout Australia. He is also convenor of a ministry and research project among ex-pastors. He and Jan are a 'clergy couple' with four children.

Arthur Cundall, who retired in 1989 as Principal of the Bible College of Victoria, has had considerable pastoral and lecturing experience in Australia, England and elsewhere. He is a convention speaker, and the author of many books and articles. He is married to Jan, and has three adult children in England.

Rod Denton has been a member of the Blackburn Baptist Church (Victoria) pastoral team since 1980. He is married to Sue and has two daughters, Sarah and Kathryn. Prior to his ministry at Blackburn, he was the project manager of a new coastal development project in Adelaide. He is currently a full-time student at Fuller Theological Seminary, U.S.A.

Owen Dowling has been Anglican Bishop of Canberra and Goulburn since 1983. A former schoolteacher, church organist and choirmaster, Owen was ordained in Melbourne in 1960, and has served his present diocese since 1965. He is Australian Warden of the Order of St Luke the Physician, episcopal adviser to Anglican Renewal Ministries of Australia, and Chairman of the Liturgical Commission of the Anglican Church of Australia.

Margaret Dwyer has worked in primary and secondary schools in various Australian States. At present her ministry is in retreats, spiritual direction and in assisting groups in personal development and communication. She is a member of a Sisters of Charity community, and is spiritual director of 'Currajeen' Retreat House at Eltham, Victoria.

Graeme Garrett is a tutor in Theology at St Mark's School of Ministry in Canberra. He is an ordained minister of the Baptist Church and was formerly a pastor at Collins Street and Box Hill Baptist churches in Melbourne. Prior to taking up his present position he was, for nine years, Professor of Theology at Whitley College in the University of Melbourne.

Ron Ham has been pastor at Collins Street Baptist Church, Melbourne since 1982. He has had previous pastorates in Victoria and New South Wales, and has been a lecturer in theology. Janice and he have two adult children.

Jim Harrelson is pastor of the United Methodist Church of St Francis, Kansas (USA). Trained as a teacher with an MA in history, he has studied at several seminaries, taught New Testament Greek at university level and is currently working towards the DMin at Fuller Theological Seminary. He is married to Sue and has two sons.

John Harris has spent much of his life as a teacher and lecturer, mostly in cross-cultural contexts. He has a particular interest in Aboriginal culture and Christian faith. John has academic qualifications in science, education and linguistics. He has been Director of the Zadok Institute for Christianity and Society for four years and is to take up a position as Master of New College, University of NSW, in 1991. John and Judy have three teenage children.

Greg Headington has been associate pastor at First Presbyterian Church in Houston, Texas (USA) since 1981. After working as a professional tennis instructor and petroleum landman, he now ministers in the areas of missions and singles, and is chaplain to the three professional sports teams in Houston.

Richard Herman is now pastor of the Covenant Presbyterian Church, Sharon, Pennsylvania (USA), having served ten years as pastor to the Latta Memorial Presbyterian Church, Christiana, also in Pennsylvania. He is currently working on a DMin degree from Fuller Theological Seminary. He and his wife, Lissa, have one eight-year-old daughter, Elisabeth.

David Hewetson, an Anglican, has ministered for over thirty years in a number of capacities — as parish minister, teaching missioner, missionary administrator and principal of a theological college in Tanzania, and writer. He and his wife, Ann, have three children.

Lorna Jenkins is a pastor's wife with three adult children. She is a writer and lecturer with a special interest in Christian education. She and her husband are now working in Touch International Ministries in cooperation with Dr Ralph Neighbour Jnr. They are developing ministry in the area of advanced and specialist education for pastors and Christian workers.

Peggy Jones has been a librarian at Whitley Baptist College in Melbourne, Victoria and, more recently, secretary/research assistant with Compassion, a child-development mission. She is currently working towards a BA, majoring in English. She and Don have four children.

Ross Kingham is married to Valmai. They have three children, and live in Duffy, ACT. Ross is full-time director of Barnabas Ministries Incorporated, an ecumenical ministry of encouragement and renewal for Christian leaders in Australia. He is a minister of the Uniting Church in Australia.

John Lane is a member of the national staff of Scripture Union in Australia, serving as Publishing Manager. He lives in Melbourne with his wife, Wendy, and family. He is an elder and lay preacher of the Uniting Church.

Ken Manley is Principal of Whitley College, the Baptist college of Victoria, having previously pastored various churches and lectured at the Baptist colleges in Adelaide and Sydney. He is author of books and articles on church history. He is married to Margaret and they have two teenage daughters.

Jill Manton has been a secondary and adult migrant teacher. The greater part of her teaching has been with adults in churches during the years when she was a pastor's wife. Since her husband's death, she has been working as part of the pastoral team at a Baptist church in Melbourne and has particular responsibility for spiritual formation. She is the mother of three children.

Peter Newall is a retired Uniting Church minister, and a member of the South Australian Synod's Spiritual Development Task Force. He is involved in prayer and spirituality, spiritual direction and the publishing of cassettes on scripture and prayer.

Alan Nichols has been Anglican Archdeacon of Melbourne since 1986, after serving as executive director of the Mission of St James and St John for eight years. Alan belongs to several organisations concerned with social justice. He and his wife have five children.

David Penman was appointed Archbishop of Melbourne in 1984, following missionary and pastoral ministries in New Zealand, Pakistan, the Middle East and Melbourne. Until his death in October 1989, he served as patron or member of various church, social and educational agencies, with special concern for multicultural issues, the needs of the underprivileged and the role of women in the church. He was husband of Jean and father of four adult children. David contributed 'Joy in the morning' to this volume.

Gordon Preece, previously a youth worker, has been Anglican minister at Malabar in Sydney's eastern suburbs. He has also been lecturing part-time at the Baptist Theological College of New South Wales in Ethics. He is now working on a doctoral thesis at Fuller Theological Seminary under Robert Banks in the area of Faith and Work. He and Susan have three children.

Bronwyn Pryor, a trained infants teacher with subsequent studies in Arts and Theology, especially appreciates helping multi-handicapped children. She enjoys working as a team with her husband Robin in the Blackburn Uniting Church parish, and leading retreats for clergy and spouses. Bronwyn concentrates on children's ministry, especially with puppets and musicals, and leads women's prayer and Bible study groups. The Pryors have three teenage children. Her husband worked with her on her contribution.

Robin Pryor is a Uniting Church parish minister in Blackburn, Melbourne. He has a special concern to build up eldership, and a socially-aware spirituality. Robin is also involved in his synod's Commission on Continuing Education for Ministry, where he is involved in research and publication on ministry, and leadership of retreats. He was formerly a demographer in Australian universities, and with the United Nations. His wife worked with him on his contribution.

John Reid, bishop in the Anglican Diocese of Sydney since 1972, is in wide demand as a Bible teacher and speaker, both in Australia and overseas. He is chairman of welfare and social-issues committees in Sydney, and a member of the Lausanne Continuation Committee. He and Alison have a grown family of two sons and four daughters.

Julie Renner lives with her husband, Geoff, and three children in Melbourne. As a trained group worker, she has been involved with many growth groups and seminars and is committed to spiritual formation and the discovery of gifts for ministry in the whole church and especially among women.

Stuart Robinson has worked in Brisbane, Bangladesh and Melbourne as a missionary and pastor. He is married to Margaret, has three children, and is currently the senior minister of Blackburn Baptist Church in Victoria.

Owen Salter was until recently editor of the monthly Australian Christian magazine, *On Being*. He is part of an inner-city Baptist community in Melbourne which he serves as an elder. He and his wife Jane have two children.

Darcy Taplin is Lecturer in Practical/Pastoral Studies and

Director of Field Education at Morling College, the Baptist theological college of New South Wales, following more than twenty years of pastoral ministry. Married to Ann, the Taplins have two married sons, one daughter and one grandchild.

Steve Troyer graduated from Moody Bible Institute, has worked with Youth for Christ, has pastored in central western New South Wales and is now pastor at Wallsend Baptist Church. He is a freelance writer. He is married to Elaine and they have four sons.

Grace Thomlinson currently divides her time four ways: looking after her husband, Geoffrey; working at World Vision as co-ordinator of the Church and Christian Relations Unit; teaching Christian Ethics and Old Testament at the Bible College of Victoria; and contributing to the music ministry at Blackburn Baptist Church.

Ian Webber, whose background is in education and theology both as teacher and administrator, is a consultant with World Vision of Australia and is responsible for seminars and workshops, domestic projects and church and mission societies liaison. He is chairman of the council of elders of Ringwood Uniting Church. He and Lorraine have six children.

Claire Wilkinson has been a primary school teacher for many years. She retired early to coordinate a counselling and healing centre and bookroom at Blackburn Baptist Church in Victoria. She and her recently deceased husband have five children.

Emlyn Williams has worked for Scripture Union in both England and Australia. At present he serves in Victoria as Schools Work Coordinator. He has written a number of books of group study material and youth resources. He lives with his wife, Tricia, and their children, Anna and Tom, in Croydon in Melbourne's outer suburbs.